Musical Instruments
of the Bible

Musical Instruments of the Bible

Jeremy Montagu

Praise him in the sound of the trumpet:
Praise him upon the lute and harp.
Praise him in the cymbals and dances:
Praise him upon the strings and pipe.
Praise him upon the well-tuned cymbals:
Praise him upon the loud cymbals.
Let everything that hath breath; praise the Lord.

Scarecrow Press
Lanham, Md., & London
2002

SCARECROW PRESS, INC.

Published in the United States of America
by Scarecrow Press, Inc.
A Member of the Rowman & Littlefield Publishing Group
4720 Boston Way
Lanham, Maryland 20706
www.scarecrowpress.com

12 Hid's Copse Road
Cumnor Hill, Oxford OX2 9JJ, England

British Library Cataloguing in Publication Information Available

Library of Congress Cataloging-in-Publication Data

Montagu, Jeremy.
    Musical instruments of the Bible / Jeremy Montagu.
      p. cm.
    Includes bibliographical references (p.) and index.
    ISBN 0-8108-4282-3 (alk. paper)
    1. Musical instruments. 2. Music in the Bible. I. Title.

 ML166 .M66 2002
 220.8'78419—dc21   2002021202

In memory of

Bathja Bayer
(1928–1995)

Mishnah, Sēder Nᵊzīqīn,
Pirkēi Avōt (Ethics of the Fathers),
2:16

Contents

Illustrations

Transcription

While a few words are sufficiently familiar that we use them without diacritical signs, on the whole we follow *The Chicago Manual of Style*. The Greek η and ω carry macrons, *ē* and *ō*, to distinguish them from ε and ο. The υ, a short *u* sound, has been transcribed as *y* since Roman times.

In Hebrew, the silent א is indicated by ' and the almost-silent guttural ע by '. The ח is transcribed as *ch* (a guttural sound as in Scots loch, German *achtung*, and colloquial yeccch), as is כ (and also Greek χ). For most people there is no difference in sound between ח and כ, though in some communities כ is pronounced further back in the throat than ח. For the alternative form, כ, found at the beginning of a syllable, we use *k* as simpler than *kh*, with, to distinguish them, *q* for ק, though both sound the same. ס and שׂ also sound the same and are each transcribed *s*, whereas שׁ is transcribed *sh*. The only other two-letter equivalent is *ts* for צ. פ is transcribed *f*, not the old-fashioned *ph* and following normal modern Israeli pronunciation, both ת and ט are transcribed *t*, not *th* for the latter nor *s* for the former. For the vowels, the long *qāmats, tsēre, chīrīq, chōlām,* and *shūrūq* carry a macron, as in their first syllable here, whereas for the short vowels the normal English equivalents are used, as for all the other consonants. The "silent" vowel shᵊva is transcribed as here when it is vocalized (a slight, breathy sound as with the definite article "th' book") but for simplicity is ignored when actually silent. Finally, the consonantal ו is transcribed *v*, not the Germanic *w*, and when used as a vowel letter, the וֹ and וּ simply as *ō* and *ū* respectively. The וֹ and וּ have been thus pointed in the Quadrilingual Index to assist reading; other vowels and points have been omitted there as in modern Israeli convention.

Since there is no standard pronunciation of vowels in English (tom*ah*to, tom*ay*to, tom*a*tto, etc.) it is difficult to give any guidance. It might help to say that the vowels with a macron are close to the Italian sound for each vowel, whereas those without one are lighter or shorter. The Greek η is an *ee* rather than an *ey*.

Acknowledgments

Many people have helped in this work, which began thirty or more years ago as an illustrated lecture to music clubs and societies of all sorts. Dr Bathja Bayer of the Hebrew University of Jerusalem, whom I had met while lecturing there, recommended to Stanley Sadie that I should write the relevant articles for *The New Grove Dictionary of Musical Instruments* which he edited (London: Macmillan, 1984). She, to whose memory this book is dedicated, was the leading scholar in this field, though publishing comparatively little herself, especially in English. She wrote the major article "Nᵊgīnāh vᵊzimrāh" in the *Entsīqlōpedyāh Miqra'īt* (*Encyclopaedia Biblica*) (Jerusalem: Mōssad Bī'ālīq, 1964– , Vol.5, 1968), as well as seminal articles in *Yuval*, the occasional publication of the Jewish Music Research Centre at the Hebrew University. From those *Grove* articles, again with her encouragement, stemmed a handbook for the Bate Collection of Historical Instruments in the University of Oxford, of which I was the Curator, and then after I retired thence, a slightly larger self-published booklet. Bruce Phillips encouraged me to expand that further to this larger book.

Living in Oxford one is surrounded by libraries, scholars, and book-dealers and I am indebted to many for their patience and their help. An essential aid has been Shlomo Hofman's *Miqr'ey Musica* (Tel-Aviv, Israel Music Intitute, 1989), a polyglot musical concordance to the Hebrew text of the Bible.

Several people have read this book and made valuable comments, among them my son Simon and his wife Heftsibah Cohen-Montagu, who was also most helpful in securing some of the illustrations. My quondam-student and unofficial god-daughter Brenda Neece provided essential guidance on American usage, though I fear that I have not always followed her advice. My wife Gwen has been, as always, a tower of strength with help, criticism, and correction, and has intercepted innumerable interruptions and intrusions, to the detriment of her own interests and work.

To all, and especially her, my thanks.

Chapter 1

Introduction

The intent of this book is to identify those musical instruments which are named in the Bible. We know what we mean by harp and organ, but what did Moses mean by harp and organ in Genesis 4:21? What did the Psalmist specify for praising the Almighty? And what were all those instruments in Nebuchadrezzar's orchestra and those which St. John the Divine said should never more be heard in Babylon?

The Bible was compiled over a very long period. In Genesis 'In the Beginning', the first book of the Bible, Moses, who led the Exodus from Egypt around 1250 B.C., narrates the stories of a time much older still.[1] The last book, that of Revelations, is less than two thousand years old, nearer to our own time than to the events that are recounted in Genesis. Instruments change with time, and so do their names and so do the meanings of those names. To take an example from our own more recent history, what was meant by harp in Anglo-Saxon England, from around A.D. 600 to 1000, was what we would now call a lyre, very different from the instrument known as an harp from 1200 on. That in turn was different from the instrument that sang in Tara's halls, one of which survives in Trinity College Dublin from around 1400. That was different again from the harp for which Mozart wrote at the end of the eighteenth century, still more different from Debussy's and Ravel's harps around 1905, for which the one wrote the *Danses Sacrées et Profanes* and the other the *Introduction and Allegro,* and even more different from ours today. And all those changes came in only a thousand years. So it is not surprising if some of the biblical instruments changed from one part of the Bible to another, over a period more than twice as long.

What complicates the whole issue, the reason why we know less than we would wish about the biblical instruments, is that the Bible, as most of us know it in English, is a translation. The Old Testament was written in Hebrew, with a little in Aramaic, and the Apocrypha survives only in Greek, though much was probably originally written in Hebrew or Aramaic. Parts of the New Testament were also probably originally written in Aramaic, the language that Jesus and his disciples spoke, but the earliest version that we have is in Greek. Even for those who can read the Bible in the original languages, there are many words which appear only a few times, and some appear only once. As a result their meanings may have to be guessed. For those which concern us, their context makes it a reasonable guess that they are the names of musical instruments, but there may be no indication at all of what sort of instrument they were. When the Psalmist writes "Praise the Lord on the xxx", the xxx is more likely to be a musical instrument than, for example, an axe or a basket, but that may be as far as we can go with any certainty. However, a readable text needs more than that; one cannot leave gaps, nor can one write xxx. As a result, translators have had to resort to guesswork and to probability, and this has been true for all translators, for over two thousand years, whatever language they were translating into.

The first translators of all were living in the Holy Land itself. By the sixth century B.C. Hebrew had become a literary language, read perhaps by those best educated, but little used for speech or even for reading by most of the people. The common language was Aramaic. This was written in a script that was adopted for Hebrew also while the Israelites were in exile in Babylon and has been used ever since. Pre-exilic, or 'Old Hebrew' script was very different.[2] While the two languages are clearly related to each other, both vocabulary and grammatical constructions are different. Some words are similar enough that their meanings are easy to guess from one language to the other, but others are quite different and required then an interpreter, today a dictionary, to be understood.[3] It seems probable that, when the remnants of the two tribes of Benjamin and Judah returned from the seventy years of Babylonian exile in 516 B.C., those who were children of the original exiles, the first generation born in Babylon, would still have had some command of spoken Hebrew, learned from their parents. Their children and their grandchildren, on the other hand, would have spoken only Aramaic, the language of the Exile, which they would have used for day-to-day communication with the peoples who surrounded them in Babylon. We see the same process today. Immigrants come with their own language and many learn ours with some success. Their children are brought up with both languages, ours to speak at school and their own at home. Their children, a generation later, speak only our language and often have difficulty talking to their grandparents and would usually find it almost impossible to read any books they had brought "from the Old Country." As a result, when services and regular readings from the Bible were resumed in the Holy Land, at Ezra's behest the Levites translated the reading as it went along and "caused the people to understand the Law . . . they gave the sense and caused them to understand the reading" (Nehemiah 8:8).

Although an approved version of this translation must surely have existed, it seems never to have been written down, but was passed orally from generation to generation among the priests and scribes as part of their training. Only when, after the destruction of the Temple by the Romans in A.D. 70, there was neither role nor function for the priesthood, was it realized that these texts must be codified and written down lest they be lost as the Jews were dispersed across all the known world. The results are called Targumin or Interpretations. The first two known to us, dating from the end of the first century and referred to as the Palestinian and as Jonathan's, survive in only fragmentary form and are anyway very free translations. The third, Targum Onkelos, so-called from the name of its reputed author, was compiled early in the second century, and is still widely used today. While on the whole it is close to the standard Hebrew text, not only are there some variants which can be useful clues to original meanings now lost, but the vocabulary of the Aramaic itself, in relation to other languages of that part of the world, can be helpful in interpreting some words.

The first written translation is several centuries earlier than the Targum, dating from about 250 B.C. It was made in Alexandria in Egypt, from the Hebrew into Greek, at the request of the Egyptian King, Ptolemy Philadelphus, who reigned from 265 to 240 B.C.[4] According to legend, seventy-two scholars were sent from Jerusalem to prepare the text for him, which is why this translation is known as the Septuagint, abbreviated as LXX, from the Latin word for seventy.[5] There was initial opposition from the large Jewish community of Alexandria to the idea of a translation but, once completed, it became accepted and even valued, especially by those who had lost any practical knowledge of Hebrew or Aramaic and for whom Greek was their common tongue. They needed a translation if they were to understand the weekly Bible readings, just as many members of Jewish congregations today follow the text in their own languages while the Hebrew is being read to them. Many small details in the Septuagint show that the translators were working from a slightly different Hebrew text from that which was to become accepted as the standard or Massoretic text and which has come down to us.

This standard Hebrew text, which is read and studied in all Jewish communities, was codified by the learned rabbis (which means teachers—a rabbi has no priestly function even though today he, or she, is expected to act as a cleric) known as the Massoretes, deriving from a word meaning tradition or that which is handed down. It is difficult to be certain when this codification took place, but it is generally accepted that it was not long after the Roman destruction, perhaps by the end of the second century A.D., probably shortly after Onkelos had completed his Targum. One reason for the uncertainty regarding the date is that the earliest surviving copy of the Massoretic text dates from around 900, considerably later than some surviving copies of the Latin text.

This Latin translation came some three hundred years later than Onkelos, and has become the most influential of all the Christian texts. It was made by Eusebius Hieronymus, known universally as St. Jerome, and completed by around A.D. 405. It is known as the Vulgate because Latin became the common (Latin *vulgo*) language of the Church. It was, until recently, still in daily use in the Roman Catholic church and it remains to this day their basic text, from which any translations into other languages are made.

By this time, of course, the Gospels and other books of the New Testament had long been written. Like the Septuagint, these were in a Greek rather different from the classical language of ancient Greece, a Greek known as κοινη, *koinē* or common, that was used as a common tongue or *lingua franca* over much of the Near East. It is thanks to the monastic traditions of the Church, small communities living together in their own buildings with their own libraries of sacred texts, carefully preserved and copied from scroll to scroll, that we have earlier Latin and Greek texts of the Bible than we have of Hebrew, save for such portions that were found in settlements around Qumran and other Dead Sea sites.

When the Romans had destroyed the Temple and razed the city of Jerusalem to the ground, there were two results which concern us here. The first was that if there were no Temple, there was no need for priests. The only essential function of a priest is to perform a sacrifice, and God had commanded that sacrifices should only be offered in his appointed place (Deut.12:14), and from Solomon's time onwards that place was the Temple. Along with the priests, the Levites, who manned the Temple orchestra as well as performing many other functions in the sanctuary, also became redundant. There is a distinction between priests, *Cohanim,* and Levites, vestiges of which survive to this day in Jewish practice. Aaron, his brother Moses, his sister Miriam, and all their family were of the tribe of Levi, descended from one of Jacob's twelve sons (Genesis 29:34), and when tasks were assigned in the desert (Exodus 38:21), the Levites were assigned the duty of serving the Tabernacle, from which the Temple derived. The priests, however, the Cohanim, were the sons of the first High Priest, Aaron himself (Ex. 28:1), and their descendants, as distinct from the rest of the tribe of Levi.

The other result was the dispersion of the population of Jerusalem, including its scholars and teachers. Some settled in other parts of the Holy Land, initially in Yavneh and then in the Galilee. Many returned to the center of the former Exile, to Babylonia, where some communities had remained, not returning to but in contact with the Land of Israel. There they set up academies, part of whose function was to record all those practices and customs which had been lost, part simply to study and teach, and part, perhaps the main part, to establish and record all the commandments of the Oral Law which had been given to Moses on Mount Sinai during the forty days he spent alone there with God, and which had until that time been passed down through the generations from mouth to mouth.

After over a century of discussion and debate, the initial codification of this Law was compiled around A.D. 200 by Rabbi Yehudah haNasi, Judah the Prince, and is called the Mishnah. Copies of its text were widely disseminated to all the centers of rabbinic study and teaching and were discussed, argued, and debated for some three hundred years. Eventually these debates also were recorded, and the result was the Gemara.

Together, the Mishnah and the Gemara make up the Talmud, of which there are two versions, as it were a majority and a minority report. The majority is the *Talmud Bavli,* the Babylonian Talmud, and

is that used here. The other is the *Yerushalmi,* the Palestinian or
Jerusalem Talmud, shorter, less authoritative, and rather less informative for our purposes.

The Talmud, in its many volumes, always quotes the passage from
the Mishnah that it is about to dissect in Gemara. Its discussion on
that passage will quote the opinions of many of the rabbis and may
also ramble widely through the Bible and other parts of the Talmud,
as well as citing legend and secular literature, but it will always
return to the relevant tractate of the Mishnah in the end. The Mishnah is also published as a separate text, for it can be studied by itself,
with or without later commentaries. There are six Orders of the
Mishnah and, within these orders, many Tractates. The order most
relevant to this study is the second, Mō'ēd 'Appointed times'. Passages from the Mishnah are cited by its own enumeration within
each tractate. Passages from the Talmud are cited, again by the name
of the tractate (for example Rōsh haShānāh), and then by the *daf*
(*blatt* in Yiddish) or folio, with *a* for *recto* and *b* for *verso*.

The English versions of each used here are, for the Mishnah, Jacob
Neusner's recent translation, though Herbert Danby's older translation is also referred to, and for the Talmud the Soncino edition
which, along with a partial text of the Mishnah and the full text of
the Babylonian Talmud as well as the whole of the Tanach, the
Hebrew Bible, all with English translation, has been made available
on CD-ROM by the Davka Corporation of Chicago, with all the con-
comitant advantages of search and index.[6] Tanach, incidentally is an
acronym: T for Torah 'Law', the Pentateuch given to Moses on
Mount Sinai, N for Nᵊvī'īm 'Prophets', which includes the historical
as well as the prophetical books, and CH for Kᵊtūvīm 'Writings', all
the more literary books, such as Psalms.

Our concern in this book is with the texts that we read, and therefore with later translations into English rather than other languages.
Because all the early Christian clergy, of course, read Latin, as did
most of such few of the laity who could read anything at all, for the
first thousand or so years of the Christian era translations were fairly
spasmodic. Ælfric translated the Pentateuch, the first five books of
the Old Testament, and several of the historical books into Anglo-
Saxon at the end of the tenth century, and he was followed by the
West Saxon Gospels.[7] Many early manuscripts of the Latin text have
translations, known as glosses, written, often scribbled, between the
lines or in the margins, but these were only available to the individ-

ual owner. The general population had to be content with such portions of the Bible as the clergy thought it good for them to hear, often only paraphrased as narrations or explanations of the stories which were pictured on the walls and in the roofs of their churches.

It was the gradual move towards reform, along with the slowly growing spread of literacy, which drove the demand in the fourteenth century for translations, once again, into the common tongue. The first major English translation was that of John Wyclif, working from the Vulgate rather than from the original, and compiled early in the 1380s, with a second edition revised by his assistant and secretary, John Purvey, in 1395. Even though these translations were proscribed by the Church, they were still widely available as late as the early 1500s, indeed, according to Partridge, they were the only English text available as late as 1528.[8] Wyclif was followed by William Tyndale, who worked to a much greater extent from the original texts. His New Testament was published in 1526 and most of the Old in 1530, including the Pentateuch and the Narrative Books, as they are called here.[9] Much of his translation survived in the so-called Matthew Bible of 1537, the only one licensed by Henry VIII after his repudiation of Papal authority in 1534 which marked the beginning of the Church of England, and through the Matthew into the King James. The last of the famous translators of this period was Miles Coverdale, whose first Bible appeared in 1535, portions of which were revised for the Matthew Bible to cover those parts not provided by Tyndale. His translation of the Psalms, part of one of which is used on the title page here, survives in the Book of Common Prayer, which was first published in 1549.[10]

The Authorized Version, abbreviated AV, is still generally the best-loved English translation, and it is therefore that which will be used here as our basic English text. A group of Puritans, who were dissatisfied with all the available translations, met King James VI of Scotland during his progress from Edinburgh to London, where, after the death of Queen Elizabeth, he became King James I of England, and appealed to him to commission something better.[11] It is called Authorized because it was compiled under his authority between 1603 and 1610, and because it was he who authorized it, it is also often called the King James Bible. There have been innumerable English translations since then.

The Authorized Version was "translated out of the original tongues and with the former translations diligently compared and

revised" by fifty-four learned scholars. The "original tongues" are
the Massoretic Hebrew text for the Old Testament and the κοινη
Greek for the New Testament. The "former translations" were, in
addition to the earlier English versions, principally Jerome's Vulgate
Latin text and the Greek text of the Septuagint. Learned and schol-
arly as the fifty-four translators were, they were not musicologists,
and while, as we suggested initially, it was often clear from the context that they had reached the word for a musical instrument, they
frequently had no idea what the instrument in question might be.
They were not alone in this. The seventy scholars of the Septuagint
had often had the same problem, as had Jerome, so the "former
translations" were seldom of any practical help in our area. So sometimes they guessed, and sometimes, especially in the Book of Daniel,
they gave up altogether, as we shall see later, and simply used the
names of instruments that might have appeared in a royal orchestra
of their own time. Even the original author of that book, who is
thought to have codified the present text some centuries after the
events it chronicles, was patently unsure of the instruments of King
Nebuchadrezzar's court, and he appears to have adopted the same
policy as did the authors of the AV, simply listing the Aramaic equivalents of his own time.

Because this book is not a translation, we are not obliged to produce an answer, right, wrong, or guessed, in every case. We are at lib-
erty to say that we do not know. We can, by using all the evidence
available, including archeology, linguistics, and ethnomusicology,
produce some quite definite answers as to what instrument was
meant, what it looked like, perhaps even what it sounded like. We
can produce, in other cases, some probable answers. We can produce
some possible answers. And with some we can only say that we do
not know. Of the biblical instruments, only one, the ram's horn, is
still in use. The instructions for making another are clear enough to
identify it as a metal trumpet. Two, the cymbals and a drum, can be
identified with reasonable certainty from the etymology of their
names, and one, bells or jingles, is reasonably identifiable from its
purpose and its use. Others are less certain. We shall meet each
below.

It seems most sensible to refer to instruments in the order in which
they first appear in the Bible though, when it is convenient to do so,
we shall follow each to further appearances. We are therefore working our way through the Bible in the order in which it appears in

most English texts, save for those of the Roman Catholic Church, who accept the Apocrypha as a part of the canonical text and therefore absorb it into the normal running order.

Some passages are referred to more than once, and an Index of Biblical Citations will assist in locating these correspondences. Because so many of our problems of identification arise from the guesswork in translations, we frequently provide the original texts, for the benefit of those who can read them, with transliteration as an aid. There is also a Quadrilingual Index which includes, I hope, every reference, giving in parallel columns the Hebrew, Greek, Latin, and AV. These citations have sometimes been simplified, especially in the Greek and Latin, since we may not need to know whether the word was plural or singular, and seldom whether it was accusative, genitive, dative, etc. Where we lose the Hebrew, in the New Testament, we have used that vacant column to include Tyndale's translation, in some ways the most beautiful, for general interest and to show how heavily King James's translators lent upon him.

NOTES

1. The date is taken from John Bright, *A History of Israel* (London: SCM Press, 2nd ed., 1972), 121 and chronological table, 478. The traditional date, in the King James Bible margin, within the 40 years in the wilderness between 1491 and 1451 B.C., is somewhat higher than is probable.

2. Numerous examples of both can be found in Hershel Shanks, *Jerusalem: An Archaeological Biography* (New York: Random House, 1995), specifically 86–7. A few letters of Old Hebrew can be seen on the coins on plate 8, which deliberately used an archaic style.

3. Marcus Jastrow, *Dictionary of the Targumin, the Talmud Babli and Yerushalmi, and Midrashic Literature* (London: Luzac, 1903; reprinted New York: Judaica Press, 1989) is that most commonly used.

4. Nina L. Collins, "Who Wanted a Translation of the Pentateuch into Greek?" in *Journal of Semitic Studies,* Supplement 11: *Jewish Ways of Reading the Bible,* ed. George J. Brooke (Oxford: Oxford University Press on behalf of the University of Manchester, 2000): 20–57, citing the Letter of Aristeas, c. 150 B.C.

5. J. Weingreen, *Introduction to the Critical Study of the Text of the Hebrew Bible* (Oxford: Clarendon Press, 1982), 30.

6. *The Mishnah,* translated Herbert Danby (Oxford: Oxford University Press, 1933); *The Mishnah, A New Translation,* Jacob Neusner (New Haven: Yale University Press, 1988); *The Babylonian Talmud.* The Soncino edition

(London: Soncino Press, 1965ff.), on CD-ROM (Chicago: Davka Corporation, 1991–6).

7. A. C. Partridge, *English Biblical Translation*, The Language Library, ed. Eric Partridge and Simeon Potter (London: André Deutsch, 1973), 20. There are several accepted spellings of Wyclif's name.

8. Partridge, 24.

9. The original text of his New Testament has been reprinted by the British Library (London, 2000). His Old Testament is unfortunately only available today in modernized form.

10. Much of this information, including all the dates, comes from Partridge.

11. Partridge, 106.

Chapter 2

The Pentateuch

GENESIS

The first reference in the Bible to musical instruments comes in Genesis 4:21: Jubal "was the father of all such as handle the harp and organ" (AV); *ipse fuit pater canentium cithara et organo* (Vulgate); ὁ καταδείξας ψαλτήριον καὶ κιθάραν, "who invented the psaltery and harp" (LXX); כָּל־תֹּפֵשׂ כִּנּוֹר וְעוּגָב, *kol-tōfēs kinnōr vᵃʿūgāv*, "all who handle *kinnōr* and *ʿūgāv*" (Hebrew).[1]

And so confusion starts. Whatever the *kinnōr* was, it was certainly not a psaltery and probably not an harp; whatever the *ʿūgāv* was, it was certainly neither an harp nor an organ. The psaltery is a type of zither, a flat, wooden box with wire strings, running horizontally across the upper surface, which are plucked with the fingers, fingernails or plectra. Instruments of this type were known in the Middle East by the twelfth century A.D., and perhaps earlier, and traveled both east and west, to Persia, India, and China, coming into Europe, like many other instruments, with the Crusaders and over the Pyrenees from Moorish Spain. There is no evidence for the existence of any such instruments as early as the biblical period. About the organ we can be more definite, for we know the name, place, and date of its inventor, a Hellenistic Egyptian named Ctesibius in Alexandria, around 250 B.C., many centuries after Jubal's time.

David's "Harp", Kinnōr

So, what was the kinnōr? By the time that 1 Samuel 16:16 and 23 were written, some centuries later than Genesis, it was the instrument which the Psalmist, David, played (translated as *citharam* (Vulgate);

κινύραν (LXX)—the Greek *kinuran* is clearly a verb formed as a transliteration of Hebrew kinnōr) to his sheep and to King Saul with his hand. All the texts agree that he played with his hand, but whether this is a distinction between his bare hand and a tool such as a plectrum, we cannot tell. The Greek, followed by the Latin, uses the verb *psallein* 'to pluck' and so makes it clear that the kinnōr was a string instrument. A plectrum, a quill from a bird or a blade of wood, bone, horn, ivory or stiff leather, can pluck the strings much more forcefully than can the hand unaided. The player's hand, though, is more subtle as well as gentler, and is therefore more likely to have soothed King Saul's angry moods. With all five fingers and thumb, and perhaps both hands, rather than a single plectrum, David could have used a more elaborate and flowing playing technique than he may have done when playing to the sheep, as well as a quieter sound than that of a plectrum, more suited to playing soothing music indoors.

Playing to King Saul, though, may not have been so different from playing to the sheep. One does not play to animals for fun, though it may be pleasant to while away the lonely hours in the field. Animals can become restless, and music soothes and calms them. The singing cowboy is not a Hollywood invention. Many a stampede has been prevented by playing or singing, and there are several references to the practice in the Bible, for example in Deborah's Song (Judges 5:16). In 1 Samuel, it is surely significant that of the four references, all stress the use of the hand. 16:16 and 16:23 mention both harp and playing with his hand, whereas 18:10 and 19:9 mention only playing with his hand (16:17 and 18 refer only to playing well without mentioning either the instrument or how it was done). It was clearly of prime importance that he should use his hand (though see Chapter 4 for a different interpretation).

Certainly there was no question of rubbing the string with a bow at that date, for the fiddle bow only appeared around A.D. 800.[2] The fact that today, some 3,000 years after King David's time, and far longer after Jubal's, kinnōr is the modern Hebrew word for the violin is just one more example of the way that names change to mean different instruments over the centuries, and this is how confusion arises.

Whether David's kinnōr was identical with Jubal's, is, with so many centuries between them, unlikely. What either of them was, we do not know for certain, but it is very probable that the kinnōr was a lyre of some form, rather than an harp. We know from carvings, statues, and wall paintings that the lyre was played over much of that part of the world around that time, but while harps were used in Egypt and in Mesopotamia, no evidence for them has been found in the Holy Land. The lyre was the most important instrument of Classical Greece, the *kithara*, the instrument to which Orpheus and Homer sang their poems and lays. More relevantly to us, a group of nine lyres was found in one of the Royal Tombs of Ur (the Chaldean city from which Abraham came), dating from around 2450 B.C., much the period with which Jubal might be associated. Some of these lyres are in the University of Pennsylvania Museum in Philadelphia, some in the British Museum in London, and some in Baghdad.[3]

This type of lyre had a wooden soundbox, approximately trapezoidal in shape, the parallel longer sides horizontal. Two wooden arms projected upwards, with a crossbar linking their upper ends. From this crossbar or yoke the strings ran down across the front of the soundbox, held away from its surface by a bridge. The strings were wound round the yoke enough times to maintain a secure grip, and then each was wound around a small wooden rod or lever. The levers helped to turn the coils round the yoke and thus tune the strings. Lyres with this same tuning system survive still in Ethiopia as the *beganna* (plate 1). Lighter lyres, with gourd bodies, are still

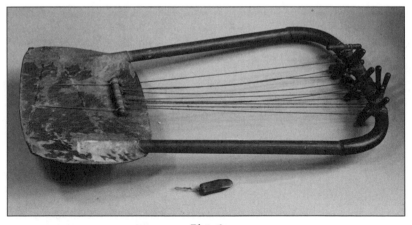

Plate 1
Lyre, beganna, from Ethiopia, perhaps a descendant of the kinnōr. The bridge is missing and its wooden plectrum lies beside it. Montagu Collection I 46.

used in the Sudan, Kenya, and Uganda (plate 7), as well as Ethiopia
and must be very like whatever David used as a shepherd, even if he
used a larger wooden lyre when he sang to King Saul.

The traditional Ethiopian beganna is illustrated here for two reasons. One is that it has the same type of tuning levers as the lyres
from Ur so that there is some slight justification for suggesting that
this is a Semitic type of lyre. The David mosaic from A.D. 509 in the
synagogue at Gaza shows him playing a lyre with the same type
of levers, though one must add that there are no other points of
resemblance.[4] The other reason is the well-known legend that the
Ethiopian royal house descended from the Psalmist's son King
Solomon and the Queen of Sheba. There is thus a remotely possible
connexion between the Psalmist and Ethiopia.

One of the best known representations of an ancient Israelite lyre
is that used today on the Israeli half-shekel coin (plate 2), though as
we shall see below the source from which this was taken is of very
dubious authenticity. An older Israeli coin from about 1972, which is
shown beside it, copies a much more credible kinnōr, taken from one
of the Bar Kochba coins of around A.D. 130.[5] Other illustrations from
that area show a variety of forms, none of them very clear or very
detailed, and, as is almost inevitable with ancient iconography, none
is identified on the representation as a kinnōr, leaving us only with
the Hellenistic-period iconography showing King David playing the

Plate 2
Lyres on modern Israeli half-shekel (R) and quarter-shekel (L) coins, the half-shekel
based on a probably spurious seal, the quarter-shekel on the kinnōr on a Bar Kochba
coin shown on plate 8. Montagu Collection X 240.

lyre and the knowledge, from the text of the Bible, that he played the kinnōr, and thus the assumption that kinnōr was the name for the lyre. The tradition that the Sea of Galilee is called Kinneret in Hebrew because its shape is the same as that of the kinnōr is, to anyone who has seen Kinneret either on the ground or on a map, less than helpful. We shall discuss lyre typology in more detail in the next chapter, and playing techniques more fully in Chapter 8.

If we are to believe the association with Jubal, the kinnōr is the instrument with the longest history in the Bible, for we find it also in the last book of the Hebrew bible, that of Maccabees in the Apocrypha, dating only a century or two before the Christian era. Can it still be the same instrument? It would seem improbable, but we must not discount the power of tradition when wondering how much instruments might have changed over the biblical period. The lists of the musical establishment of the Temple, recorded in 1 Chronicles 15 when compared with the parallel passages after the return from Exile, are evidence for the lack of change despite the availability of a wider choice of instruments. Certainly the list of instruments which we shall encounter in Daniel had become familiar to the Children of Israel while they were in Babylon, for the events recounted there all occurred during the Exile. And yet there is no trace of any of those or any other new instruments when the Temple service was re-established under Nehemiah and Ezra. The service was more elaborate, perhaps, but still with the same equipment. One might find an analogy in Japan, where instruments preserved from the sixth century A.D. in the Shōsōin in Nara show astonishingly little difference from those used today, especially those used in the *gagaku* ensemble of the court.[6] Even much of the music is the same today, though so much changed in speed and character that it took a scholar of the caliber of Laurence Picken to recognize it.[7] Regrettably, since the Temple orchestra died with the Romans, whereas the *gagaku* ensemble survives still, there can be no comparable source for the recovery of Temple music. Nor do we have any repository like the Shōsōin to preserve the instruments of King David's, or even the Maccabaeans' time.

Jubal's other Instrument

The *'ūgāv*, עוּגָב, may well have been some kind of woodwind instrument. The Targum translates it as *abuva*, a word which is used elsewhere for a reed instrument, the *chālīl*. The word *'ūgāv* appears only four times in the Bible: here, in Psalm 150, to which we shall return in due course, and twice in Job (21:12 and 30:31). None of these four references gives us any concrete evidence of what it was, but its coupling in Gen. 4:21 with kinnōr as the two archetypal instruments, and its combination with *minnīm*, which simply means 'strings', in Ps. 150 suggests that it may represent woodwind in general.

There is no agreement even as to the origin of the word, so that etymology is of little help. It has been suggested that there is a link with עגב, meaning lust or sensuous love, but since various instruments have been accused of this connexion throughout history, this etymology is of no help. The origin of the Aramaic *abuv* is hollow, and we know from other contexts that *abuv* and *abuva* were always recognized as flutes or reed instruments, so this remains the likeliest interpretation. Of one thing we can be certain: that, as we said above, it was not an organ, as the AV translates it, for that instrument is far too late in date.

The Tabret, *Tōf*

The only other musical reference in Genesis comes in 31:27, where Laban is reproving Jacob for his precipitate flight with his two wives and all the flocks he had gained by selective breeding. Laban says, "Wherefore didst thou flee away secretly, and steal away from me; and didst not tell me, that I might have sent thee away with mirth [Hebrew, שִׂמְחָה, *simchāh* still used for any joyful occasion], songs [שִׁרִים, *shirīm*, the word used for the Song of Songs and for many psalms], with tabret [תֹּף, *tōf*; LXX τυμπάνων, *tympanōn*, and *tympanum* in Latin] and with harp [kinnōr]?".

Tabret, meaning a small tabor or small drum, appears here, but the more usual word is timbrel as it is here in Tyndale's translation or, for example, in Ps. 150 in the AV. It is the old English name for what we now call the tambourine, a small drum with a shallow shell, held in one hand and struck with the other. The old English timbrel, like our tambourine, had pairs of miniature cymbals set in slots cut in the side of the shell to add a pleasing jingle to the sound, and so does the modern Arab *duff*, a word clearly cognate with Hebrew *tōf*. Such jingles are unlikely to have been used in biblical times but it may then have had a snare, a strand or two of gut, running across the underside of the skin inside the shell, like the modern Moroccan *bendir* illustrated here (plate 3).

Plate 3
Frame drum, bendir, from Morocco, similar to the tōf, with snares running
across the underside of the head. Montagu Collection VIII 70.

Frame drums, as these instruments are called typologically, are widely used in all sorts of celebrations all over the Middle and Near East and throughout North Africa. As we shall see in a moment, they are the instruments most frequently played by women, but they are also played by men, especially on joyous occasions. One can understand Laban's frustration at being deprived of a lavish party to say farewell to his nephew and daughters.

EXODUS

The first reference here is again to the timbrel, or as Tyndale spells it, 'tymbrell.'[8] After the Children of Israel had crossed the Sea, Moses and all his host sang a song, of which we have every word (Exodus 15:1–18). Then (15:20) "Miriam, the prophetess, the sister of Aaron, took a timbrel in her hand; and all the women went out after her with timbrels and with dances", but we only have the first sentence of Miriam's song. The word for song and sing, incidentally is the same as with Laban.

This is the tōf's most typical use, throughout the Bible and still today, as an instrument for women to accompany dance and song. The tōf and dance are coupled in Psalm 150:4, again as תֹף וּמָחוֹל, *tōf ūmāchōl*. They are together, too, when Jepthah's ill-fated daughter comes out to greet him (Judges 11:34) "with timbrels and dances". They are again coupled, and again with women, who came "from all the cities of Israel", with singing, dancing, and rejoicing, when David had won battles against the Philistines (1 Samuel 18:6). "All the house of Israel played" them and sang and danced when David brought up the Ark of God from Gibea to his new capital of Jerusalem (2 Sam. 6:5 and 1 Chronicles 13:8). The tabret accompanied the prophets whom Saul met after he was anointed (1 Sam. 10:5) but it could also be used by the wicked as Job pointed out (Job 21:12). Many other references associate the timbrel or tabret with mirth and joy.

In all these citations, the Hebrew word is the tōf and we have no doubt at all as to what it was: a frame drum like our tambourine but almost certainly without the jingles. Māchōl, the word translated as dance, we shall discuss in the next chapter. We have many clay figurines from the area, dating from biblical times, holding such a drum, most of them female (plate 4). While it is sometimes suggested that they may be Astarte figures, one of the pagan goddesses, holding a moon, enough of them have one hand on the face of the disk as in our illustration, just as one does when playing a frame drum, that we can be certain that most, at least, are players of the timbrel or tōf.

There are no visible jingles in any of the early iconography, not on these figurines, not on any of the Mesopotamian carvings, not on any of the Greek vases. It would seem unlikely that if there really were jingles they would not be shown on at least some of these examples if they were as large as those on our modern tambourines, still more if they were as large as those, nearly twice the size of ours, to be seen in European medieval illustrations. What would not be visible on any of the early iconography are the internal iron rings fixed to the sides of the frame, characteristic of frame drums today from Central Asia, nor the internal snares, lying under the skin inside the frame, instead of outside it as on our side drum, which are usually fitted on North African and Near Eastern frame drums today (plate 3). It is very probable that some such rattling elements did exist, for all the peoples who use them say that they sweeten the sound. Because there is no way to adjust the skin tension of such

Plate 4
Clay figurines of women with frame drum, tōf, and double pipes, chālīl,
from a Phoenician cemetery at Achziv, 8th to 6th centuries B.C. Israel
Antiquities Authority.

drums, save by holding them to the fire or rubbing the skin hard
with the hand to heat it by friction, these rings and snares are the
only way to ameliorate the somewhat dull thud of hand on skin as
evening falls and humidity rises with the dew.

The Ram's Horn Trumpet, Shōfār

The next instrument to be mentioned is very different, as was
its player. As God prepared to give the Ten Commandments on
Mount Sinai, there came thunders and lightnings, and a thick cloud
upon the mount, "and the voice of the trumpet exceeding loud"
(AV); *clangorque buccinæ vehementius perstrepebat* (Vulgate); φωνὴ τῆς
σάλπιγγος ἤχει μέγα, *phōnē tēs salpingos ēchei mega* (LXX); וְקֹל שֹׁפָר
חָזָק מְאֹד, *vᵊqōl shōfār chāzāq mᵊʾōd* (Hebrew) and then "when the voice
of the trumpet sounded long and waxed louder and louder, Moses
spake, and God answered him by a voice" (Ex. 19:16 and 19). In both

verses, the Hebrew for trumpet is שׁוֹפָר, *shōfār*. That this is the ram's horn is confirmed by verse 13, "when the trumpet soundeth long, they shall come up to the mount", for the Hebrew word there is יֹבֵל, *yōvēl*, which means ram. In the Targum the word is *shofara* in all three verses, thus equating shōfār with yōvēl.

A possible reason why verse 13 says a ram is recounted by Rabbi Hanina ben Dosa.[9] The shōfār heard on this momentous occasion, ringing out from heaven, was made of the left horn of the ram which Abraham had sacrificed instead of Isaac (Gen. 22:13). No part of that ram went to waste, for it had been one of God's ten special creations in the last moments of the Sixth Day, before the advent of the Sabbath on which God "rested from all his work which he had made" (Gen. 2:2). Its sinews became the strings of David's lyre, its skin girded Elijah's loins, and the right horn, which is larger than the left, will be heard "in times to come" (Isaiah 27:13, which is normally equated with the Last Trump, 1 Corinthians 15:52).

Save for those two occasions, the shōfār is blown on earth, rather than from the heavens, and it is widely used throughout the Bible. It is the only biblical instrument still in use today, and modern examples are shown on plate 5. One reference suggests that there may have been more than one variety. In Joshua 6, שׁוֹפְרוֹת הַיּוֹבְלִים, *shōfᵉrōt hayōvᵉlīm* are specified almost throughout the passage. In verse 5 we have "that when they make a long blast with the ram's horn [*keren hayōvᵉl*], and when ye hear the sound of the trumpet [*qōl hashōfār*], all the people shall shout." Yōvēl, as we said above, means a ram, which is the normal animal used and the Targum uses *shofaraya dᵉkeren dikhraya*, "shōfār from the horn of a ram". We have no idea how the shōfār hayōvēl differed from the ordinary shōfār, or even whether it did, but the repeated specification of hayōvēl suggests that it may have done. Yōvēl also came to mean the jubilee (the English word derives from the Hebrew), the advent of which was signaled every fifty years by a call on the shōfār (Leviticus 25:8 ff.). Tyndale says in Joshua "trompettes of rammes hornes" but adds a marginal note: "After the Hebreu. The cōmen Transl readeth /of the yere of iubelye", referring thus to Coverdale's first translation of 1535.[10] Was the jubilee signaled by a call on a special form of shōfār, the form that was used at Jericho? We do not know. When the Mishnah was compiled, the first section of the Talmud, only about 200 years after the last jubilee had been proclaimed by the sound of the shōfār in the Temple, there was already disagreement about what

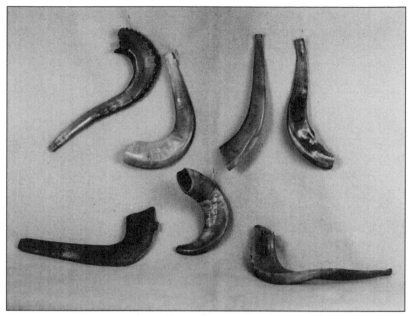

Plate 5
*Shōfᵉrōt, clockwise from upper left, from Eastern Europe (XI 264—Richard Koch
Bequest), Morocco (X 202), Israel (XII 154), North Africa (VII 210), Israel
(III 216), Persia (VII 212), and Germany or Poland with engraved inscription
(V 234). Montagu Collection.*

sort of shōfār had been used on what occasion, so it is not surprising
that we cannot answer the question today.

The word shōfār is thought to derive from the Akkadian word
shapparu, a wild goat, and goat horns are also permitted to be used,
as are the horns of any kosher animal save for that of a cow, which is
prohibited because of the episode of the Golden Calf. Perhaps this is
why the Bible specified shōfār hayōvēl at Jericho, the special shōfār
which would be used to signal the jubilee. On all other occasions
goat, ibex, antelope such as the oryx and kudu, etc., are permitted as
well as ram, but perhaps on those two occasions only the ram.

The Talmud is quite specific about what renders a shōfār kosher,
allowed, and what renders it *pasul*, prohibited.[11] If it was too long
and has been shortened, it is allowed. Even if it has been scraped
thin, it is allowed. While the mouth (which we would call the bell)

may be overlaid with silver or gold, the mouthpiece must be left plain so that nothing comes between the player's lips and the natural horn and nothing interferes with the sound.[12] Equally, whatever is overlaid on the bell may only be on the outside and then only if it does not change the sound. If it were overlaid on the inside, it would not be permitted, for then the gold or silver would be making the sound, not the horn. This is emphasized by the prohibition on using a shōfār that has been cracked and stuck together again or that has a hole in it unless the hole has been stopped up.[13] Even if the hole has been stopped, if it affects the sound, it is not permitted to be used, and the Rabbis of the Gemara say that it should not be used in any case.[14] If it is split lengthwise it is not permitted, but if it is split across, the horn can be shortened to cut off the split part and then, if enough is left to allow it to be held in the hand, with some of the horn showing on each side of the hand, it is allowed.

The shōfār was used in biblical times for many purposes. It was a ritual trumpet. What is now celebrated as the Jewish New Year was specified in Leviticus 23:24 as *zichrōn tᵊrū'āh*, "a memorial of blowing of trumpets", and in Numbers 29:1 as *yōm tērū'āh*, "a day of blowing the trumpets". While that verse does not specify whether it was the shōfār or the silver trumpets which were to be used, the Talmud makes it very clear that it was the shōfār, though with considerable, and contradictory, discussion on whether it was the rams' horn or a straight antelope horn.[15] Psalm 81:3 is another example of use in a ritual, as of course is Ps. 150:3.

It was a war trumpet. When Gideon rescued the people from the oppression of Midian, "he divided the three hundred men into three companies, and he put a trumpet into every man's hand," trumpets in the hand of all of them in Hebrew, as the AV margin points out (Judges 7:16). Job 39:25 is another well-known example.

It was a signal instrument, for giving commands, in a number of references, and also for ceremony, for example at the proclamation of King Solomon (1 Kings 1:34 and 39). It was also an alarm (Ezekiel 33:3, and very specifically Joel 2:1, Amos 3:6, and Zephaniah 1:16), a use which has persisted through the centuries.

In both Joshua and Judges we find the use of massed ram's horn trumpets, and each has an extraordinary effect. In Joshua 6:20, "So the people shouted when the priests blew with the trumpets; and it came to pass . . . that the wall fell down flat." And in Judges 7:20 and 21, "And the three companies blew the trumpets, and brake the pitchers, and held the lamps in their left hands and the trumpets in their right hands to blow withal: and they cried, The sword of the Lord and of Gideon . . . and all the host ran, cried, and fled."

The shōfār seems also to have been in general a means of confounding evil, of averting catastrophes, of frightening away demons. Certainly Mishnah Ta'anīt provides a list of the occasions when the shōfār should be sounded, such as when crops grow in strange ways and when rain ceases for forty days in the midst of the rainy season, or if the rainfall is insufficient to fill the cisterns and pits.[16] It was also blown for pestilence, blasting (of crops), mildew, locust, caterpillars, wild beasts, and the sword, drawing some of these from Solomon's prayer in 1 Kings 8:37 and the last two from Leviticus 26:6.[17] Rain was, and still is, a critical matter throughout that part of the world: enough rain and people eat, insufficient and there is famine. The only disaster for which the shōfār was not blown was an excess of rain![18]

An elaborate water ceremony took place on the last day of the Festival of Succoth (Tabernacles, the autumn harvest festival which lasts for eight days), to the accompaniment of the Levites with those instruments which are laid down in 1 Chronicles 15:16–24 (and will be discussed in more detail in that section). It was clearly a highly joyful occasion, for "pious men and wonder workers would dance before them with flaming torches in their hands and they would sing before them songs and praises. Levites beyond counting playing on harps, lyres, cymbals, trumpets, and [other] musical instruments."[19] The instruments in the original Hebrew of the Mishnah are *kinnōrōt*, *nᵊvālīm*, *mᵊtsiltayīm*, *chatsōtsᵊrōt*, and *clēi shīr*, the lyres which we met above, probably a second type of lyre, cymbals, metal trumpets, and the tools of song.[20] The shōfār was repeatedly blown. Some traces of this survive in the modern synagogue service, with a prayer for rain again on the last day of that festival and, among Sephardi communities, repeated shōfār blowing, sometimes by a number of shōfᵊrōt together, on the penultimate day, Hoshanah Rabbah.

So, why was the shōfār blown on these occasions? Ostensibly, of course, as a cry to God for relief, analogous perhaps with Elijah's mocking commands to the prophets of Baal (1 Kings 18:27), but Judaism does not encourage the idea that God needs to be awoken, to have his attention drawn to the troubles of mankind. Other interpretations have been closer to the idea, frequently encountered in the New Testament and perhaps typical of that period, which is also that of the Mishnah, that many troubles are caused by the machinations of devils, demons, and evil spirits. It is an almost universal human concept that loud noises frighten such spirits and drive them away. Few of the world's cultures are free of this superstition, and the remedy is often strengthened by the use of instruments which are associated with sanctity. Church bells, for example, are often credited with the power to avert thunderstorms, especially in the harvest season when they could beat down the crops. Thus it is all the more appropriate that the shōfār should be used in this way.

The practice continued into modern times. There are many legends in medieval and later sources of the shōfār being used for these and similar purposes, but we are already straying beyond the remit of our subject, and perhaps we should leave the matter here.

The shōfār was the one ritual instrument to survive the destruction of the Temple by the Romans in A.D. 70. This was partly because it was also a secular signal instrument, and not specifically a priestly one, and partly because it still had a part to play in the ritual life of the synagogue, especially for Rosh haShanah. To this and other more recent aspects of the instrument's use we shall return in chapter 8. Other instruments fell out of use, unless they were useful for general musical purposes, because once the Temple was destroyed, there could no longer be any Temple music. Instrumental music was banned from the service of the synagogue, both because it was a different type of service from that of the Temple, a service of prayer rather than of sacrifice, and as a sign of mourning for the Temple's destruction.

Golden Bells, Pa'amōnīm

Only one other instrument is referred to in Exodus. In 28:33–35 Moses is commanded to "make pomegranates of blue, and of purple, and of scarlet, round about the hem [of the high priest's robe]; and bells between them round about. A golden bell and a pomegranate, a golden bell and a pomegranate, upon the hem of the robe round about. And it shall be upon Aaron to minister; and his sound shall be heard when he goeth in unto the holy place before the Lord." In 39:25, when this commandment is carried out, the text is amplified to state that the pomegranates are bobbles of twined linen. As a minor sidelight revealing how international trade expanded rapidly in Europe in the last decades of the fourteenth century, it is interesting that while Wyclif in the 1380s uses powmgarnettis, his spelling of pomegranates, a European fruit, his successor, John Purvey, who produced the second edition a decade later, used piyn applis.

The word translated as bell is פַּעֲמֹן, *pa'amōn*, which derives from פַּעַם, *pa'am*. This is used with numbers for times, once, twice, etc., and can also, by extension, mean stroke or footfall. These verses are the only appearances of *pa'amon* in the Bible, so some guesswork has always been necessary. What would enable "his sound shall be heard" when attached to the skirt of his robe and related to his footsteps? According to the Talmud, "our rabbis taught that 72 bells containing 72 clappers were brought and hung thereon, 36 each side, but R. Dosa said, on the authority of R. Judah, 'There were 36, 18 on each side.' "[21] The obvious answer is indeed a small bell or a rattle such as a pellet bell, a vessel containing a loose pellet to jingle, with which we are familiar as a child's toy. We know them, also, strapped on a dancer's legs, or attached to horse harness and to sleighs. The Targum has *zaga* which relates to words which can also mean a nutshell, and which could describe either small clapper bells or pellet bells. Many very small clapper bells, made of bronze and measuring from 20mm in diameter to about twice that size, have been found archeologically in the Holy Land. These are similar to those which are attached to the *rimonīm* 'pomegranates', as they are called, on the Scrolls of the Law in synagogues today. Pellet bells seem not to have turned up archeologically so frequently, and may have been rarer in ancient Israel, though they appear on horse trappings in Mesopotamia.

LEVITICUS

There are only two musical references in Leviticus, both to the use of the shōfār. The first, in 23:24 as quoted above, specifies "a memorial of blowing of trumpets" on the first day of the seventh month, Rosh haShanah, the New Year. The other, 25:9, also discussed above, in the AV says "Then shalt thou cause the trumpet of the jubile [sic] to sound." The Hebrew, however, does not mention yōvēl for 'jubilee' until the next verse, referring only to shōfār tᵊrū'āh, or loud shōfār, which is used in the Aramaic, Greek, and Latin, and in the AV margin. It is not as illogical as it might seem to begin the jubilee year at the end of Yom Kippur, the Day of Atonement, rather than on the

New Year itself. On Rosh haShanah, the first of the year, the shōfār is sounded to call Israel to repentance, to begin to recollect all the sins committed during the past year so that ten days later, on Yom Kippur, a 25-hour fast with evening and all day spent in synagogue, one can then ask for forgiveness. That period of the Ten Days of Repentance would be no time for claiming ancient rights, the return into property and so forth, whereas after Yom Kippur with, one may hope, divine forgiveness, one can turn one's attention to such matters.

NUMBERS

The Silver Trumpets, Chatsōtsᵊrōt

The first reference in Numbers is to the one instrument which we can identify with absolute certainty from the prescription of how it was to be made and the purposes for which it was to be used. From 10:2 onwards, Moses was commanded: "Make thee two *chatsōtsᵊrōt* of silver, of an whole piece shalt thou make them: that thou mayest use them for the calling of the assembly, and for the journeying of the camps . . . (verse 9) And if ye go to war in your land against the enemy that oppresseth you, then ye shall blow an alarm with the *chatsōtsᵊrōt*" (AV). Of a whole piece is an inaccurate translation of the Hebrew כֶּסֶף מִקְשָׁה, *kesef miqshāh*, which is better as silver of beaten work. The Greek, *ἀργυρᾶς ἐλατὰς*, of silver beaten with a hammer, is accurate enough; so is the similar Latin, *argenteas ductiles*; so too are Wyclif's "two beten out silueren trompes" and Tyndale's "two trõpettes of beaten syluer". The AV is not only inaccurate but is positively misleading because "of a whole piece" suggests casting, whereas the original text specifically prevents that by demanding beaten work: silver raised (the technical term) from sheet into a tube by hammering it.

There is only one type of instrument which fits this description. The facts that the chatsōtsᵊrōt were made from hammered silver and were used to signal movement of the camp and for blowing alarms, makes it plain that they were indeed trumpets, *σάλπιγγης* in Greek (*salpingēs*, the plural of *salpinx*) and *tubae* in Latin. This is confirmed by the fact that the words used for sounding them in the Hebrew are those which always refer to trumpeting and which are still used today as the names of the calls of the shōfār.

It is a reasonable assumption that the trumpets which Moses made in the desert, only a short while after leaving Egypt, would have been similar to those with which the Children of Israel had been familiar in that land during their centuries of servitude. Josephus's description of them, many centuries later, as being slightly less than a cubit long, the distance from the fingertip to the back of the elbow, much the length of the trumpets seen in Egyptian wall-paintings and carvings, bears this out.[22] Certainly the trumpets carved on Titus's Arch in Rome, which purport to be those captured after the fall of Jerusalem, are much longer than a cubit. They are clearly ordinary Roman trumpets, presumably modeled on the only ones which the carver had available, and they are not evidential for the appearance of the Israelite trumpets of Josephus's time, contemporary with Titus, still less for the biblical instruments some 1,300 years earlier.

The Exodus from Egypt was within a couple of centuries or so of the reign of the Pharaoh Tutʿankhamūn, two of whose trumpets were found after his tomb was opened in 1922, the only surviving ancient Egyptian trumpets so far discovered. The alleged third trumpet, in the Louvre in Paris, is the top of an incense stand.[23] Tutʿankhamūn's trumpets match the description in Num. 10:2 in all respects save for the material of the smaller, which has a bronze or copper body and a gold bell instead of being made of silver. I was permitted to examine, though not to touch, that trumpet when it came to London with the Tutʿankhamūn Exhibition in 1973.[24] Briefly, it was indeed made of beaten work, unlike the Louvre object, which is cast.[25] The body is made of sheet bronze or copper which has been hammered to raise or curve it into a slightly conical tube with a longitudinal seam in the normal meander pattern for such work, where each side of the tube lies alternately over the other and, after soldering, is burnished to a smooth finish.[26] The joint was left slightly rough on the inside of the tube and the indentations of the meanders are clearly visible when looking down the interior. The bell had been separately made and hammered, and burnished, as one can with gold, so that the two edges had simply flowed into each other, making the use of solder unnecessary. It had then been riveted over the end of the tube, with a sleeve of very thin gold, hardly more than gold foil, over the joint both to conceal it and to render it airtight—the head of one of the rivets can be seen beneath the foil as a highlight in the detail photograph of the bell in the British Museum catalogue. The mouthpiece was simply a strengthening ring of metal rod at the top of the tube, with the end of the tube swaged out over it. The total length, given by Hans Hickmann and the British Museum, is 494 mm; the silver trumpet, which is not now in its original state (it shattered when it was blown in the 1930s), was, according to Hickmann, 582 mm long.[27] Whiston gives the length of Josephus's cubit as 21 inches (533 mm); my cubit is 500 mm.[28] Reconstructions of the two trumpets are shown in plate 6.[29]

Some of the specified occasions in Num. 10 when the chatsōtsᵊrōt were to be blown were (verse 10) "in the day of your gladness, and in your solemn days and in the beginnings of your months" (AV). It is interesting to compare that with Ps. 81:3 "Blow up the trumpet in the new moon, in the time appointed, on our solemn feast day", where the Hebrew word in the psalm for the AV's trumpet is shōfār. Clearly custom and practice had changed between the forty years in the wilderness, of Numbers 10, and the time, at least some centuries later, when that psalm was written.[30] The use of one instrument had given way to that of another.

King James's translators wrote trumpet each time in English, but in the Hebrew we have two very different instruments: chatsōtsᵊrāh in Numbers and shōfār in the Psalm. This is why it is essential to refer to the language of the original text, as we do throughout here, and not to rely on a translation, where so often the same word is

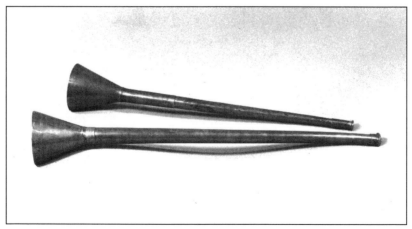

Plate 6
Reproductions of Tutʿankhamūn's trumpets by Peter Holmes, presumed to be similar to the chatsōtsᵊrōt. Montagu Collection I 164.

used for two different instruments. The LXX occasionally has *keras*, the Greek for a natural animal horn, for the shōfār but normally uses salpinx indiscriminately for either, and twice (in the story of Gideon) we get *keratinas salpizein*, to hornly salpinx. St. Jerome occasionally uses *buccina* for the shōfār, but more often uses tuba for either instrument, and these distinctions are not always in parallel with those in the Greek. There is no perceptible system in this and it seems entirely a matter of the whim of the moment which word is used. The one thing that can be said in their favor is that neither ever uses keras or buccina for the metal chatsōtsᵊrāh.[31] With this very casual use as a background one can hardly blame the AV translators for not making it clearer which instrument was being used. It might be of interest to note that among the earlier translations into other European languages, Martin Luther seems the only one to have distinguished between the two, using *Trompete* for chatsōtsᵊrōt in Numbers and *Posaun* for shōfār in the psalm.[32] It is because of Luther's constant use of Posaun for shōfār that composers such as Mozart wrote solos for trombone (the modern meaning of Posaun) when setting the "Tuba mirum" of the Requiem. Posaun derives from Latin *bucina*, one of the Roman military trumpets which, as Renato Meucci has recently proved, was made of animal horn, normally bovine.[33] The Roman tuba, on the other hand, also a miliary instrument like the Greek salpinx, was straight, slightly flared, made of bronze, and about one and a half meters long, so corresponding exactly with the instruments on Titus's Arch. The incorrect double-*c* in the Vulgate's and church Latin's buccina probably arose through a false etymology from *bucca*, cheeks, instead of from Greek βυκάνη, *bukanē*, a crooked horn.[34]

Following the command in Numbers 10:8-9, "And the sons of Aaron, the priests, shall blow with the trumpets. And if ye go to war . . . then ye shall blow an alarm . . . and ye shall be saved from your enemies," when they went to attack the Midianites (Num. 31:6), Moses sent the chatsōtsᵊrōt with the priests.[35] The chatsōtsᵊrōt remained exclusively the priestly trumpets, but this did not mean that priests could not blow the shōfār—that instrument was available to all, but the silver trumpets only to the descendants of Aaron. So far as ceremonials were concerned, there was clearly a mixture of use. In 1 Kings 1:34, 39, and 41, when King Solomon was anointed, the origin of most later coronation ceremonies in those Christian countries which have kings or queens, the shōfār was blown. But by

2 Kings 11:14, when Jehoash was crowned, the chatsōtsᵊrōt had become the accepted instruments for such ceremonies.

When King David established the orchestra which would become that of the Temple once his son King Solomon had built it, the priests were assigned the chatsōtsᵊrōt (1 Chronicles 15:24). Levites sang and played the other instruments, presumably including the shōfār, translated as cornet in 1 Chronicles 15:28 (LXX σωφὲρ, *sōpher*, an obvious attempt at shōfār, and buccina in Latin). This is one of only three recorded biblical occasions when both types of trumpet were used together. Another is Ps. 98:6 where the Hebrew is simply בַּחֲצֹצְרוֹת וְקוֹל שׁוֹפָר (*bachatsōtsᵊrōt vᵊqōl shōfār*, with the chatsōtsᵊrōt and the voice of the shōfār), whereas the LXX, and following it the Vulgate, are much more complex: ἐν σάλπιγξιν ἐλαταῖς, καὶ φωνῇ σάλπιγγος κερατίνης, (*en salpinxin elatais kai phōnē salpingos keratinēs*) and *in tubis ductilibus et voce tubæ corneæ*, both meaning with hammered metal trumpets and trumpets of horn. The AV adheres more closely to the Hebrew: "with trumpet and sound of cornet".

Coverdale has a quite different interpretation in his Psalter, which survives in the Book of Common Prayer, translating it as "with trumpets also and shawms". The shawm was the leading loud woodwind instrument of the European Middle Ages and Renaissance, played with a double reed. It is still used over much of the world, sometimes as the chanter of a bagpipe, as in Scotland, and also mouthblown over much of southern Europe, all round the Mediterranean, and throughout the east, as far as China. In Europe it gave way to the oboe, a much quieter and more domesticated instrument, from the 1650s onwards. We shall meet the *chālīl* in the next chapter, which might be a shawm, though on general grounds of date this is unlikely. It is more probable that we can say that the shawm was unknown in most, at least, of the biblical period and that Coverdale was simply trying to make some distinction between buccina and tuba.

The third time both appear is 2 Chron. 15:14 where "they sware unto the Lord . . . with trumpets and cornets." The LXX uses salpinxi for the chatsōtsᵊrōt and κερατίναις (*keratinais*) for shōfᵊrōt, meaning, reasonably enough, something made of horn, and the Vulgate has tubæ and buccinæ.

The AV's cornet is spelled nowadays, and sometimes was then, cornett with double-*t* to distinguish it from the modern band instrument. It was used from the late fifteenth century through King

James's time, into the eighteenth century. It was made of wood, slightly curved, with fingerholes, and it was played with a very small trumpet mouthpiece, almost as small as that of the shōfār. Players therefore set the mouthpiece in the side of the lip, exactly as shōfār blowers do, where the lips are thin enough to control so small a mouthpiece. It was the great virtuoso instrument of the Renaissance and early Baroque, excelling in ornate divisions, as variations were then called.

It is in this passage in 2 Chronicles 5:12 to 14 that we get an idea of what music in the Temple may have been like. There were singers, who also had cymbals, "psalteries" (nᵊvalīm, probably another type of lyre, to which we shall return), and kinnōrōt, "and with them an hundred and twenty priests sounding with trumpets", trumpeting with trumpets in the Hebrew. In the next verse, "the trumpeters and singers were as one", but with only two or three notes available on either trumpet it seems unlikely that they were actually in unison, all on the same pitch, and one suspects that the sound must have been both deafening and probably discordant. They were, it seems from verses 13 and 14, actually within the Temple, rather than in one of the courtyards, and the shattering noise, not to mention the smell of blood from the sacrifices and the flies, must have meant that such occasions were rather different from any modern conception of religious observance.

Although they appear in the same verse, Hosea kept the two instruments some miles apart (5:8), blowing the shōfār in Gibeah and the chatsōtsᵊrāh in Ramah. The Talmud, though, goes into great discussions of how, according to Rabbi Hisda, the one substituted for the other after the destruction of the Temple, and, in discussing Mishnah Rosh haShanah 3:3 and 3:4, their joint use.[36]

As a postscript, it should perhaps be stressed that the broadcast of the Tutʿankhamūn trumpets in 1938, a recording of which has often been rebroadcast since, gave a very false impression of their potential, and thus of that of the chatsōtsᵊrōt. Bandsman Tappern, who blew them on that historic occasion, was not aware that the plain metal ring was the only mouthpiece that there had been in Pharaonic times, and he therefore put his normal trumpet mouthpiece into the end, wrapped with cloth to make a good fit. That is how he was able to play the "Grand March" from *Aida*, the *Posthorn Gallop*, and some other well-known calls. The original instruments, judging from the behavior of the reproductions illustrated here, and the reports of Hickmann and Kirby, produced even less range than the shōfār, a low note, somewhat vague and indistinct though it can be improved with practice, an excellent middle note, which can be inflected up and down a little, and a high third note, attainable with some effort.[37] The design of the mouthpiece is such that it seems unlikely that that third uppermost note was used; it requires enough pressure that some distortion of the material, and probably some damage to the player's lip, would result, and the low note is of limited use for military purposes. There is no doubt at all, from the iconography, that in ancient Egypt these were military instruments, normally used singly. Nor is there any doubt that Tutʿankhamūn's trumpets were not a pair—they are different in material, in size, and in decoration. Simply he had two trumpets just as he had two or more of many other wonderful things. It was only Moses who was commanded to make a pair. Their playing technique, with that of the shōfār, is discussed further in Chapter 8.

DEUTERONOMY

There are no references to instruments in Deuteronomy.

NOTES

1. N.B. that Hebrew is written from right to left; thus the first word here, *kol-tōfēs*, is the right-hand one of the three.

2. Werner Bachmann, *The Origins of Bowing and the development of bowed instruments up to the thirteenth century*, translated Norma Deane (London: Oxford University Press, 1969), 24 ff.

3. Subhi Anwar Rashid, *Mesopotamien*, Musikgeschichte in Bildern II/2 (Leipzig: Deutscher Verlag für Musik, 1984), 28–45.

4. Illustrated by Shlomo Hofman, *Music in the Talmud* (Tel-Aviv: Israel Music Institute, 1989), plate 6.

5. Simeon Bar Kochba led a revolt against the Romans and for a few years issued coins from Free Judea. Two of his coins are shown on plate 8.

6. Kenzō Hayashi, Shigeo Kishibe, Ryōichi Taki, and Sukehiro Shiba, for the Shōsōin Office, *Musical Instruments in the Shōsōin* (Tokyo: Nihon Keizai Shimbun Sha, 1967).

7. Laurence Picken, *Music from the Tang Court* (London: Oxford University Press, 1981).

8. *The Matthew Bible*, as it is now usually known, which was mostly translated by William Tyndale and partly by Miles Coverdale, and sponsored and edited by John Rogers [A. C. Partridge, *English Biblical Translation*, The Language Library, ed. Eric Partridge and Simeon Potter (London: André Deutsch, 1973), 69–70] but which was published as *The Byble, translated by Thomas Matthew* ([Antwerp?]: for R. Grafton and E. Whitchurch, 1537).

9. *Pirke de Rabbi Eliezer*, 31. The translation by Gerald Friedlander was published in various editions, initially London: Kegan Paul, Trench, Trubner & Co; New York: Bloch Publishing Company, 1916, and recently New York: Judaic Studies Library 6, Sepher-Hermon Press, 1981. The story is also recounted, along with other legends regarding the shōfār, by S. Y. Agnon in *Days of* Awe (New York: Schocken, 1948), 67; by Louis Ginzberg in *The Legends of the Jews*, translated Henrietta Szold, (Philadelphia; Jewish Publication Society of America, 1909; on CD-ROM Chicago: Davka Corp., 1998), Vol. 1, 283, and doubtless in other sources.

10. *Biblia the Bible, that is, the holy Scripture of the Olde and Newe Testament, tr. out of Douche and Lat.* ([Cologne?], 1535), reprinted as *The Coverdale Bible 1535* (Folkestone: Dawson, 1975).

11. Talmud, Sēder Mōʿēd, Rōsh HaShānāh 27b.

12. Herbert Danby has misinterpreted this in his translation of *The Mishnah* (Oxford: Oxford University Press, 1933), 191, Rosh ha-Shanah, 3.3 & 3.4, reading mouthpiece where the Hebrew text says mouth and thus reversing the sense of the text. Jacob Neusner, *The Mishnah: A New Translation* (New Haven: Yale University Press, 1988), 303–4, translates it correctly.

13. Neusner, *Mishnah*, 304, Rosh Hashanah 3:6.

14. Talmud, Rōsh HaShānāh 27b.

15. Talmud, Rōsh HaShānāh 26a–27a.

16. Mishnah, Sēder Mōʿēd, Taʿanīt 3:1–3:2; Neusner, *Mishnah*, 311.

17. Mishnah, Taʿanīt, 3:5; Neusner, *Mishnah*, 312; he cites, incorrectly (a misprint), 1 Kings 8:27.

18. Mishnah, Taʿanīt, 3:8; Neusner, *Mishnah*, 312.

19. Neusner, *Mishnah*, 289.

20. Mishnah, Sēder Mōʿēd, Sukkāh, 5:4.

21. Talmud, Sēder Kādāshīm, Zᵊvāchīm 88b. The translation is that of the Soncino edition. This sort of argument and contradiction is typical of talmudic discussion, as is its location, the debate on animal sacrifices. Almost any subject can turn up almost anywhere. *R.* is the normal talmudic abbreviation of *Rav* or Rabbi.

22. Flavius Josephus, *The Works of Josephus*, translated William Whiston (London: Printed by W. Bowyer for the Author to be sold by John Whiston,

Bookseller, 1736; reprinted Peabody, Mass.: Hendrickson, 1987), *The Antiquities of the Jews*, 99, book 3, chapter 12, paragraph 6 (291).

23. Christiane Ziegler, *Catalogue des instruments de musique égyptiens, Musée du Louvre, Département des antiquités égyptiennes* (Paris: Éditions de la Réunion des Musées Nationaux, 1979), 97, IDM 117 = N 909.

24. I. E. S. Edwards, *Treasures of Tutankhamun* (London: British Museum, 1972), exhibition catalogue, 45.

25. Details and sketches of its construction will be found in my brief article, "One of Tutankhamon's Trumpets," *Galpin Society Journal* XXIX (1976): 115–7, which was reprinted with the same title in *The Journal of Egyptian Archaeology* 64 (1978): 133–4.

26. The material is always given as "bronze or copper"; nobody is going to file a bit off to analyze it!

27. Hans Hickmann, *La Trompette dans l'Égypte Ancienne* (Cairo: Institut français d'archéologie orientale, 1946), 19. Note that none of the mouthpiece patterns drawn as fig. 25 there bears any resemblance to that of the bronze trumpet. See my sketch with the articles in *Galpin Society Journal* and *Journal of Egyptian Archaeology*, above.

28. Josephus, *Works*, 887, an appendix on Jewish weights and measures.

29. These were made for me by Peter Holmes long before the British Museum Exhibition took place and, because they were based on Hickmann's description, are slightly inaccurate in detail, especially in regard to the mouthpiece and the attachment of the bell. Unfortunately vol. VI of the Tutʿankhamūn's Tomb Series, Lisa Manniche, *Musical Instruments from the Tomb of Tutʿankhamūn* (Oxford: Griffith Institute, 1976), 7–13 and plates V–XII, adds little to our knowledge, save for its excellent photographs, and is certainly incorrect in some details of construction of the bronze trumpet.

30. While the psalms as a whole are traditionally attributed to King David, it is generally accepted that they vary quite widely in date and that the authorship of many is unknown; few can be dated to any specific period. Thus one cannot be any more precise than "some centuries later".

31. The Quadrilingual Index here may be found useful for checking such details. The author has found it invaluable and therefore reprints it for others to use.

32. Luther was a Hebrew scholar (Partridge, *English Biblical Translation*, 35), but then according to the same source so was Tyndale, who normally used trompette for either, though occasionally distinguishing between the two.

33. Renato Meucci, "Roman Military Instruments and the *Lituus*," *Galpin Society Journal* XLII (1989): 85–97, 86, citing and restoring Vegetius, *Epitoma rei militaris*, 3,5.

34. Charlton T. Lewis and Charles Short, *A Latin Dictionary* (Oxford: Clarendon Press, 1879), s.v. *bucina*.

35. The word used for "blow an alarm" is from the same root as *tᵊrūʿāh*.

36. Talmud, Sēder Mōʿēd, Shabbāt 36a for the first and Mōʿēd, Rōsh haShānāh 27a for the second.

37. Hickmann, *La Trompette*, ch. 7; Percival Kirby, "The Trumpets of Tut-ankh-amen and their Successors," *Journal of the Royal Anthropological Institute* 77 (1947): 33–45; Percival Kirby, "Ancient Egyptian Trumpets," *Music Book: Volume VII of Hinrichsen's Musical Yearbook* (London: Hinrichsen, 1952), 250–5. N.B. that Kirby's third trumpet in the Louvre is that identified above as part of an incense stand.

Chapter 3

The Narrative or Historical Books

JOSHUA

The only references in Joshua are those in chapter 6 to the shōfᵊrōt which brought down the walls of Jericho. These were covered in the previous chapter.

JUDGES

In chapter 5, Deborah's song celebrates the defeat of Sisera. In it comes a passing reference to an instrument which was unrecognized by the AV translators. In verse 16 Deborah asks the tribe of Reuben "Why abodest thou among the sheepfolds, to hear the bleatings of the flocks?" This is another of those passages where it is essential to check the original text, in the Hebrew שְׁרִקוֹת עֲדָרִים, *shᵊriqot 'adaraym* and Greek συρισμοῦ ἀγελῶν, *surismou agelōn*. Here it is not the sheep which are bleating but the shepherds who are whistling or piping for the flocks. שרק (*shāraq*) is a verb meaning whistle or hiss, and the Greek συρισμοῦ is "a late and poor form of συριγμός, *syrigmos*," meaning also to pipe, whistle, or hiss, and itself related to the syrinx or panpipe.[1] The Latin is *sibilos*, again whistling or hissing, the origin of our 'sibilant'. Hebrew *shāraq* we shall meet again in Chapter 5 with Daniel and Zechariah, again with this meaning of whistling or piping. Surely this is another example, to add to David looking after his flocks in 1 Samuel 16:16, to which we referred in the last chapter, of the singing cowboy or shepherd. A complication is that there is no certainty that Hebrew *mishpᵊtayim* means sheepfolds. The only other time it appears in the Bible is in Genesis 49:14, where it is translated as two burdens. Here it is the presence of the flocks which has influenced the translation, for a common place for flocks is in sheepfolds. There are in Hebrew two letters sounded as *t*—had it been the other one here, it would have meant "between two judgements", and there is here a strong suspicion of a pun, with Deborah accusing the Reubenites of being unable to make up their minds whether to come and help or not.

What was the instrument? Presumably some form of flute or whistle, perhaps even the panpipe, though we have no archeological evidence for that instrument in ancient Israel.

Gideon's attack on the Midianites in Judges 6 and 7 was discussed in Chapter 2. In Judges 11 we have the tragedy of Jephthah's daughter. This is a curious story, not only because of its reminiscences of the Greek legend of Iphigenia, but also because his daughter, whose name we never learn, asks for a two-month suspension of her death so that she "may go up and down the mountain . . . I and my fellows". This, like the sacrifice itself, has strong pagan resonances, as has the custom (verses 39–40) that "the daughters of Israel went yearly to lament" her fate. It sounds very much as though she became the center of a shrine cult, and the clay figurines illustrated in plate 4 may have been part of such a cult.

RUTH

The book of Ruth is one of our disappointments. Despite two occasions where music and instruments might well have been involved, there is no mention of them at all. In Ruth 3:2–7, it is clear that Boaz and his workers are celebrating the end of the harvest, an occasion often marked with a barn-dance or similar festivity, but although Boaz's "heart was merry", no such celebration is mentioned. We know from other cultures of the musical use of at least one harvest implement for such an occasion. In the Museum of Welsh Life there are three winnowing trays, each a roughly oval wooden frame covered with a skin to produce an object apparently identical with a frame drum or tōf.[2] The wheat or barley is threshed, beating the grain from the ears and straw, and it is poured by handfuls into a tray. This is moved up and down to toss the grain so that the wind blows away the lighter chaff, all the loose bits of ears and straw still mixed with the grains, leaving just the heavier grains behind. At my suggestion, evidence was sought through the Museum's records, and it was found that these Welsh trays had indeed been used as drums for end-of-harvest dancing.[3] Further investigation by a colleague in Dublin showed that similar trays had been the origin of the Irish bodhran, now a drum popular with folk musicians worldwide.[4] It would have been very probable that Boaz, who "winnoweth barley to night in the threshingfloor" (3:2) would have been using something very like what the Welsh Museum calls a semmet to separate the grain from the chaff, and also very probable that, like similar trays which are used for winnowing in many areas, he would have used them as drums also.

We are deprived, too, of a possible musical occasion when in the next chapter he and Ruth are married, for we are not told of any musical accompaniment, any more than we are at the marriage at Cana (John 2:1–11). There is wine at Cana, enough of a feast to have a ruler (verse 9), but alas no music or dance, despite these being almost universally associated with weddings throughout that part of the world, a particular vexation for, as we shall see, we have much less information about musical instruments in the New Testament than in the Old.

FIRST BOOK OF SAMUEL

In 1 Samuel 10:5 we meet two of our more problematic instruments. After Samuel has anointed Saul, he tells him that he will meet "a company of prophets coming down from the high place with a psaltery, a tabret, and a pipe, and a harp before them", נֵבֶל וְתֹף וְחָלִיל וְכִנּוֹר, with a *nēvel vᵊtōf vᵊchālīl vᵊchinnōr* (the *vᵊ* means and). Both kinnōr and tōf we have already encountered. *Nēvel*, translated as psaltery, and *chālīl* as pipe are new to us, and clearly they were instruments which were new to the Israelites at this period, according to the AV margin around 1100 B.C. This is also the first time we encounter ecstatic prophecy. The nēvel appears here, in Chronicles, and Nehemiah, and also in a number of psalms, almost always as psaltery, and certainly wherever psaltery appears in the AV, it is always as a translation of nēvel. However, in Isaiah 5:12 and 14:11

and in Amos 5:23 and 6:5 it is translated as a viol There is good reason to say that the nēvel was not a psaltery and, as we shall see in chapter 5, we can be absolutely certain that it was not a viol.

A Mystery, the Nēvel

So, what was the nēvel? We have to admit that we cannot be certain. Earlier scholars were sure that it might have been one of those small bow harps which one sees Egyptian musicians carrying on one shoulder as they play, and which survive today in Central Africa and Uganda (plate 14), but there is no evidence at all for the use of any form of harp in biblical Israel. Current thought is that it might have been a different form of lyre from the kinnōr. Certainly the Greeks had their concert lyre, *kithara*, which one equates with kinnōr, as the Septuagint and Vulgate often do, and they also had the lighter *chelys* or *lyra*, whose body was often made from a tortoiseshell and which was used for less formal music such as songs around the supper room. Again such instruments survive in Africa, with the large beganna in Ethiopia (plate 1) and also the lighter *kissar* over much of

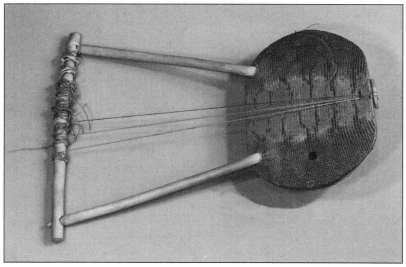

Plate 7
Small lyre, kissar, from Kenya. Montagu Collection II 32b.

East Africa (plate 7). Various types of lyre appear throughout the biblical area, but we cannot be certain whether they were differentiated by name, for no illustrations have captions attached.

We can say, however, as we did in Chapter 2, that the psaltery did not exist in the ancient world. It was widely used in the European Middle Ages as a flat wooden box with wire strings running horizontally across its surface and plucked with the fingers or a pair of quill plectra. In the thirteenth century the *qanun*, which is still used in Turkey and Egypt, came into Europe from the east and its name qanun became *canon* in medieval Latin. It seems to have acquired the name psaultrie or sawtrey by guesswork from the biblical references to *psalterium*, which were already well-known from Jerome's Latin.

Psalterium derives from the Greek *psaltērion*, so what was that? Here again the answers are vague. The word means something plucked with the fingers and, although it was applied to the harp, an instrument which was rarely used in Greece, from the late fourth century B.C. onwards, this does not help us within the biblical area.[5]

More to the point, the Septuagint uses the word psaltērion very selectively. In Genesis 4:21, Job 21:12, and Ezekiel 26:13 it is a translation of kinnōr. There they may have been using it in its literal sense of something that was plucked, without any specific implications, particularly so in Isaiah 38:20 and Ezekiel 33:32, because no instrument name appears there in the Hebrew. In the Psalms, Isaiah, Nehemiah, and Daniel psaltērion is always a translation of nēvel, but all the other translations of nēvel into Greek are as νάβλα, nabla. This may be a matter of different translators using different terms. The later narrative books, Samuel, Kings, and Chronicles have nabla; an exception is Daniel, but one would expect Greek psaltērion to be used for Aramaicized-Greek *pᵊsantērīn*. All the poetical and prophetical books have psaltērion. This distinction does suggest a division of labor, and the best evidence for this is the repetition of Nehemiah 12:27 in 2 Chronicles 5:12. The story is the same, the Hebrew is the same, nēvel in each case, but the Greek is psaltērion in Nehemiah and nabla in Chronicles.

The equation of nēvel and nabla may be by correspondence: the three letters of nēvel, נבל, nūn-vēt-lamed, are the same as νβλ, nu-beta-lamda, the three consonants of nabla. One has to remember also that Hebrew is a consonantal language—the vowels were not written until a very late period—and also that vēt and bēt are the same letter, ב and בּ, the latter sounding *b* at the beginning of a sylla-

ble and the former *v* within a syllable or even at the beginning after a
strong vowel. Without vowels or other points the two words are
identical.

And perhaps the nēvel really was a nabla. So what was a nabla?
Here, as so often, we have a problem. According to Martin West it
was a Phoenician "harp" (more probably a lyre—there is no evidence for harps in the Phoenician area either) that arrived in Greece
about the end of the fourth century B.C., far too late for any of the
references in the Bible, but in good time for the Septuagint.[6] Of
course, this does not tell us how much older it was in Phoenicia, and
so it remains possible that it was the same as the nēvel—the Phoenicians were neighbors of the Israelites in Lebanon and it was from
them that Solomon got his skilled workmen and much of the material to build the Temple.

Let us for a moment accept the supposition that the Israelites did
acquire the nabla from the Phoenicians in the eleventh century B.C.
They would have taken the n-b-l of its name and inserted whatever
vowels were convenient between them, just as they inserted the
appropriate vowels between the *tāf* of Torah, the *nūn* of Nᵊvī'īm, and
the *kaf* of Kᵊtūvīm to form Tanach. This is how Hebrew works.

Bathja Bayer has gone into the problems of the *nēvel* in considerable detail, suggesting quite convincingly that it was a different type
of lyre.[7] She quotes two somewhat rudimentary descriptions from
the end of the biblical period. The first comes from Flavius Josephus,
who was born Joseph ben Mattitiyahu, the son of a priest, in A.D. 37.
Initially he led Jewish troops in the revolt against the Romans, but
once it became clear that the Romans were going to be the winning
side, even before the destruction of Jerusalem, he decided to join the
erstwhile enemy. He became a protégé of Titus, the Roman general
and conqueror of Judea, who later became emperor.[8] He produced
two major books, in addition to his life story and other shorter
works, one *The Jewish Wars* and the other *The Antiquities of the Jews*.
Both date from the closing years of the first century A.D., between
A.D. 73, when the fortress of Masada fell and the Romans finally
conquered Judea, and 97 to 100, between which dates Josephus died.
He wrote, in the *Antiquities*, that King David made musical instruments and that their forms were: the κινύρα δέκα χορδαῖς ἐξημμένη
τύπτεται πλήκτρῳ—kinyra deka chordais exēmmenē typtetai plēktrō:
"the *kinyra* [which we assume to have been the kinnōr] had ten
strings fixed on it (which were) struck with a plectrum".[9] He goes on:

νάβλα δώδεκα φθόγγους ἔχουσα τοῖς δακτύλοις κρούεται—*nabla
dōdeka phthongous echousa tois daktylois krouetai*: "the *nabla* [which we
assume to have meant the nēvel] had twelve strings played with the
fingers". Finally in this paragraph, for his last description of biblical instruments, Josephus says that the κύμβαλά τε ἦν πλατέα καὶ μεγάλα
χάλκεα—*kymbala te ēn platea kai megala chalkea*: "the cymbals were
large plates of bronze", something with which nobody would argue.

Dr. Bayer's second description is from the Mishnah, where Rabbi
Joshua ben Hananyah says that a ram's voice, when dead, is seven-
fold, its two horns for trumpets, two of its leg-bones for pipes, its
skin for a drum, its large intestines for the nēvel, and its small intestines for the kinnōr.[10] Ben Hananyah had been a singer in the Temple
in his youth, when these instruments were still in use.

If we may assume that the nabla, the word that both Josephus and
the Septuagint use, was the same as the nēvel, and it would be very
difficult to argue otherwise, then we should also accept Bayer's various references from Greek literature to the nabla which give a continuous sequence from the biblical references, through the Septuagint
and the Apocrypha, to Josephus's time and thence to the Mishnah.[11]
She is suggesting, on the basis of these various texts, that the nēvel is
a larger, or at least lower-pitched instrument than the kinnōr, with
thicker strings (hence the use of the large intestines) and a lower tes-
situra. It does seem probable that she is correct, and that it was
because the nēvel had thicker strings that it responded better to the
fingers than to a plectrum, as Josephus tells us. She reminds us also
of something on which Joachim Braun lays rather more stress, that
the other use of the word nēvel, to mean a leather bag, sack, or wine-
skin, seems also to appear at much the same period as does the musical one.[12] Both she and Braun survey illustrations of different types
of lyre on the coins of the Bar Kochba Rebellion to establish which
might be the nēvel and which the kinnōr. As well as views of the
Temple (merely a somewhat indeterminate portico), his coins show
chatsōts³rōt, the temple trumpets, and two very distinct types of lyre
(plate 8). One is a somewhat squat and clumsy looking instrument
which does indeed look as though its body might have started life as
a leather bag or wine-skin, and the other is a much more elegant
instrument.[13] The assumption is that the squatter, with its sack-like
body, is the nēvel and the longer and more elegant the kinnōr. This
may well have been so, but it is still difficult to be certain, and it is
still only an assumption even that both nēvel and kinnōr were differ-

Plate 8
Coins from the Bar Kochba Revolt, showing what we assume to be the kinnōr,
the longer instrument, and the nēvel, the squatter, c. A.D. 130.
Israel Antiquities Authority.

ent forms of lyre. As Dr. Bayer says in conclusion, "The problem of the *nebel* remains open", something with which one can only agree.[14]

A further complication arises in three of the psalms, 33:2, 144:9, and 92:3. In the first we have AV: "Praise the LORD with harp; sing unto him with the psaltery *and* an instrument of ten strings", *bᵊkinnōr; bᵊnēvel ʿāsōr zammᵊrū-lō*, more literally praise the Lord with kinnōr; with nēvel ʿāsōr make music to him. This is clarified in the Targum by *bᵊchinara bᵊnivla daʾasartey nimin*—with kinnōr with nēvel ten-stringed. Ps. 144:9 is the same, save that there is no kinnōr, just the nēvel ʿāsōr—this is the only time in the Bible that there is any suggestion that any form of nēvel might play by itself rather than with other instruments. In both psalms the AV has split the nēvel ʿāsōr into two separate instruments, "the psaltery, *and* an instrument of ten strings".[15] They were perhaps encouraged to do so by Ps. 92, where the Hebrew also separates them, *ʿalēy ʿāsōr vaʿalēy nāvel*, "upon the ʿāsōr and upon the nēvel". The Targum, somewhat unhelpfully reverses matters in this psalm and agrees with Josephus, with whom it is more or less contemporary, by inserting the kinnōr and giving it the ten strings: *al pum kinnara daʿasretey nimin vᵊal pum nivla*, "with the voice of the kinnōr ten-stringed and the voice of the nēvel". This is still only two instruments, if confused, but the AV adds to the confusion by turning it into three instruments, for it translates the passage as "upon an instrument of ten strings and upon the psaltery; and upon the harp."

None of this helps us in the identification of the nēvel and complicates the next question, which is: were there two types of nēvel, the ordinary one which turns up in many places, and the ten-stringed one which appears only in Ps.33 and 144? And if so, do we have both appearing together, once and once only, in Psalm 92? Or was the ʿāsōr something different, in which case what was it?

Does this contradict what we have accepted above from Josephus and other evidence? Bathja Bayer stresses that ʿāsōr in this sense appears only these three times in the Bible, only in these three Psalms, 33, 92 and 144, always with nēvel, and that there is no evidence that it does in fact mean ten-stringed.[16] It appears otherwise in the Bible as בְּעָשׂוֹר *beʿāsōr*, usually as the phrase on the tenth day of the month. The ordinal meaning ten has been assumed from this even though the normal spelling for ten is different: עֶשֶׂר, *ʿeser*, or sometimes with objects of which there are ten עָשָׂר, *ʿāsār*, or עֶשְׂרֵה, *ʿesrēh*, which is usually the compound -teen, as in *shᵊmōnēh-ʿesrēh*, eighteen.

So we have, it would seem, three possibilities:

1. that the nēvel in the Psalmist's time did have ten strings –
2. that ʿāsōr means something quite different but we do not know what—
3. and that while the nēvel did in the Psalmist's time have ten strings, by the first century A.D., when both Josephus and the Targumist were writing, it had acquired two more strings and now had twelve, while the kinnōr had ten. This last seems perhaps the likeliest, for there are many other instances we could adduce for instruments changing in this way. Our own lute, when Tinctoris described it around 1480, had five or occasionally six strings or courses.[17] Within fifty years or less it always had six, and by John Dowland's time, around 1600 in the great lute-song period of the late Renaissance and early Baroque, it had up to nine or ten and, when extended, twelve or fourteen. If the lute could change as much as that in little over a century, surely the nēvel could do so over more than a millennium.

There is a well-known Talmudic expression for cases which remain insoluble: *tēykū*, "it remains standing", and according to legend these will be resolved only when the prophet Elijah returns. It is perhaps the logical term to use here, for Elijah lived in the time when both nēvel and ʿāsōr were in common use and he, at least, may have known what they were.

Meanwhile here we shall follow the opinion of the leading scholar of our time in this area of biblical instruments, Dr. Bathja Bayer, and take kinnōr for the more elegant lyre and nēvel for the other, squatter, sack-like lyre—both of them lyres and neither of them a harp, neither of them a psaltery.[18] Relevant playing technology will be described in Chapter 8.

The Pipe, Chālīl

The other instrument new to us in this reference, 1 Sam.10:5, the *chālīl*, seems, as here, to have been an ecstatic instrument. It was used also for King Solomon's coronation as in 1 Kings 1:40. The word means pierced or hollow, confirming that it was a pipe of some sort, as the AV translates it, and its use in these two examples suggests that it was a fairly loud one. It is therefore likely to have been reed-blown.

It might have been a shawm, a double-reed instrument of conical bore, producing a very loud sound, but this seems unlikely because the earliest representation of a conical shawm so far discovered is on a pot from the Faliscans, who were one of the Etruscan tribes of the early fifth century B.C., five or six hundred years later than the period we are discussing.[19] From what one knows of the instruments of that period it is more probable that it was an instrument of the *aulos* type, which is the Greek word the LXX uses to translate it. Both the Greek $\alpha\dot{v}\lambda o\varsigma$, and the Roman *tibia*, the word always used for it in the Vulgate, were a pair of pipes held together in the mouth. The pipes were cylindrically bored, thus producing a lower pitch than might otherwise be assumed from their length. The reeds were normally double-reeds, rather larger than our bassoon reeds. The pipes were held divergently, in a narrow V, one with each hand, as may be seen on many Greek pots and with the pottery figurine on plate 4 here. They were often played by dancers in Greece, frequently by girls who appear to be less than respectable, but they were also used by men, including soldiers, and also on formal occasions similar to King Solomon's crowning. The *monaulos*, the single aulos, was also used in the ancient world, and that instrument survives today, as a single cylindrical pipe still played with a large double reed. In

Turkey it is called the *mey*, in Iran the *balaban*, in Iraq the *karnata* or *pik* among the Kurds, in many of the Central Asian republics as *duduk* and *balaban*, in China the *guan*, in Korea the *p'iri*, and in Japan the *hichiriki*, all the way down the Silk Route from Europe to Asia, a trade route already well-traveled long before the end of the biblical period. A small selection, each with their very large double reeds, is shown in plate 9.

A further possibility is that the chālīl might have been the well-known instrument with two parallel single-reed pipes called *zummāra* in some Arabic languages and shown on plate 10. Hickmann illustrates a wall-painting of a player from the Fifth Dynasty in Egypt's Old Kingdom, around 2500 B.C., and refers to another from the Fourth Dynasty a century or two earlier.[20] Examples have been

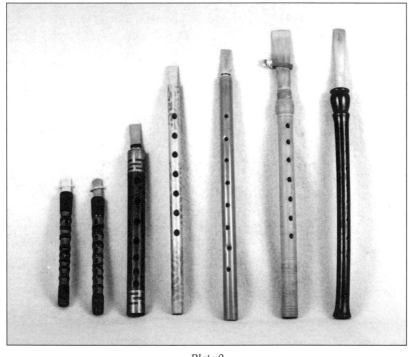

Plate 9
Cylindrical shawms probably similar to the chālīl (L to R) hichiriki from Japan (X 60 & I 194), guan from China (I 196, VII 166b, & VIII 176), balaban from Iran (VIII 40), and mey from Turkey (VI 118). Montagu Collection.

found archeologically in Egypt from New Kingdom times, which includes the period when the Israelites were in Egypt. Two of these ancient pairs are illustrated by Hickmann, with two modern examples beside them, for they are still endemic throughout the Near and Middle East.[21] Almost anywhere from Tangier to the Euphrates little boys will appear from nowhere trying to sell them to unwary tourists.

Evidence that the divergently-held pairs of double-reed cylindrically-bored pipes are the most likely is that bronze and clay portrayals of players of these instruments have been found in Israel from almost precisely the correct dates. Joachim Braun describes and illustrates several from 1200–1000 B.C. onwards and one appears here in plate 4.[22] The AV margin gives 1095 B.C. for this chapter in

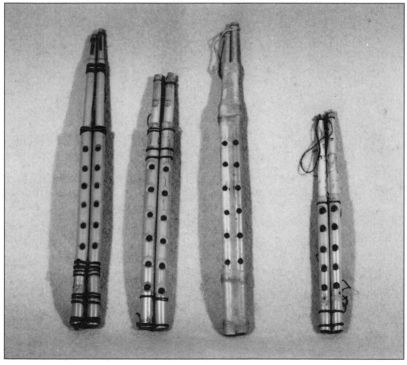

Plate 10
Geminate double-pipes, zummāra, (L to R) from unknown area in the Near East
(XII 134), and Israel (IV 226, VIII 122, & I 150c). Montagu Collection.

Samuel, but a convenient, if approximate and fictional, mnemonic is that around 1000 B.C. King David could have met Ulysses (Odysseus) on his way to or from Troy, a potential coincidence, with an easily-remembered date, of which more than one author has made fictional use.

All that we can say for certain is that the chālīl was a pipe of some sort and a fairly loud one. We shall discuss the playing technique of the aulos in more detail in chapter 8.

When Saul blew the trumpet throughout all the land, in 1 Samuel 13:3, it was, as one would expect, the shōfār.

The other references in the latter part of 1 Samuel, from 16:16–23 and through 19:9, are to the search for one who can play with his hand to soothe King Saul, and thus the introduction to the royal court of David the son of Jesse to which we have referred above; his instrument "played with the hand" is always the kinnōr, which we discussed in connexion with Genesis 4:21.

Another Mystery, Māchōl

In 1 Samuel 18:6 we meet yet a third problem instrument, if indeed it is an instrument at all. After David had slain Goliath "the women came out of all the cities of Israel, singing and dancing" (we shall continue the verse below). The words translated singing and dancing are *lāshīr vᵊhamᵊchōlōt*, literally to sing and the *māchōls*. In several other references the word māchōl is coupled with tōf, which we already know to be a drum (see above under Exodus 15:20). Two examples are the story of Jephthah's daughter (Judges 11:34) and Psalm 150, and tōf also appears here in Samuel in the plural, *tuppīm*, a few words later. When discussing tōf in Exodus we left the translation of māchōl as dance, but Psalm 150, as we shall see below, is a list of instruments on which one praises the Lord. If māchōl were not an instrument, it would be the only implement of praise listed there which was not. An instrument which one might expect to find in the psalm is chālīl and it may be that māchōl is there in its place, especially as both share a common linguistic heritage in the syllable *chāl/chōl*, meaning hollow or pierced.

Whenever māchōl appears in the Bible, both LXX and Vulgate usually translate it as *choros*, which in the Greek and Roman theater meant dancers rather than singers, and the AV has followed suit. This is a possible interpretation, for many of the dances of that part of the world are round dances, rather more often than line dances, square dances, or pair dances. People dancing in a ring make a pattern which could be regarded as hollow.

It is even possible that we have to consider both interpretations. We are dealing with a span of centuries and maybe at one time the word meant a dance and at another an instrument! Examples such as Psalm 150 do suggest that māchōl was an instrument, whereas 2 Samuel 6:14 and 16, where David "danced with all his might" and is "leaping and dancing" do, quite strongly, suggest that it meant dance. Others could be interpreted either way, such as the two references, 1 Sam. 21:11 and 29:5, to "singing in dances". These refer back to 18:6 and again leave us questioning the meaning of māchōl, for the Hebrew, *ya'anū bamᵉcholot* might be better 'singing with māchōls'. It could, of course, mean singing as they danced as well as singing with pipes—as so often we are left uncertain. Both the Latin and Greek, incidentally, make it clear that it is women who are doing it, as in 18:6.

If it were an instrument, what was it? While the drum is very frequently used to accompany the dance, it is also very commonly coupled with a pipe. The European medieval pipe and tabor, still surviving in parts of France and Spain, and in South America, as a one-man dance band, is by no means the only example of such a combination. Many commentators have suggested that in at least some contexts in the Bible, a pipe of some sort might be a more likely translation than a dance. As just two examples, Stainer points out how much more beautiful Lamentations 5:15 would be if mᵉchōlēnū were our pipes rather than our dances and that what Moses heard when he came down the mountain with the tablets of the Law in his hand (Exodus 32:19) was pipes not dances. He is sure *ha'ēgel ūmᵉchōlōt*, calf and māchōls, was piping round the calf.[23] The one problem with that reference is that Moses *vayar* as he approached the camp, which means "and he saw," not "and he heard." But it does remain a possibility, of which we should take account, that at some times and in some contexts, māchōl could be a pipe. What sort of pipe we cannot tell. Perhaps a duct flute such as our tin- or penny-whistle—bone flutes of that type have been found—perhaps a reed-blown pipe such as the chālīl. All that we can say is it would have been a tube of some sort because of the root meaning, hollow.

There were many attempts in the Middle Ages to establish what all the biblical instruments were. Many of these were based on the illustrations to a letter which Jerome was purported to have sent to Dardanus, but the letter is a forgery, dating some centuries after Jerome's time, probably around A.D. 800.[24] Nevertheless, from the ninth century until well into the eighteenth century, one music historian after another reprinted these pictures as factual illustrations of the instruments of the Bible. Several of the pictures are improbable, and that of the choros is one of the odder (plate 11). It is shown as a blend of trumpet and doughnut or bagel, an oval or sometimes circular ring, with a projection for a mouthpiece at one end and a trumpet bell projecting at the other, with the air column presumably going both left-about and right-about round the ring.

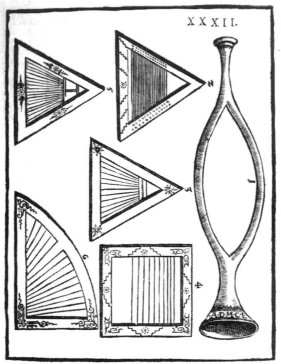

1. Ghorus. 2. Pſalterium; 3. 4. Pſalterium Decahordan. 5. 6. Cithara Hieronimi

Plate 11
Biblical instruments illustrating the Pseudo-Jerome Epistle to Dardanus.
The right-hand double-tube "trumpet" purports to be the Choros. From Michael
Praetorius, Syntagma Musicum II: De Organographia, Wolfenbüttel, 1619.

A Rattle? Shalishīm

Returning now to the rest of 1 Samuel 18:6, "the women came out of all the cities of Israel singing and dancing to meet King Saul [to meet David in LXX] with tabrets [tuppīm], with joy [*simchā*, a word used today also for any party or other joyous occasion], and with instruments of musick [*shalishīm*]". Shalishīm, used in this sense, appears nowhere else in the Bible, so one should not blame King James's translators for evading the issue. Neither LXX nor Vulgate do any better. LXX has κυμβάλοις, cymbals, and the Vulgate has *sistris*, the plural of sistrum, an Egyptian rattle with bars in a hooped frame which either slid to and fro, striking the frame as they did so, or had discs or small bars, rattling as they slid along the rods. The Vulgate may be nearer the truth, for the root meaning of shalishīm might be threes, and some sistra had three bars. However, Bathja Bayer stresses that only one fragment of a sistrum, the handle, has been found in biblical Israel.[25] It is five or six centuries earlier than this period, clearly Egyptian, decorated with the head of Hathor, an Egyptian deity and thus with no Israelite relevance.[26] More recently Bayer has suggested that the women might have been dancing in threes.[27] However, it seems much more probable that shalishīm has no connexion with three and that the word is onomatopoeic, meaning something which goes *shlshlsh*, and this again might suggest some form of rattle. As we shall see below, there is good archeological evidence for pottery rattles and we have already encountered in the previous chapter small jingles of some sort on the High Priest's robe. Alfred Sendrey says that the Talmud equates these with shalishīm, but this is due to misreading *shᵊlōshīm vᵊshishāh*, the thirty-six bells on each side of the robe, as the name of the bells, which is actually *zaggin* in Aramaic.[28] The Targum translates shalishīm into Aramaic as *tseltsᵊlin*. The verb *tsiltsel* has the primary meaning to ring clearly or to clap, and clearly relates to *tsil*, a word which, as we shall find below, undoubtedly means cymbal.[29]

SECOND BOOK OF SAMUEL

In 2:28 Joab's trumpet was the shōfār, the context suggesting that this was as much a ritual use as a signal or military one.

We have already discussed some of the instruments in the story in 2 Samuel 6, which tells how David brought the Ark of the Covenant from Gibeah to Jerusalem. Before returning to it, to examine the rest of them, it is worth trying to see it in its context, for it is a story that resonates down the centuries, to such an extent that it is affecting present-day politics. David brought the Ark to Jerusalem, to his city on the slopes of the mountain towards the Ophel, just to the south of what is now the Old City. The summit of that mountain was in legend where Abraham had nearly sacrificed his son, Isaac (Gen. 22), and where Jacob had seen the angels ascending and descending the ladder (Gen. 28:17—"this is none other but the house of God"—and 28:22).[30] There Solomon, David's son, was later to build the first Temple, which was destroyed by the Babylonians. It was rebuilt by Nehemiah on the return from the Exile and, after the dilapidation of centuries, rebuilt again by King Herod on the same site. Herod first constructed a tremendous platform, many acres in size, to level up much of the mountain's slopes, a great plateau which now forms almost the whole eastern side of the Old City. This platform is known today as the Temple Mount, Har haBayit in Hebrew, and as Haram esh-Sharif in Arabic. It was in Herod's Temple that Jesus when yet a child debated with the rabbis (Luke 2:46), and it was from that Temple that he drove the dealers and money-changers (Matthew 21:12 and Mark 11:15). It lay waste for many centuries, because the Romans destroyed it utterly in A.D. 70, only a few years after the Crucifixion. Once more in legend, for the place is not named in the Koran any more than it is in Genesis, it became the site whence the Prophet Mohammed journeyed to heaven. The hoofprint of his horse can be seen to this day on that same rock on which Isaac had lain, bound for sacrifice. On that same site, to shelter and honor that rock, Caliph Abd al-Malik built the Dome of the Rock around A.D. 700, and Caliph al-Wahid some ten years later built the El Aqsa mosque further along the platform, on its southern edge, overlooking the remains of David's city. All three of the great monotheistic religions thus have equal claim to regard it as sacred, and one day may share it in peace.

David's Band

The AV says, 2 Samuel 6:5, "And David and all the house of Israel played before the Lord on all manner of instruments made of fir wood, even on harps, and on psalteries, and on timbrels, and on cornets, and on cymbals." The first question is what is meant by "all

manner of instruments made of fir wood", *bᵊchol 'atsēy vᵊrōshīm*.
Scholars debate whether *bᵊrōsh*, בְּרוֹשׁ, means a fir or a cypress, with
cypress coming out slightly ahead. Whichever it was, and they are
not so different from the instrument maker's point of view, we still
have the difficulty that not all the following list of instruments could
be made of either of those woods. The standard dictionary of biblical
Hebrew, universally known as the BDB, points to the parallel text
in 1 Chronicles 13:8, where the Hebrew is *bᵊchol 'ōz ūvᵊshīrīm*, "with
all their might, and with singing" (AV).³¹ They do not go so far, because to do so would be heretical in Orthodox Jewish circles, as to
say that a scribe got things muddled when writing 2 Samuel 6:5, but
it is just the sort of slip that is very easily made. To confuse עץ, *'ats*,
woods, with עז, *'ōz*, strength, is not difficult. Remember that the original text had no written vowels and if one were muttering to oneself
as one wrote, the sounds *ts* and *z* are not so different. And ברשם,
vᵊrōshīm, only differs from בשרם, vᵊshīrīm, by reversing two letters.
The other letters in each word are so-called vowel letters added,
probably at a later stage, to help readers by indicating the correct
vowels. If one were to admit that possibility, it would make things
very much easier, not only here but for two other instruments named
in this verse.

The Vulgate is much the same as the Hebrew and the AV, save that
it just says made of all woods in Samuel, *in omnibus lignis fabrefactis*,
and in Chronicles *omni virtute*, with all strength.³² The Septuagint,
has an entirely different version of the passage. It has, for Samuel,
παίζοντες ἐνώπιον Κυρίου ἐν ὀργάνοις ἡρμοσμένοις ἐν ἰσχύϊ, καὶ ἐν
ᾠδαῖς, *paizontes enōpion Kyriou en organois hērmosmenois en ischui, kai
en ōdais*, were playing before the Lord on well-tuned instruments
with strength, and with songs. One wonders what Hebrew word the
LXX were translating as ἡρμοσμένοις, which comes from the same
root as our harmony, and thus means well-tuned, but it suggests that
the LXX were working from a different Samuel text from ours, one
closer to that of Chronicles. This is but one of the number of indica-
tions that the LXX had access to a somewhat different Hebrew text
from that which has come down to us, and this is why it is important
to consult it. The LXX text in Chronicles is much closer to the
Hebrew, with ἐν πάσῃ δυνάμει, *en pasē dynamei*, with all strength—
dynamei is the origin of our dynamic. Unfortunately, the Targum cannot help for there is none to Chronicles, and that to Samuel is the
same as the Hebrew.

The full list of instruments, all plurals, in 2 Samuel 6:5 is in Hebrew kinnōrot, nevālīm, tuppīm, mᵊnaʿanᵊʿīm, and tseltsᵊlīm, in Greek ōdais, kinyrais, nablais, tympanois, kymbalois, aulois, in Latin citharis, lyris, tympanis, sistris, cymbalis, and in English harps, psalteries, timbrels, cornets, cymbals. Of these, the LXX is the only one to have six terms and the only one to mention ōdais, songs (as in our odes). Kinnōr, kynura, cithara, harp, is a normal sequence of translation, but nēvel, nabla, lyra, psaltery is less usual. Why did Jerome suddenly go for lyra instead of psalterium? Tōf, tympanon, tympanum, timbrel, is a familiar sequence and again presents no difficulty. The next, however, raises considerable problems: mᵊnaʿanᵊʿīm, aulos, sistrum, cornet.

Cornets here is not a translation of shōfār as previously, but of mᵊnaʿanᵊʿīm. This is the only time in the whole Bible that the word is used. The root from which the word is thought perhaps to stem, though this also is uncertain, means tremble, vibrate, or sometimes shake.[33] If this derivation is correct, then we presumably have some sort of rattle. The Targum is unhelpful, using a word which means square blocks, and LXX substitutes cymbals, the next word in the Hebrew, and adds auloi or pipes. The probable answer is a rattle, though as we have just seen the sistrum, which the Vulgate uses for it, is improbable. Some other sort of rattle, of which there is a multitude in every culture, is more likely. Bathja Bayer makes a strong and acceptable case in favor of vessel rattles of pottery, to which we shall return in more detail in chapter 8.[34]

The last instrument in this verse, cymbals in English, Latin, and Greek, is certainly correct as a translation of Hebrew tseltsᵊlīm. *Zil* is to this day the Turkish, Armenian, and Arabic word for cymbal. The name of Zildjian, the firm that makes the world's best orchestral and band cymbals today, originally in Istanbul but now mainly based near Boston, simply means cymbal-maker or cymbaler in Armenian. In our parallel passage, in 1 Chronicles 13:8, we have even stronger proof that cymbals is correct, for the word there is *mᵊtsiltayim* (the *mᵊ* is a grammatical prefix commonly used when forming nouns from verbs). In Hebrew there are three forms for nouns, singular, plural, and dual. The dual, which ends a word with -*ayim* is used only for things that always come in pairs such as the parts of the body: hands, eyes, ears, feet, and so on. It is also used for Egypt, which was historically Upper and Lower, Jerusalem, which has also been two cities, again upper and lower, and the heavens, which in the Bible are often the heavens above and the heavens beneath. It is never used for things that usually but not invariably come in pairs such as parents (the Bible is very realistic). Here mᵊtsiltayim is a dual, and indeed before the orchestral suspended cymbal was first used in the nineteenth century, and the rock band's ride cymbal in the twentieth, cymbals did always come in pairs. Many cymbals have been found archeologically in the Holy Land, some large enough that they must have been hand-held, others small enough to have been held on the fingers, as is still done over much of northern Africa and the Near East, or fixed on the ends of a pair of wooden or metal tongs, as in a number of Egyptian finds.[35] Diameters vary from 40 mm to 105 mm and the latter corresponds, as nearly as one can judge, with those held in the hands of pottery figurines, many of which have also been found in the area. A mosaic from the synagogue at Sepphoris (Tzippori), where Rabbi Judah haNasi compiled the Mishnah, not far from Nazareth, shows a pair of cymbals linked by a chain, and therefore certainly played in the hands.[36] Cymbals are often seen for sale in the shops of antiquity dealers in Israel, looking convincingly corroded and ancient (plate 12). To achieve such a state can take anything from a week to a millennium, depending on the probity of the dealer or his supplier.

Plate 12
Cymbal, allegedly antique but perhaps no older than medieval, bought in Israel but perhaps Persian from the objects associated with it. Montagu Collection VIII 124.

Chronicles adds chatsōts³rōt to the list, and these, as the AV correctly states, are the trumpets which we have already met in Numbers 10 and which are translated as usual as salpinx and tuba, so that here there is general agreement.

David Dancing

On David's second attempt to bring up the Ark, later in 2 Samuel 6, in verses 14 and 16, we have David dancing. This is not the ordinary dancing which may have been meant by māchōl, but מְכַרְכֵּר, *m³charcher*, from כָּרַר, *khārār*, to whirl about. David was leaping and whirling like an over-excited child at bringing the Ark to his new city at last, with the skirt of his robe flying high in the air (verse 20), and it is not surprising that the well-brought-up, and somewhat stuffy daughter of King Saul was shocked at what she saw and at such behavior. But dancing is still a sign of rejoicing in the Jewish communities, and Samuel Pepys, the seventeenth-century English diarist, was equally shocked when on Simchat Torah (Rejoicing of the Law, the day immediately following the last day of Succoth, when the annual reading of the Pentateuch reaches the final chapter of Deuteronomy and immediately begins again with the first chapter of Genesis) he saw elderly and respected scholars dancing around the synagogue with scrolls of the Law in their arms.[37] Still today in synagogues worldwide, people dance on that occasion, "leaping and whirling before the Lord".

There are several further references in this second book of Samuel to trumpets (15:10, 18:16, 20:1 and 22), and they are in all cases the shōfār.

A Horn is a Horn

In 2 Samuel 22:3, we find the word horn used in quite a different sense: "the horn of my salvation". The Hebrew word is קֶרֶן, *qeren*, which means horn as the horn of an animal; the ram which Abraham sacrificed, for example, was caught by its horns, *b³qarnāyv*, in the thicket (Gen. 22:13). Qeren (also often transcribed keren) is used in five quite different ways. First as the horn of an animal, in Genesis and elsewhere. Second, deriving from that, for a container: the Lord says to Samuel (1 Sam. 16:1) "fill thine horn [*qarn³chā*] with oil". Clearly this is the same use as, for example, a powder horn in later times, simply as a bottle. Third, for the altar. In Exodus from 27:2 onwards the altar always has horns, *qarnōt*, one on each of its corners. Many stone altars survive, in the Israel Museum in Jerusalem and elsewhere, and in every case they have a triangular conical projection on each corner. The outer edge is straight, an extension of each corner of the altar, but the side edges, rising from each side towards the corner, curve to the point, as does the side of the horn contained by those edges (the hypotenuse, though curved, in Euclidian terms). These four projections are the horns referred to. Fourth, the reason why Michelangelo's statue of Moses has small horns on his forehead, as do many other Renaissance representations, is that when Moses came down from the mount with the second set of tablets in his hands (Exodus 34:29) he "wist not that the skin of his face shone," in the Hebrew עוֹר קָרַן, *qāran ʿōr*. Jerome mistook the verb qāran, shone, for the noun qeren, horn, and translated it as *cornuta*. More surprisingly Jerome confused עוֹר, ʿōr, skin, with אוֹר, ʾōr, light, which added to the muddle. There are one or two occasions in the Bible where qeren (not qāran) is used as a beam of light, for instance Habakkuk 3:4, and it may have been that which led to Jerome's confusion. And fifthly, we have the sense with which we began, when David refers to "the horn of my salvation", just as Hannah (1 Sam.2:1) had greeted the birth of Samuel with "mine horn is exalted".

There is much discussion of that last use of horn, and certainly it is a common use throughout the latter part of the Bible, but equally certainly it is not a musical sense and therefore need not concern us here. Qeren is used musically only once in Hebrew, in Joshua 6:5: "when they make a long blast with the ram's horn . . .", *bᵊqeren hayōvēl* 'with the horn of a ram'. One has to say "in Hebrew" because in the book of Daniel, which is written in Aramaic, *qarna* is, as we shall see below, used throughout as a horn in the musical sense.

FIRST BOOK OF KINGS

The two books of Kings continue the history related in Samuel. 2 Samuel ends with the political problems of succession in a kingdom with an ageing king and too many sons. This problem is quickly resolved with the coronation of Solomon in 1 Kings 1:39, a paraphrase of which became the text of *Zadok the Priest*, the best-known of Handel's Coronation Anthems, written for George II in 1727, and sung at every British coronation since then. In verses 34, 39, and 41 of 1 Kings 1, the instrument is in each case the shōfār. The text is unclear (the wording is "blow ye the trumpet" and "And they blew the trumpet"), so that we do not know whether it was the people who were blowing or the priests—the only priest named is Zadok—but since it was the shōfār, the ram's horn, rather than the priestly trumpets of silver, we may assume that it was the people. Certainly in verse 40 it is written that it is the people who *mᵊchallᵊlīm bachālīlīm*, who piped with pipes on the chālīl, the instrument we discussed above in 1 Samuel.

Mentioning Handel suggests that it might perhaps be as well to emphasize that there is no connexion between chālīl and *hallel*. The latter word, meaning praise and the first part of hallelujah, praise the Lord, stems from quite a different root. The initial letter *he*, ה, for hallel is quite different from the *chet*, ח, of chālīl, even though the latter is sometimes transcribed as an *h* with a dot under it. The etymology of chālīl, as noted above, is from a root meaning 'hollow', whereas that of hallel is from a root *alalu* meaning shout aloud. It is very probable that it was onomatopoeic, coming from the ululation, the cries of joy, especially of women, produced by a high-pitched vowel interspersed with movements of the tongue akin to those used to pronounce the letter *l*.

The Arrival of the Queen of Sheba

When the Queen of Sheba came to visit King Solomon she brought many gifts, among them what seems to have been the ideal wood for the pillars of the Temple and the royal palace, and also for "harps and psalteries", kinnōr and nēvel. Unfortunately, the AV translation in 1 Kings 10:12 of *'atsēy hā'almuggīm*, trees of almug, is "almug trees". Nor are we helped by the parallel reference in 2 Chronicles 9:11, because the tree there has become algum, due to a transposition of letters as in 2 Sam. 6:5. The BDB, the main Hebrew dictionary, suggests that the *al* part of the name is the Arabic definite article, familiar to us in English as the beginning of algebra, alchemy, alcohol, and so forth.[38] No suggestion is given for the identity of gum or mug wood (certainly not the Australian eucalyptus or gum-wood which we know today). The Vulgate each time has *thyina*, citrus wood, which one suspects is as much guesswork as some modern translations such as sandalwood. The LXX were at least logical and used πελεκητὰ, *pelekēta*, hewn, in Kings but in Chronicles they used πεύκινα, *peukina*, fir-wood, which would be possible in Israel but much less likely as a wood from Africa, whence the Queen of Sheba was supposed to have come. It was probably this *pelekēta* which became transmuted erroneously into *ēlektron* (an amalgam of gold and silver) in Josephus's wholly implausible account of Solomon's furnishings of the Temple. 40,000 nabla and kynura are improbable enough, but 200,000 salpinges exceed all possibilities of belief.[39] Electrum can also mean amber, but neither that nor the metal are likely materials for building instruments, irrespective of their number, and Bathja Bayer suggests that scribal error is the solution.[40]

We know very little of the materials used for making string instruments in antiquity because so few survive, with none at all from the biblical area. A small number of Egyptian instruments has survived, due to the dry conditions there. Of these, the harps and most of the lutes have wooden bodies, though some lutes use a tortoise carapace. All have skin bellies, as do most such instruments from that area, and the rest of North Africa, today. The ideal material, in our culture, for the belly or soundboard of such string instruments is spruce or some similar wood, the peukina or fir-wood which we have just encountered in Chronicles. However, this is a wood which grows mostly in northern latitudes and, for musical purposes, ideally in the mountains where it will be slow-growing and close-grained. This, in medieval Europe was the difference between the *rebab* of southern Spain and the North African Maghrib and the rebec of the rest of Europe. The rebab had a skin belly and the rebec a wooden one. The nearest approach in biblical lands for suitable woods is the cedar and fir from Lebanon which other references (e.g. 1 Kings 9:11) state that Solomon did use for the pillars of the Temple and his palace.

Unfortunately the catalogs of the various museums which possess wooden instruments from the neighboring areas (none has yet been found in ancient Israel itself) mostly just say wood. An exception is the Louvre catalogue of Egyptian instruments, which gives tamarisk as the wood of two asymmetric lyres.[41] Whether this identification applies to the whole instrument, the arms and yoke as well as the planks of the soundbox, or only to some parts, is not specified. Tamarisk is not a wood commonly associated with instrument making. Certainly wood of some sort was normally used for the back and front of the soundbox of the lyre in Egypt, and this was also certainly true for the Greek kithara, the large concert lyre. It is a reasonable assumption that wood was used in ancient Israel for the kinnōr. The nēvel, with its association with a leather bag, and the rather sloppy appearance on the Bar Kochba coins, might have had a skin body. Much as we would like to know what woods were used, we only have the information above, so that we can only say cypress or fir and, after the arrival of the Queen of Sheba, almug.

SECOND BOOK OF KINGS

2 Kings has less information for us. What Elisha's minstrel may have played in 3:15 is not revealed in the English or the Hebrew, but the Targum gives him a kinnōr. LXX has *psallon*, plucking a string, as has the Vulgate.

Jehu's coronation in 9:13 is, as one would expect, accompanied by the shōfār, but Jehoash's, in 11:14, very surprisingly is with the silver trumpets, the chatsōtsᵊrōt.

The final reference, in 12:13, to the ritual appurtenances of the Temple, is, as one would expect with such things, to the silver trumpets.

FIRST BOOK OF CHRONICLES

The two books of Chronicles (originally almost certainly a single book) were allegedly compiled by Ezra and Nehemiah after the return from the Babylonian Exile, but more probably they are later still, perhaps from the fourth to second century B.C. It has also been suggested that it was the Chronicler who wrote the books of Ezra and Nehemiah rather than vice versa, which could mean that they also came from this later period.[42] Chronicles is a slightly revised and somewhat elaborated version of the history recounted in Samuel and Kings, as is indicated by the Greek name for the book, *Paraleipomenon*, Matters omitted, which was transcribed into Latin. A particular feature of the additions is names, including the names of David's singers (1 Chron. 6:31 ff.). These are often shown surrounding him in medieval psalters, often with instruments in their hands, frequently as a frontispiece, as it were, accompanying Psalm 1,

Beatus vir, "Blessed is the man". This is a somewhat puzzling translation, for the Hebrew is *ashrēy haīsh*, "Happy is the man", a rather
different concept. Wyclif, rather closer to the Hebrew, has "Blissful
the man".

The instrumental accompaniment to moving the ark in 13:8 has
already been discussed, but David's formal establishment of the
Temple choir and orchestra in chapter 15, verse 16 onwards, is new.
It is clear that it was the singing which was the more important
element, for while the AV has "with instruments of musick", the
Hebrew has *bichlēi-shīr*, "with tools [the root meaning of instru-
ments] of song". To this day in the synagogue, it is the song, the
words, which are of primary importance. When one is learning to
lead the services, and especially to read from the Bible, it is emphasized again and again that if one loses or forgets the melody, this is
not too serious (though it is desirable that one gets it right, and even
essential in some circles), but that every word must be pronounced
clearly and correctly—whenever a verbal error is made, members of
the congregation will call out a correction and the reader must go
back and repeat it correctly. Clearly this tradition went back at least
far as the Chronicler's period, even perhaps to David's own time.
The later medieval and renaissance church practice of obscuring the
text with melismatic ornamentation and elaborate polyphony would
never have been permitted in the Temple any more than it has been
in more modern synagogue and church practice. The three instruments named in 15:16, "psalteries and harps and cymbals" are those
that we have already encountered under those names, nēvel, kinnōr,
and mᵊtsiltayim. Some at least of the singers were expected to double on cymbals, as musicians say today for those who have to cope
with two instruments, for (15:19) "the singers, Heman, Asaph, and
Ethan, were appointed to sound with cymbals of brass", and (in 16:5)
it was Asaph who was the chief of the musicians and he "made a
sound with cymbals".

"Cymbals of brass," is מְצִלְתַּיִם נְחֹשֶׁת, *mᵊtsiltayim nᵊhōshet* in
Hebrew, κυμβάλοις χαλκοῖς, *kymbalois chalkois* in Greek, and *cymbalis æneis* in Latin. The AV normally translates nᵊhōshet and its
equivalents, *chalkos* and *æs*, as brass or brazen, but it is much more
likely that the metal was bronze. Certainly it cannot always have
meant brass for in Job 28:2 we have "brass *is* molten *out of* the stone,"
a passage which must refer to copper since brass does not exist in a
natural state in rocks. Bronze is an alloy of copper, the basic meaning

of nᵊhōshet, chalkos, and æs, with tin and it was sufficiently well-known in antiquity that today we use Bronze Age for the first main archeological era to use metal. Brass was little-known and a rather more hit-or-miss alloy of copper until the early Renaissance, with calamine as the main hardener. Zinc, the normal material later, seems to have been unknown as a metal, and even where it was known its very low boiling point, compared with that of copper, would have made any combination of the two metals very difficult to achieve. What little brass existed in the later antiquity seems to have been produced in small quantities in crucibles by combining crushed calamine ore with copper.[43] Copper, by itself, is an unlikely material for cymbals, being too soft to give a good ringing sound.

In 15:20 and 21 the players of the psalteries and harps (nēvel and kinnōr as usual) are playing on "Alamoth" and "the Sheminith" respectively. These terms, which appear also in the titles of Psalms 46 and 6, are both obscure and the cause of much debate. Sheminith has as clear or as tenuous a link with eighth as ʿāsōr had with ten and shalishīm had with three, but we have no idea whether people sang in octaves or not, or whether this might imply women singing parallel with the men. More seriously we have no idea whether the Israelites had, as we do, a seven-note scale and so might have thought of the quasi-unison which today we call the octave as the eighth note, a matter we shall discuss again in the next chapter.[44] Any meaning of Alamoth is even less clear, though ʿalmah, the singular form of the word, means a young woman, and thus just possibly soprano-voiced or anyway high-pitched.[45] A more probable solution is that advanced by Bathja Bayer, that the author of Chronicles was using terms obscure even by his time to add a "convincing patina of High Antiquity" to his text.[46] Added to the nēvel and kinnōr were the silver trumpets, chatsōtsᵊrōt (15:24) and a choir-master (verses 22 and 27). The "master of song" in verse 27, הַשַּׂר הַמַּשָּׂא, hasar hamassā, is quite different from מְנַצֵּחַ, mᵊnatsēach, which the AV translates as "The Chief Musician" in a number of psalm titles and to which we shall return in our next chapter.

This gives us an orchestra of eight nēvel players (verse 20), six on kinnōr (verse 21), seven trumpeters, all of them priests (verse 24), and three cymbal players who were also singers (verse 19), plus other singers and their choir-master. It would seem probable that this was a temporary band, assembled for the special occasion of moving the ark, which was then brought up in 15:28, with all these instruments, plus the shōfār, here translated as cornet, as we noted above when discussing the book of Numbers.

In the next chapter, 16:5, King David establishes what we presume to have become the permanent, or at least the regular Temple orchestra, a rather smaller band of eight string players, two trumpeters, and one cymbal player. The cymbal player is to be the chief, presumably giving stop and start signals with his cymbals or perhaps marking the rhythm, a somewhat daunting thought. The numbers of each string instrument are not specified, but if one conflates the players names in 15:20 and 21 with those in 16:5, we appear to have Zechariah, Shemiramoth, Jehiel, Eliab, and Benaiah on nēvel, and Mattithiah, Obed-Edom and Jeiel on kinnōr, though Benaiah is also named as a trumpeter. Thus we have either four or five nēvel to three kinnōr.

At the end of the chapter there seems to have been some redistribution of roles and in 16:42 we have two people responsible for both chatsōtsᵊrōt and cymbals.

In 23:5 we have an example of the exaggeration characteristic of the writer of Chronicles, who is always keen to stress the importance of the Levites, and suddenly we have an orchestra of four thousand, something which we can take with a large pinch of salt, just as we did with Josephus's numbers. We return to the more reasonable number of twenty-five on kinnōr, nēvel, and cymbals in 25:1, 3, and 6, to a total ensemble of 288 including singers (verse 7). Note that the horn, which is lifted up in verse 5, is not a musical one; this is the qeren which is exalted here and elsewhere.

SECOND BOOK OF CHRONICLES

This recounts the history of King Solomon's reign and the gradual disintegration of the House of Israel into rival and often warring segments. We also have more contradictory information about the Temple orchestra. Just as we thought we knew the numbers of the musicians, we reach 2 Chronicles 5:12 and 13. In addition to the singers with cymbals, psalteries (nēvel as usual), and harps (kinnōr), there are now "with them an hundred and twenty priests sounding with trumpets" (chatsōtsᵊrōt as usual with priests).

2 Chron. 7:6 is again the metal trumpets, as are 13:12 and 14 and 23:13. The instruments of musick in 7:6 and 23:13 are, as they were in

1 Chron. 15:16, the tools of song. That "David the king had made [them] to praise the Lord because his mercy endureth for ever" and "the singers with instruments of musick and such as taught to sing praise", emphasizes again and again the importance of words—the phrase "because his mercy endureth for ever" comes repeatedly in the Bible, especially in this part of it, and it is the refrain for every verse of Psalm 136, known as the Great Hallel, the great song of praise.

9:10 and 11, with its scribal transposition of algum instead of the almug in 1 Kings 10:11 and 12, has been covered above. We have also already discussed 2 Chron. 15:14 as one of the three occasions when shōfār, the ram's horn, and chatsōtsᵊrāh, the metal trumpets, appear together.

When looking at Joshua and Judges, we considered the miraculous effect of massed shōfᵊrōt.⁴⁷ In 2 Chron. 20:21 to 28, we find a similar effect produced by what appears to be (20:28) the Temple orchestra. Note that in verse 21 we have the same phrase of praise that we just quoted. In verse 26, by the way, "Berachah" literally means a blessing.

Hezekiah's Temple band in 29:25 to 28 is the normal combination. One wonders slightly whether 30:21 represents any change, whether the use of loud instruments, in the Hebrew *bᵊchlēi oz*, with tools of strength, suggests outdoor instruments such as the chālīl, with the cymbals and trumpets, instead of the quieter nēvel and kinnōr. However, there is no evidence for this. What we do have in 35:25 is evidence for women singers, so far only mentioned very much in passing in 2 Samuel 19:35, and hinted at above as a possibility when we were discussing the mysterious Sheminith. Ezra (2:65) also mentions the singing of women, but whether these were in the choir or whether they were hangers-on or entertainers is not clear. He is describing the people who were returning from exile, where they might well have adopted foreign practices. Nehemiah (7:67) tells the same story but improves on Ezra by having a choir of 245 instead of 200. We cannot, regrettably from the point of view of the more progressive modern Jewish communities, be certain that these "singing women" were any part of the Temple choir, though it would seem odd to pick them out in these ways if they were not. The author of Ecclesiastes, who may or may not have been Solomon, "gat me men singers and women singers" (2:8), but if it were Solomon, who encouraged or anyway allowed his wives to worship strange gods, this may not have been to any good purpose. It is perhaps an indication of a different purpose when he continues "and the delights of the sons of men". The authors of the AV may have felt a difference also, because they said men singers and women singers whereas every other reference is to singing men and singing women—the Hebrew uses the same words throughout as does the Vulgate. The Septuagint does distinguish, using chief men and chief women in Chronicles only, but this is almost certainly due to a misreading of the Hebrew, reading שׂ instead of שׁ, easily done in those days when there was no superscript dot to distinguish *s* (for chief: *hasārīm vᵊhasārōt*) from *sh* (for singing, *hashārīm vᵊhashārōt*).

EZRA AND NEHEMIAH

With one exception, all the entries in these two books are the same as in the two books of Chronicles, such as one would expect if the assumption is true, that the authors of all four were the same.[48]

The exception is Nehemiah 4:18 and 20, where the shōfār is used for one of its routine purposes, as an alarm signal. The Israelites, on their return from captivity in Babylon, were under constant attack, much as were the farmers in the early days of the resettlement and the kibbutz movement in the late nineteenth and early twentieth centuries, when "every one with one of his hands wrought in the work, and with the other hand held a weapon" (4:17).

The other points of interest in these two books, to which we referred in our Introduction, is that Ezra (3:12) says that while there were some elderly people who had been in Jerusalem before the exile, the majority had either forgotten or never learned Hebrew (a familiar story today!) and that Nehemiah (Neh. 8:7 and 8) arranged for Ezra's colleagues to provide a running translation as Ezra read from "the book of the law of Moses" (Neh. 8:1 and 2). This stresses the importance of understanding the words of the Law, and the reason that the Bible today is available in almost every tongue on earth.

With these two books we end the sequence of historical narrative which began with the creation of the Universe (allowing for the knowledge of the time, Genesis 1:1–5 is as good a description of the 'Big Bang' theory of creation as one would expect to find in antiquity) to the return of the remnant of the Children of Israel from captivity in Babylon and the rebuilding of Jerusalem and the Temple.

Hereafter, while some books are historical, others are poetic, allegorical, moral, or prophetic and are arranged in no particular order. Esther, the next book in the AV, certainly recounts a history of events in Persia, as does the following book, that of Job, in Uz, but neither is datable with any certainty. The AV margin says that "Moses is thought to have written the Book of *Job*, whilst among the *Madianites* [presumably a misprint for Midianites and corrected thus in some printings], Before Christ cir. 1520," but this not a theory which would be acceptable to modern scholars. The one thing which would lend some credence to such an idea is that it is only in Job (21:12 and 30:31) and in Genesis (4:21) that we find kinnōr linked with ʿūgāv. Ahasueras, the Persian king who made Esther his queen, appears also in Ezra 4:6 and Daniel 9:1, though as some concordances suggest, and it would seem chronologically more probable, he may have been three different rulers of that name.[49]

ESTHER

There are no musical references in Esther, although when it is read in the synagogue, on the Festival of Purim in the early spring each year, an instrument is used in every Jewish community. The story tells of the machinations of a villain who is so evil that his name, Haman, should be blotted out. Children and adults alike whirl a *gregger*, a ratchet such as are used at football matches, or by farmers to scare birds, or by night watchmen a century or two ago, and for many other purposes. A small selection is shown on plate 13.

JOB

In Job 21:12 and 30:31 the harp and organ are as they were in Genesis 4:21. The timbrel in 21:12 is the tōf. The war-horse in Job 39:24 and 25 hears the ram's horn trumpet, the shōfār, and saith Ha, ha, in Hebrew הֶאָח, *he'ach*.

NOTES

1. Henry George Liddell and Robert Scott, *A Greek-English Lexicon* (Oxford: Oxford University Press, 4th ed., 1855), s.v. σύρισμα.

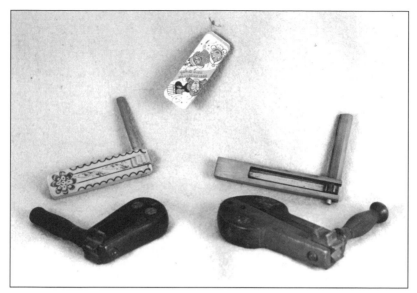

Plate 13
Greggers and other ratchets, clockwise from the top, tin-plate from Israel
(VII 168), made for use on Purim by Simon Franks (XI 84), nineteenth-century
England (IX 256), eighteenth-century England (VIII 126), Czechoslovakia
(VIII 172).

2. Museum of Welsh Life, St. Fagan's, Cardiff, cat. nos. 98.331, 04.282, and 67.7/1, all of mid-nineteenth century date.

3. Thanks to E. Roy Saer, then responsible for the musical instruments in the Museum.

4. Micheál Ó Suilleabháin, "The Bodhran," *Treoir*, vol. 6 no. 2 (1974): 4–7, and no. 5 (1974): 6–10.

5. M. L. West, *Ancient Greek Music* (Oxford: Clarendon Press, 1992), 74.

6. West, *Greek Music*, 77.

7. Bathja Bayer, "The Biblical Nebel," *Yuval* I (1968): 89–131.

8. Josephus tells his story slightly differently, Flavius Josephus, *The Works of Josephus*, translated William Whiston (London: Printed by W. Bowyer for the Author to be sold by John Whiston, Bookseller, 1736; reprinted Peabody, Mass.: Hendrickson, 1987): 1–26.

9. This translation is a conflation of that given by Bayer, "Nebel," 121, and that in the Loeb Classical Library, *Josephus Jewish Antiquities* Books VII–VIII, translated Ralph Marcus (Cambridge, Mass.: Harvard University Press, 1998), 166–7. The reference in Josephus's system is book VII, chapter 12, section 3,

paragraph 306. The pages in Whiston's version are 203–4, but his translation is grossly misleading, with viol for kinyra and bow for plectrum. Bayer cites the *Antiquities* in an earlier edition, translated H. St. J. Thackeray and R. Marcus, *Josephus*, London–Cambridge, Mass., 1941–65.

10. Bayer, "Nebel," 127. Mishnah, Sēder Kādāshīm: tractate Qinnīm, 3:6 III. I have abridged her quotation. Jacob Neusner, *The Mishnah* (New Haven: Yale University Press, 1988), 889 translates slightly differently, as does Herbert Danby, *The Mishnah* (Oxford: Oxford University Press, 1933), 602, but both to the same effect though both using lyre for nēvel and harp for kinnōr.

11. Bayer, "Nebel," 108–10 for the Greek, 110–15 for LXX, and 115–16 for the Apocrypha.

12. Joachim Braun, *Die Musikkultur Altisraels/Palästinas: Studien zu archäologischen, schriftlichen und vergleichenden Quellen* (Freiburg: Universitätsverlag; Göttingen: Vandenhoek & Ruprecht, 1999), 44–5.

13. Bayer, "Nebel," plate I for the nēvel, plate II for the kinnōr. Braun, *Musikkultur*, Abb. V/7–2c, –3d to g for a number of different examples of the nēvel, V/7–2a and b, –3a to c for several of the kinnōr. Note that his V/7–1b, from the modern Israeli half-shekel coin (our plate 2), is based on a seal of very dubious authenticity, which is shown on his Abb. IV/3–12.

14. Bayer, "Nebel," 131.

15. One must remember that the AV uses italics to show that those words were not in the original and have been added by the translators to clarify, though in this instance to confuse, the text.

16. Bayer, "Nebel," 100.

17. Anthony Baines, "Fifteenth-century Instruments in Tinctoris's *De Inventione et Usu Musicae*," *Galpin Society Journal* III (1950): 19–26, 22. A course is one or more strings tuned to the same nominal pitch and treated as one string.

18. There are various spellings here of Dr. Bayer's first name. In the text we follow her own usage when writing to me in English; in footnote references and in the bibliography we use that of the relevant article or book. The letter ׳, *yōd*, is normally transliterated *y* in English but *j* in German (with identical results—they sound the same). Her family came from Germany, which is why she used *j*, whereas anglophone publishers sometimes used *y*.

19. Berkeley 8935. Illustrated in Heinz Becker, *Zur Entwicklungsgeschichte der antiken und mittelalterlichen Rohrblattinstrumente* (Hamburg: Musikverlag Hans Sikorski, 1966), 50 and Abb. 3.

20. Hans Hickmann, *Ägypten*, Musikgeschichte in Bildern II/1 (Leipzig: Deutscher Verlag für Musik, 1961), 118, Abb. 85.

21. Hickmann, *Ägypten*, Abb. 86.

22. Braun, *Musikkultur*, 111–16, Abb. IV/2.

23. John Stainer, *The Music of the Bible with some account of the Development of Modern Musical Instruments from Ancient Types*, revised edition with Addi-

tional Illustrations and Supplementary Notes by Francis W. Galpin (London: Novello, 1914, reprinted New York: Da Capo Press, 1970), 111.

24. Christopher Page, "Biblical Instruments in Medieval Manuscript Illustration," *Early Music* 5:3 (July 1977): 299–309; reprinted with the same pagination in Christopher Page, *Music and Instruments of the Middle Ages: Studies on Texts and Performance* (Aldershot: Variorum, 1977).

25. Bathyah Bayer, *The Material Relics of Music in Ancient Palestine and its Environs: an Archeological Inventory* (Tel-Aviv: Israel Music Institute, 1963), 8, no. 29.

26. Illustrated by Braun, *Musikkultur*, Abb. III/3–3, and discussed on his p. 88.

27. In her comprehensive article "Nᵊgînāh Vᵊzimrāh," *Entsīqlōpedyāh Miqra'īt Ōtsar Hayᵊdiōt 'al HaMiqra Ūtᵊqufātō* (*Encyclopaedia Biblica, Thesaurus Rerum Biblicanum Alphabetico Ordine Digestus*) (Jerusalem: Mōssad Bī'ālīq, 1964–) vol. 5, 1968, 755–82, 775.

28. Alfred Sendrey, *Music in Ancient Israel* (New York: Philosophical Library, 1969), 383 and note 576, citing Sēder Kādāshīm, Zᵊvachīm 88b. It is said that Sendrey did not himself read Hebrew, which is how this sort of error can arise, and that is the reason that his book, though well-known, is seldom cited here.

29. Marcus Jastrow, *Dictionary of the Targumim, the Talmud Babli and Yerushalmi, and Midrashic Literature* (London: Luzac, 1903; reprinted New York: Judaica Press, 1989), 1286.

30. Louis Ginzberg, *The Legends of the Jews*, translated Henrietta Szold (Philadelphia: Jewish Publication Society of America, 1909, and on CD-ROM Chicago: Davka Corp., 1998), Vol. 1, 283. Chapter 2, footnote 8, cites several other legends concerning the mount.

31. Francis Brown, S. R. Driver, and Charles A. Briggs, *A Hebrew and English Lexicon of the Old Testament* (Oxford: Clarendon Press, 1907; reprinted 1975), 141, s.v. ברוש.

32. One should perhaps point out that both LXX and Vulgate, and translations which follow them, name the two books of Samuel as 1 and 2 Kings and the Hebrew's and AV's two books of Kings as 3 and 4 Kings. We are using the AV names throughout.

33. Brown, Driver, Briggs, *Lexicon*, 631, s.v. נוע.

34. Bathja Bayer, "Mena'an'im—Pottery Rattles," *Tatzlil* 4 (1964): 19–22, in Hebrew with English summary on p. 65.

35. Bayer, *Material Relics*, 6–8, nos. 3–28.

36. Ze'ev Weiss and Ehud Netzer, *Promise and Redemption: a Synagogue Mosaic from Sepphoris* (Jerusalem: The Israel Museum, 1996), 24 of the English section and illustrated on p. 28 of the Hebrew section.

37. Samuel Pepys, *Diaries*, 14 October 1663: ". . . more like Brutes than people knowing the true God . . ." The original manuscript is in the Pepys

Library, Magdalene College, University of Cambridge; there are numerous modern editions, the best of which is ed. Robert C. Latham and William Matthews (London: G. Bell and Sons, 1971; reprinted London: HarperCollins, 1995). The relevant passage is in vol. 4, 335.

38. Brown, Driver, Briggs, *Lexicon*, 38, s.v. אל.

39. Josephus, *Antiquities*, bk. VIII, 3, 8, 94; Loeb, 264–7; Whiston, 218.

40. Bayer, "Nebel," 122.

41. Christiane Ziegler, *Catalogue des instruments de musique égyptiens, Musée du Louvre, Département des antiquités égyptiennes* (Paris: Éditions de la Réunion des Musées Nationaux, 1979), 118–121, IDM 126 and 127 = E 14470 and E 14471.

42. Bayer, "Nebel," 101.

43. Henry Hodges, *Artifacts: an Introduction to Early Materials and Technology* (London: John Baker, 1964), 68–9 and William Smith, ed., *Dictionary of Greek and Roman Antiquities* (London: Walton and Maberly, and John Murray, 2nd ed., 1853), 24–5 and 759–61, s.vv. *aes* and *metallum*. More recent research has made very little alteration to these older statements.

44. How other than with "quasi-unison" can one express our concept of the octave, with players or singers on the same named note but a distance above or below, in a way which does not by its very name imply eight notes?

45. Brown, Driver, Briggs, *Lexicon*, 761, s.v. עלמה. Perhaps one should add that these authors opt for women's voices as the meaning of Alamoth.

46. Bathja Bayer, "The Titles of the Psalms—A Renewed Investigation of an Old Problem," *Yuval* IV (1982): 29–123, 78.

47. Perhaps one should emphasize that shōfᵊrōt is the correct plural. Possibly the use of a normally feminine plural form on a masculine noun was influenced by assonance, by the *-ar* ending sounding like the commonly feminine *-ah*. This is one of the few occasions on which Curt Sachs was in error in his *History of Musical Instruments* (New York: W. W. Norton and London: J. M. Dent, 1940) 111–12. This would not be worth mentioning were it not that his reputation is such that others have been unwittingly led astray.

48. The Vulgate calls Nehemiah the second book of Ezra, Esdras in Latin. Perhaps for this reason it relegates the two apocryphal books of Esdras to the back of the book.

49. Robert Young, *Analytical Concordance to the Holy Bible* (Edinburgh: George Adam Young, 1879; 8th ed. 1939, reprinted by various publishers, mine Guildford and London: Lutterworth Press for the United Society for Christian Literature, 1979), 22, s.v. Ahasueras.

Chapter 4

The Poetical Books

PSALMS

As one would expect for musical instruments, the book of Psalms is a prime source, but it is a source which needs to be handled with some circumspection.

One of the most serious problems is that of the incipits which introduce a number of the psalms. Are they as they were originally? And if they are, what do they mean? Take, for example, Psalm 30, "A Psalm *and* Song *at* the dedication of the house of David", *mizmōr shīr chanukkat habayit lᵊdāvid*.[1] Most, like this example, have little or no apparent relevance to the psalm that follows. Fortunately, many aspects of these questions, fascinating though they be, are beyond the detailed constraints of our subject. There is plentiful, and essentially inconclusive, literature on the subject, a good example of which is the discussion in Sir John Stainer's well-known book.[2] A more modern, and more useful approach, is Bathja Bayer's long and thorough study.[3]

Some questions are relevant. First and foremost: how does a *mizmōr* differ from a *shīr*? Many psalms begin, like Psalm 3, מִזְמוֹר לְדָוִד, *mizmōr lᵊdāvid*, "A Psalm of David", while others are entitled shīr, "a Song". A few, like Psalm 30 quoted above, have both. More interestingly, some alternate, as, for example, some of the psalms of the sons of Korach. Psalm 46 is a shīr and 47 a mizmōr and one might expect the same of 48 and 49 were it not that 48 is shīr mizmōr. Do they differ and if so how? and if so, how can they combine? One wonders, incidentally, why the sons of Korach are singled out for more psalms than anyone else, for it was Korach who led the great rebellion in the desert of the Levites versus the Cohanim and it was Korach who was swallowed up with his followers as the earth gaped open below their feet (Numbers 26:10). Perhaps it is to emphasize the statement in Deuteronomy 24:16 that children should not suffer for their fathers' sins.

The AV translators have unfortunately failed to help us in this as much as we might desire. Shīr is translated as song, as one would hope and expect, for that is what it means. But mizmōr is translated as "A Psalm" and to add to confusion it is added to many psalms where it did not appear originally. This is sometimes encouraged by the Septuagint which uses ψαλμὸς, *psalmos* for mizmōr, often adding it when it is not in the Hebrew, though not as often as the AV does. LXX uses ᾠδῆ, *ōdē* (our ode) for shīr. In the original Hebrew text many psalms are simply headed *lᵉdāvid* or simply have no heading at all. The AV does have the great advantage over many other translations that we can always tell when something has been added or interpolated.[4]

The importance for our purposes and the relevance to this study is that the root of the Hebrew word, זמר, *zmr*, does seem to be connected with playing instruments.[5] There are to this day instruments which are called *mizmar* or *mizmōr*, *zamr* and *zummāra* or other similar terms in Arabic and related languages, instruments many of which we know existed in the biblical period.[6] Because of the derived instrument names, all of which are for wind instruments, we tend to assume a wind bias, encouraged by the fact that *zmr* today means a pipe or play on a reed in Arabic. However, Bayer points out that the Greek word used by the Septuagint to translate it, ψαλμὸς, which is obviously the origin of our word psalm, derives from *psallein*, to pluck, and therefore presumably indicates a string.[7] As a result, she prefers the possibility of the idea of string instruments rather than wind, believing that the LXX entitled them psalms because they knew that they were accompanied by plucked instruments.

So does this give us evidence that the 56 psalms whose incipit includes the word mizmōr were performed with instrumental accompaniment? And that those whose incipit includes the word shīr, "A Song", were sung? And that the fourteen psalms which have both words, were sung with instrumental accompaniment? But if that applies only to those fourteen, how were those with mizmōr performed? They have words, which must be heard somehow. Unfortunately, no such correlations wholly work and the only thing that can be said with any certainty is that we really do not know what these words imply.

As a further layer of complexity, we do not know at what stage they were attached to the psalms which have them now. It has been suggested that in some cases, at least, they were originally attached as a postlude to the psalm which preceded them rather than as a prelude to the psalm at whose head they stand today, a theory which is strengthened by the end of the book of Habbakuk.[8] And to complicate matters further, there is no certainty that the psalm which precedes any title now has always done so—the order of the psalter has almost certainly changed over time.

In Psalm 3, and in many thereafter, we have the mysterious word "Selah". What does it mean? The short answer is that nobody knows nor ever will. Guesswork is another matter and open to all, and one guess of Bathja Bayer's was that it might have been the equivalent of the Italian *tacet*, be silent, so that the voices should stop for an instrumental interlude, or vice versa.[9] Psalm 39 is a clear example of the possibility of two instrumental interludes to separate three different trains of thought, each indicated with Selah. However, no suggestion that has ever been advanced (other than "we don't know") can be made to fit all the occasions where Selah appears. One suggestion will work here, another seems logical there, but none fits everywhere.

Might we gain any other ideas of performance from any of those mysterious words, some of which survive, untranslated from the Hebrew, in the King James incipits? Again, with one exception, the answer is no. For one thing it is very improbable that the word translated as "To the chief Musician" actually meant that; even the vowels now attached to those consonants, למנצח, l-m-n-ts-ch to form *lamᵊnatsēach* are suspect.[10] Certainly there is no connexion between that word and any that were used above when establishing Chenaniah as the master of song (1 Chron. 15:22 and 27) or Asaph as the chief of the musicians (1 Chron. 16:5). What is more, neither LXX nor the Vulgate believed that that word had any connexion with music or a musician. LXX translated it as Εἰς τὸ τέλος, *eis to telos*, and the Vulgate as *in finem*, each meaning the same. Like most prepositions, both εἰς and *in* have a variety of meanings, but both mean mainly into, unto, or towards, and both το τέλος and *finem* mean the end. How so many psalms can be thought to be towards the end is unclear, though if the word appeared at the end of a psalm, as Dr. Bayer suggests it may have originally done, could it then have meant *da capo al fine*—repeat from the beginning to the end, or, as in Habbakuk 3:19, as an instrumental coda?

Some psalms are attributed to Asaph, or were for him (the Hebrew could mean either), but how or why these differ from any others we do not know. Nor do we know what words such as "Michtam" or "Maschil" mean in this context. Even more problematic are those psalms whose title is translated as upon something. This would seem to indicate some musical style or perhaps a scale or mode, but we have no any evidence at all for the sound of music at that time. We do not know what sort of scale they used nor, as we mentioned in the previous chapter, even how many notes there were to the octave. We can probably assume that the octave was known, if not by that name, because very few peoples in the world are without that concept, but while many peoples use seven steps to the octave, as we did until the rise of Schönbergian twelve-step atonalism at the end of the nineteenth century, far more use five steps, the pentatonic scale, and others use four or six. Nor are all seven- or five-step scales the same. Some use steps that are equal or nearly so. Some use tones and semitones, like our own seven-step scale. Some have greater or smaller size differences than ours between steps. Nor do we have any idea of what rhythmic modes might have been used, and even less of any melodic styles. Many people have tried to recreate the music of the Bible, but all such efforts were based on pure speculation, whistling in the dark of prehistory. We are more fortunate, for at least we have some chance of identifying the instruments, though here, too, in honesty we have to admit that some, even much, is speculation.

The one possible exception is "Neginoth", which we find in the title of Psalms 4, 6, 54, 55, 61 (here "Neginah"), 67, and 76. The Hebrew in each case is בִּנְגִינוֹת, *bingīnōt*, the *bi* more usually meaning with *nᵊgīnōt* than on them, though both are possible except in Ps. 61 where it is ʿal-nᵊgīnat lᵊdavid, unto or with the nᵊgīnāhs of David. The problem is what does nᵊgīnāh mean? The ostensible root, נגן, *ngn*, which must have this form if it is to be the root of the various words that derive from it, is taken by the BDB and other sources to mean to play a musical instrument, particularly a stringed instrument.[11] It is thought to derive from the very similar word נגע, *ngʿ*, which means touch or strike, often quite forcefully—another word using the same three letters and from the same root is used for the plagues, for example, which struck the Egyptians. The suggestion is that it is the two letters נג, *ng*, common to both, which link the two in that one touches an instrument to play it.

However, the argument is somewhat circular because, as Bathja Bayer points out, the supposed connexion with instrumental music is based solely on the fact that *ngn* is the root of the various words which were translated as play, in different grammatical forms, when Saul was looking for someone to play to him *bᵊyadō*, with his hand (1 Samuel 16:16 and 18), for which see Chapter 2.[12] She suggests that because *yad* has many meanings beside hand, for instance power and mediation, there are numerous other possible interpretations of what Saul and his counselors were seeking and that there may be no musical context at all.

It is very tempting to suggest that the Neginoth psalms were sung to the accompaniment of stringed instruments, as the AV translates Isaiah 38:20, "we will sing my songs to the string instruments," *ūnᵊginōtai nᵊnaggēn*, but it would be very rash to do so. This is partly because in some places the AV translates words from the same root as song or singing without any reference to instruments, whereas in others, for example Psalm 68:25, *ngn* is purely instrumental with no implication of singing, for that is covered there by *shārīm*. The "players on instruments," *nōgnīm*, a word which derives from *ngn*, follow after. In this psalm it does seem that we have a band of string players, people who touch, to accompany the singers. We can be clear about the damsels who followed the singers and instrumentalists in that psalm, for their timbrels are the frame drum *tōf* we have often met already.

It would be tantalizing to wonder whether touching simply stood for music in general, music played on anything, as in Lamentations 3:63 and 5:14 where musick is a translation of *minᵊgīnātām*. We have had a similar usage in our own musical history. In the Renaissance and early Baroque, a touch, *Tusch* in German, meant a fanfare of trumpets, and composers wrote toccatas (Italian for touch, in Shakespearian English tucket) for any instruments they fancied. Many toccatas, as those by J. S. Bach, were for harpsichord or organ, but in Monteverdi's *L'Orfeo*, for example, the "Toccata" was written for five trumpets *"con tutte le stromenti"*, with all the other instruments together. Maybe *nᵊgīnāh* and its plural *nᵊgīnōt*, and all the other words from that root, had the same implication, music played on anything. This is one of the fascinations of biblical references, and especially of psalms, that one can speculate endlessly—but one should only do so so long as one remembers that all is speculation and that there will never, in this world, be any certainty.

Psalms vary in their literary style and in some cases this does give us some hint of how they may have been performed. Some are clearly for call and response: surely Psalm 136 was designed for a solo half-line with a full choral second half to each line, *kī lᵊʿōlām chasdō*, "for his mercy *endureth* for ever" (endureth was supplied by the AV translators; the Hebrew has no verb which usually means that the appropriate part of the verb to be should be assumed). Psalm 145, like a number of others, seems more suited to two voices, solo or choral, singing each half line to each other. The use of complementary, sometimes semi-repetitive, phrases in half lines or alternative verses is a common feature of Hebrew poetry. Psalm 41 seems to have a choral conclusion. There are other examples of all three of these characteristics, but whether such interpretations are correct, we shall never know. Some psalms anticipate a common form of medieval Hebrew liturgical poetry, with the use of alephbetical acrostics (the first two letters of the Hebrew alphabet are *alef* and *bēt*), though with an occasional missing or misplaced letter. This may reflect a mnemonic practice rather than a musical one—if one knows the letter with which lines start it helps to remember their order and what line comes next. Or perhaps it was done for fun or as a trial of poetic skill.

Two final introductory remarks. The first is that not all the psalms can be attributed to David. Some are specifically attributed to others, for instance Psalm 90 to Moses. Others, for example Psalm 137, clearly refer to events after David's time. The second is that we are, as usual, using the AV numbering both for the psalms and for their verses throughout, and not noting the differences in other versions.

The first psalm to mention instruments, leaving aside the speculations above, is 33:2. This we have already examined in Chapter 3 when discussing the nēvel ʿāsōr and it seems only necessary here to repeat that the Hebrew lists only two instruments, not three, the lyre, kinnōr, and the nēvel ʿāsōr, probably but not certainly a different form of lyre. The next verse, "Sing unto him a new song; play skillfully with a loud noise," opens with a phrase often repeated in the psalms, *shīrū-lō* (sing to him) *shīr chādāsh* (a new song), which is occasionally used elsewhere, for instance in Isaiah 42:10. The demand for novelty has ever provided creative opportunities for poets and musicians, as all other artists. One presumes that whenever the phrase appears in a psalm it is reflecting novelty achieved, that this is a new psalm.

The second half of the phrase, *hētīvū nagēn bitrū'āh*, parallels initially 1 Samuel 16:17, "play well" or "play skillfully" as the AV has it, and adding "with tᵊrū'āh," the word that is used for a trumpet call or alarm and can also mean with a shout or other loud noise as in the AV.

In Psalm 43:4 it is the lyre, kinnōr, on which God will be praised, and in 49:4 the kinnōr with which God has gone up, again with tᵊrū'āh, a shout, whereas in Psalm 57:8 the Psalmist awakes with the "psaltery" or nēvel, the other form of lyre, as well as with the kinnōr. We have the same combination in Psalm 71:22, and the same call for the Psalmist to waken with the same two instruments in Ps. 108:2.

In Psalm 47:5 the praise is with the ram's horn, the shōfār. The next verse raises some speculation. The AV has "Sing praises to God, sing praises: sing praises unto our King, sing praises." The Hebrew uses words with the *zmr* root, *zammᵊrū elōhīm zammērū; zammᵊrū lᵊmalkēnū zammērū* (the difference between *zammᵊrū* and *zammērū* is only one of word order; the final word in a phrase or sentence is often differentiated by lengthening the penultimate vowel). So does this verse, as it might well, signify a blast of instrumental color with wind instruments?

Psalm 81:2, שְׂאוּ־זִמְרָה וּתְנוּ־תֹף ; כִּנּוֹר נָעִים עִם־נָבֶל, *sᵊū-zimrāh ūtᵊnū-tof; kinnōr nā'īm im-nāvel*, "Take a psalm, and bring hither the timbrel, the pleasant harp with the psaltery," presents an immediate problem: can one "take a psalm"? Especially when the Hebrew word translated as psalm is *zimrāh*, deriving from the same root זמר, *zmr*, as mizmōr. A more active translation would be "Strike up the band," or more literally "Lift up the *zimrāh*, hold (or give) the drum, the pleasant lyre with the other lyre" (we really do need a different name for nēvel, but unfortunately we do not have one). The word translated lift up is the same as that for "Lift up your heads, O ye gates" in Ps. 24:7 and 9 and *nā'īm* is the word one uses today for anything really nice, delicious food, and so on. Perhaps here we may succumb to temptation and translate *zimrāh* as a wind instrument.

The next verse we have already discussed in connexion with the trumpets in the books of Exodus and Numbers, for here we have the ram's horn, shōfār, usurping the role of the silver trumpets, chatsōtsᵊrōt, in one of the specific tasks for which Moses was commanded by God to make them in Num. 10:10, to announce the new moon and our pilgrim festivals, the strict meaning of יוֹם חַגֵּנוּ, *yōm chagēnū*, rather than "our solemn feast day."

The first day of the new moon was a minor festival, especially for women, and, until the days when the calendar became fixed by calculation, which was well after the biblical period, it could only be recognized when somebody actually saw the slender crescent shining and reported it to the priests or other authorities. It would then be announced to the population either by beacons, signal fires, or by the silver trumpets, in the time of Moses, but later, as we learn here, by the shōfār. This may seem to us a clumsy procedure, but before the days of calculated calendars it was the only one available. The trumpet would be blown first in the Temple. Among the debris from the Roman destruction of Herod's Temple was a large stone, shaped as a niche in which a man could stand. On its lintel was engraved in clear and well-cut letters, ... לביתהתקיעהלהכ. Adding spaces and the probable vowels, this reads *l°bēt hat°qī'āh lēhach* ... , "to the place for the trumpeting, for the ..." Judging from where the stone was found, just below the southwest corner of the Temple Mount, the place where the trumpeter stood to announce the New Moon, the festivals, and the arrival and departure of the sabbath, was on top of the gateway at the head of the monumental staircase carried on what is now called Robinson's Arch.[13] Because on festivals and sabbaths no work could be done (Ex. 20:9–11, Deut. 5:12–15, and Lev. 23:3–36), which included lighting any fire or lamp, the sound of the trumpet as sunset drew near was the necessary warning that all work must cease. After the sun sank next day and the stars had appeared, it sounded again to signal that the day of observance had departed with the sun and that work might recommence. Each community within earshot would repeat the signal and so, passed from ear to ear, it would travel across the country. Because the new moon was a festival, even if a minor one, its arrival was an occasion to "Sing aloud unto God our strength: make a joyful noise unto the God of Jacob" (Ps. 81:1) and extra psalms of praise were inserted into the service on that day to celebrate it. Still today the synagogue service on Rosh Hodesh, the beginning of the month, includes special psalms and prayers of rejoicing, to "Sing aloud to God" in thanks that we and the world continue on our way.

The AV does not mention any specific instrument in Ps. 87:7, referring to "the singers as the players on instruments", but the Hebrew uses כְּחֹלְלִים, *k°chōl°līm*, as the chālīl players, or perhaps those who māchōl, those who dance, as in Judges 21:23. Neither LXX nor the

Vulgate make any mention of either singers or instrumentalists in this psalm

In Ps. 89:15, "the joyful sound" is the translation of t³rū'āh, one of the words normally associated with trumpeting, the same word that we had for the "loud noise" in Ps. 33:3 and 49:4, but there is no other indication of a musical context. Qeren, the horn in verses 17 and 24, is also unmusical, for it is the metaphorical horn that is exalted. The last verse of Psalm 89 does read very much as though it were a choral response.

Psalm 92:3 has already been discussed in some detail in the previous chapter when we first encountered the nēvel. It is worth emphasizing again that we do clearly have two instruments here, or at least two names, "Upon the instrument of ten strings ['alēy-'asōr], and upon the psaltery [va'alēy-nāvel]", with no doubt about the and (nāvel rather than nēvel, here and in Ps. 81:2 above, is again the lengthening of the penultimate vowel due to sentence structure). In the second half of the verse, "upon the harp with a solemn sound", 'alēy higgāyōn b³chinnōr, the harp is as usual the kinnōr. The word higgāyōn, translated here as "with a solemn sound", is the same as that which is translated as meditation in the last verse of Psalm 19: v³hegyōn libī, "and the meditation of my heart". The word appears only four times in the Bible, in Psalm 9:16 where, quite sensibly for a word of doubtful meaning, it is simply ignored; in Psalm 19:14; here in 92:3; and in Lamentations 3:62, where it is translated as "their device". The fact that the English translation is so different in each place shows clearly that its meaning is wholly guesswork—the AV could hardly call it a "whatsit" and therefore uses something that will make sense in each context.

In Psalm 95:2 we have the same use of "psalms" as a translation of z³mirōt as in 81:2. In Psalm 98, one of those which begins "Sing to the Lord a new song", shīrū . . . shīr chādāsh, in verses 4 and 5 the Hebrew for "sing praise" is again zamm³rū, with the same זמר root for the "voice of a psalm", v³qōl zimrāh. A similar use comes in Psalm 105:2: shīrū-lō ("sing to him") zamm³rū-lō ("sing psalms unto him")— maybe we could say "blow an instrument to him" instead. There is a number of other instances where this word zamm³rū, especially as here as an imperative, could be translated in this way. It seems unnecessary to cite them all, when all that we have is speculation, especially since on returning to Psalm 98:5 we find zamm³rū *bᵊchinnōr ; bᵊchinnōr vᵊqōl zimrāh*, and we can hardly translate that as "blow the kinnōr!" We have another example to argue against our suggestion that zamrū might imply a wind instrument in Psalm 147:7: *zammᵊrū lelōhēnū vᵊkinnōr*, "sing praise upon the harp to our God" or in the same word order as the Hebrew, "blow a wind instrument to our God with the lyre." This is obviously nonsense, so zamrū cannot always, even if perhaps it does sometimes, refer to a wind instrument. It might do so in 149:3, for the two words translated as praise are quite different. The first is *yᵊhalᵊlū*, the praise part of hallelujah: *yᵊhalᵊlū shᵊmō vᵊmāchōl*, "praise his name in the dance"—as we have said above māchōl could possibly also be a pipe rather than a dance. The second, however, is once again, zamrū. The response half of the verse is *bᵊtōf vᵊkinnōr yᵊzammᵊrū-lō*, "let them sing praises unto him with the timbrel and harp", and surely instrumental, perhaps adding a wind instrument to the drum and the lyre. The *yᵊ*, like the doubled *m* is grammatical variation.

Returning to Psalm 98, in verse 6 we have one of the rare occasions, mentioned above, where both chatsōtsᵊrōt and shōfār, silver trumpets and ram's horn (translated here "cornet") appear together.

The Songs of Degrees, the fifteen psalms from 120 to 134, could be equally well called the songs of the steps or the stairs because while the root word עלה, *'lh*, means to go up or ascend, the derivative מַעֲלָה, *ma'alāh*, plural *ma'alōt*, means steps or stairs, often specifically those of the Temple. We found in the Mishnah the description of the Sukkot water ceremony quoted above, "the Levites beyond counting played on harps, lyres, cymbals, trumpets, and [other] musical instruments, [standing as they played] on the fifteen steps which go down from the Israelites' court to the women's court—corresponding to the fifteen Songs of Ascents which are in the Book of Psalms—on these the Levites stand with their instruments and sing their song."[14] Where those courts and those steps were, nobody knows today. The whole area of Solomon's Temple was buried when Herod built the great platform which is the modern Temple Mount, building huge retaining walls on the eastern, southern, and western sides, and filling all the hollows within them to bring the whole space level with the peak of the Mount. Herod's Temple was destroyed in its turn by the Romans in A.D. 70, the whole complex and the whole city flattened, "so thoroughly laid even with the ground by those that dug it up to the foundation, that there was left nothing to make those that came thither believe it had ever been inhabited."[15] All that was left of the Temple was Herod's plateau, gradually ascending from the northern side to the rocky peak of Mount Moriah which was now just below ground level. Herod's great retaining walls loom over what was David's City, the Ophel to the south and over what is now the Western Wall plaza to the west. That plaza is built over the Tyropoen Valley. The valley is still part-filled, perhaps with debris from the Temple, for Herod's Western Wall, often called in earlier times the Wailing Wall, but now simply *haKōtel*, the Wall, extends further below the modern ground level than it does above it. All the courts and stairs, almost all the approaches to Herod's Temple, are lost to us, for the Romans swept all away in their destruction in A.D. 70.

Two flights of steps have been uncovered in recent years, just outside the Temple Mount. Among the extensive excavations immediately outside the southern wall are the steps which lead to five great doorways, the Huldah Gates, one double, one triple, and all now blocked, which are set in the southern wall. These gates are named in memory of the prophetess who authenticated the "hidden scroll" found by the High Priest Hilkiah (2 Kings 22:8, 2 Chron. 34:14–15) in the reign of Josiah. The double gate is immediately below the Al Aqsa Mosque, which looms high above it on the southern edge of the Mount and which presumably covers the point at which the internal staircase or ramp emerged on to Herod's platform. The triple gate is further to the east. The gates led into tunnels sloping up towards the surface—the beginning of the Double Gate ramp survives.[16] Today the Waqf, the Muslim religious authorities, have prohibited all excavation within the Mount, save their own, and banned access to all such areas. But the steps are there and, being outside the Mount, are accessible, and steps leading to the Temple they undoubtedly are, and to stand on them where so many must have stood before us and to recite one of those fifteen Psalms of Ascents can be very moving.

The harps that were hung on the willows by the waters of Babylon, in verse 2 of that peculiarly vengeful Psalm, 137, were as ever the kinnōrōt. It has often been suggested that they may have acted as aeolian harps, hanging from the branches of the trees and producing soft and plaintive sounds as the wind brushed through the strings.

In Psalm 144:9 the conjunction and is in italics, indicating that it was supplied by the translators, as in Ps. 33:2. In the original there is no separation. We have just the one instrument, the nēvel 'āsōr.

The last psalm is addressed to all musicians: instrumentalists (verses 3 to 5), dancers perhaps (verse 4), and singers (verse 6) alike. All are commanded to praise the Lord, *hal°lūhū*, "praise ye Him". The shōfār, the ram's horn, leads the list, and the voice of all creation, *kol han°shāmāh*, "every thing that hath breath" ends it. In the first half of verse 3 we praise Him, with *b°tēka shōfār*, "with the sound of the trumpet", the call of the shōfār. *Tēka* is from the same root as the most common of the shōfār calls, the t°kī'āh, which we met in the inscription from the Temple. In the second half of verse 3 we praise Him *b°nēvel v°kinnōr*, "with the psaltery and harp" or, as in the Coverdale translation on our title page, "upon the lute and harp", but in the original with the two forms of lyre. In the first half of verse 4 *v°tōf ūmāchōl*, "with the timbrel and dance." This is a pair which has clearly caused constant trouble, for Wyclif in the fourteenth century had "timbre and quer", timbrel and choir rather than dance, and Coverdale in 1535 had "cymbals and daunse", preserved in the Book of Common Prayer. Cymbals was an odd choice for this verse, for they come again in the next, and Coverdale had had no previous problems in translating either tōf or the tympano which appears in both the Latin and the Greek. In the second half of that verse *b°minnīm v°'ūgāv*, "with stringed instruments and organs". *Minnīm* is a word we mentioned in connexion with Jubal's invention of the 'ūgāv in Chapter 2. It means strings, primarily in the same sense as how long is a piece of string? or the string with which one ties anything. It is clearly used here in the same way that we use it in the orchestra, strings for string instruments. It appears also in Ps. 45:8, where it is ignored by the AV but is translated as stringed instruments (out of the palaces) by the Revised Version and those later translations which follow it. The organ (the Hebrew is singular, not plural) is that same word, 'ūgāv, that we met with Jubal in Genesis 4:21, and its coupling here with minnīm is surely also orchestral and archetypal, the strings and the woodwind. Here Coverdale, with his use of pipe rather than organ, is more accurate than King James's translators.

The cymbals, *v°tsilts°lēy-shāma'*, *b°tsilts°lēy t°rū'āh*, "upon the loud cymbals, upon the high sounding cymbals", is the word we have met before. This is the only instrument which appears twice and the only one, save the shōfār, which is not paired with another instrument. So, do we have a climactic repetition for the instrumentalists, or do we have two different types of cymbal? It could be either, though the way in which St. Paul quotes the verse with some alteration in 1 Corinthians 13:1, to which we shall return, does suggest two different sounds. Certainly enough cymbals of different sizes have been found archeologically in the Holy Land to support two different sizes and thus two different sounds.[17] There is a significant cluster around 10 cm in diameter (4 inches), and a little larger, and a smaller cluster around 5 or 6 cm. As we have noted, many such cymbals are sold in Israel today, usually singly, and mostly around 10 to 16 cm in diameter (4 to 7 inches), convincingly corroded and certificated such as that in plate 12 which was bought in Jerusalem, but it would be rash to swear to any date for any of them within a millennium or so. They are instruments whose use has not ceased in the area and they could be of any age from the biblical to the recent.

The first of the two adjectives, "loud" and "high sounding", derives from the word to hear, *sh⁾maʿ*, thus audible, so that loud is certainly an acceptable translation. High sounding is more difficult, for the word *t⁾rūʿāh*, is one of those used for trumpeting, and usually interpreted as an alarm, or for a shout, so it may only be high in the sense of high meaning loud. There seems little justification for Jerome's translation, *cymbalis bene sonantibus, cymbalis jubilationis. Bene sonantibus*, well-sounding, led Coverdale to translate it as well-tuned, and *jubilationis*, jubilating, is presumably why Wyclif said of huge ioȝing [joying], which his successor turned to of jubilacioun. But certainly if there were two sizes the smaller cymbals would give a high-pitched sound and the larger a louder clang. Thus it may be that we have again a pair of instruments, for once a contrasting pair, but equally a single to match the single ram's horn because both elements of the pair are the same type of instrument.

Taking the psalms as a whole, it is quite clear that the string instruments, the lyre (in the AV harp) and the other instrument, AV psaltery, which we have accepted as another form of lyre, are in the overwhelming majority. That the lyre, kinnōr, should lead is, as King David's own instrument, appropriate enough. It was the most respected instrument of antiquity in general, not only of ancient Israel. It was Apollo's instrument, it was that with which Orpheus charmed the animals and calmed the Furies. It was the lyre to which Homer sang the *Iliad* and the *Odyssey*. It was that to which Sappho burned and sang in the Isles of Greece. It was that to which all the poets and bards sang their odes and lays. It was the instrument in the royal burials of Ur of the Chaldees, whence Abraham came, and, thousands of years later, around A.D. 600, it was the instrument of the great royal ship burial at Sutton Hoo on the English Suffolk coast, where it had accompanied the lays of Beowulf.

What did it look like? Joachim Braun includes sketches of a wide range of types and dates, ranging from the Stone Age to the Roman period.[18] He also reproduces photographs of most or all, including that from the seal of very dubious authenticity which was copied to appear on the modern Israeli half-shekel coin (plate 2).[19] All that the many types have in common, two of which appear in plate 8, is the sound-box or resonator from which two arms arise which are linked, at or near the top, by a cross-bar or yoke from which strings descend to the resonator. Within that description the range of differences and variation is wide. On some the arms are of equal length and on others unequal. One would assume that in the first the strings are all the same length, and therefore are likely to have differed in thickness to obtain different pitches, whereas the asymmetric lyres, those of the second type, would obtain different pitches by having strings of different length. However, no illustration is clear or detailed enough to show such distinctions and, as so often in this study, we are left to guess, which we shall do in more detail in Chapter 8.

The last verse of the psalm, *kol han°shāmāh t°hallēl yāh, hal°lūyāh,* "Let everything that hath breath praise the LORD. Praise ye the LORD" is clear enough. But what did it sound like? While we have already said that there is no way to recreate the music of the Bible, it must be added that there is a musical notation which is certainly well over a thousand years old and perhaps considerably older. It is used for chanting the Bible in the synagogue. The basic problem is that the notational signs, which are the same for the weekly portion of the Pentateuch and for other parts such as the narrative and prophetical books and, with some additions, for the psalms, have different traditional musical meanings in each different part of the Bible. To add to the complications, several of the signs also function as punctuation marks, the approximate equivalents of our comma, semicolon, and full stop or point, and others also indicate special emphasis.

What makes their presence quite useless as historical evidence is that every Jewish community realizes them quite differently. One aspect that is uniform in every tradition is that they show not any definite pitch but a melodic movement. Some indicate an upward movement, others downward, others melismatically both up and down or vice versa. Some indicate a similar movement to that of others but at a higher or lower pitch level. Several vary in their meaning, within a single tradition, according to their relationship to other signs. But the one constant is that each tradition will interpret them in different ways. One tradition will go up, another, reading the same sign, will go down, and a third will go around. Even within any one tradition, one reader will sing in one way while another will say "But my master sang it thus."

Jewish music, like Jewish cooking, has taken many flavors from the people among whom the Jews have lived. Northern and central European singing has a strong sub-Mendelssohn tinge, albeit always recognizably Jewish; southern European is very different. The music of the B'nei Yisrael, the Jews of India, sounds Indian and that of the Yemenite communities Southern Arabian. Even though one says "recognizably Jewish", the Jewishness of Germany is different from that of Lithuania, more different from that of Yemen and more different still from that of India.

Plainly, all these traditions have been so changed by their environment that there are no longer any common underlying strains which one could use to try to reconstruct the "original" form. Thus there is no possibility of restoring the music of the Bible even if one were rash enough to believe that any music stays constant or even recognizable over a period of two thousand or so years from the time of the Patriarchs to that of the Massoretes who wrote the signs into the text around 700 A.D.

But at least we can all agree on one thing: hal°lūyāh, Hallelujah, Praise ye the Lord.

PROVERBS, ECCLESIASTES, AND THE SONG OF SONGS

With these, despite the name of the third, shīr hashīrīm, we enter a musically barren area. There are occasional references to singing, for example that to singing men and women in Ecclesiastes 2:8 which we have already mentioned. In the same verse, where the author "gat me . . . musical instruments", the AV translators were simply guessing what "the delights [or luxuries] of the sons of men" might include. The two words shiddāh v°shiddōt, which are translated as "musical instruments, and that of all sorts", are actually the same word singular and plural, and are of unknown meaning—they appear nowhere else in the Bible. The LXX guessed a butler and female cupbearers, though both words appear to be feminine. The Vulgate opted for wine cups and jars. I suppose it is just a matter of what seems to the translator the height of luxury and the peak of delights. Perhaps the choice of "musical instruments" tells us more about the AV translators, or the availability or quality of wine in early seventeenth-century England, than it does about the Preacher. The Preacher does not tell us what he did with them, save that all was vanity and vexation. He does, in 3:4, mention "a time to dance", and here the AV has reduced the contrast with "a time to mourn", for *rᵊkōd* is no ordinary dancing, but leaping and skipping. On the other hand, when Jeremiah says (Lamentations, 5:15) that "our dance is turned into mourning," it is the more normal māchōl that he uses.

NOTES

1. Hebrew does not have capital letters, and does not distinguish between proper names and other words—one is merely expected to know that *dāvid* is a name. The preliminary *lᵊ* means to, for, or of.

2. John Stainer, *The Music of the Bible with some account of the Development of Modern Musical Instruments from Ancient Types; revised edition with Additional Illustrations and Supplementary Notes by Francis W. Galpin* (London: Novello, 1914; reprinted New York: Da Capo Press, 1970), 73–83 for Stainer and 89–94 for Galpin's additional comments.

3. Bathja Bayer, "The Titles of the Psalms—A Renewed Investigation of an Old Problem", *Yuval* IV (1982): 29–123.

4. All words added by the AV's translators are printed in *italics* in the King James's Bible.

5. Most Hebrew words stem from a three-letter root, adding letters before, after, and in the middle, according to grammatical and lexical context and meaning, and changing all its vowels according to tense, person, or case, or even just to sound pleasanter, which is why roots are cited with consonants alone. Sometimes, as in this case, the root itself does not appear in Hebrew, as with נוע in the previous chapter, but may be assumed from other forms of the word or, as here, from its use with a related meaning in another Semitic language.

6. Francis Brown, S. R. Driver, and Charles Briggs, *A Hebrew and English Lexicon of the Old Testament* (Oxford: Clarendon Press, 1907; reprinted 1975), 274, s.v. זמר.

7. Bayer, "Titles of Psalms", 96.

8. Bayer, "Titles of Psalms", *passim*.

9. Suggestion made in conversation.

10. Bayer, "Titles of Psalms", 85–7.

11. Brown, Driver, Briggs, *Lexicon,* 618–19, s.vv. נָגֶן and נָגַע.

12. Bayer, "Titles of Psalms", 96.

13. Hershel Shanks, *Jerusalem: An Archaeological Biography* (New York: Random House, 1995), 153–5, with the relevant quotation from Josephus. Also on p. 155 is a drawing of a reconstruction of the staircase and gateway, with a tiny trumpeter on its top. The photograph of the stone and a drawing of it with a trumpeter standing in it, is on p. 157.

14. Mishnah, Second Division, Appointed Times, Sukkah 5:4 in Jacob Neusner's translation, *The Mishnah: A New Translation* (New Haven: Yale University Press, 1988), 289; the square brackets are his.

15. Josephus, *The Wars of the Jews,* book 7, chapter 1, paragraph 1, section 3. In William Whiston's translation, *The Works of Josephus,* 751.

16. Shanks, *Jerusalem,* 142–9.

17. Bathyah Bayer, *The Material Relics of Music in Ancient Palestine and its Environs: an Archeological Inventory* (Tel-Aviv: Israel Music Institute, 1963).

18. Joachim Braun, *Die Musikkultur Altisraels/Palästinas: Studien zu archäologischen, schriftlichen und vergleichenden Quellen* (Freiburg: Universitätsverlag; Göttingen: Vandenhoek & Ruprecht, 1999), 222–3.

19. As most of the local archaeologists agree, one can trust any government department when given the choice between genuine and fake, to choose unhesitatingly the fake.

Chapter 5

The Prophetical Books

ISAIAH

With Isaiah we return to somewhat more explicit references but with the strong implication that music, especially instrumental music, is frivolous and distracts people from a properly religious and God-fearing life. The first mention, 5:12, is evidential of this. While in the first verse of that chapter we have the encouraging "I sing [אָשִׁירָה, *āshīrāh*] to my wellbeloved", from verse 8 onwards we turn to "Woe unto them. . . ." and in verse 12 woe to them for whom "the harp, and the viol, the tabret, and pipe, and wine, are in their feasts", *kinnōr vānevel tōf v°chālīl*. The tabret is *tōf*, the same drum as the timbrel we have frequently encountered, and the chālīl we have also met above. The harp is as usual the kinnōr, but why should the nēvel be translated as viol instead of the AV's normal psaltery?

Viols and Other Anomalies

The viol was a bowed instrument and no such thing existed in the biblical period. The bow, as a tool to scrape a string, was not invented much before about A.D. 800.[1] The viol, or *viola da gamba,* Italian for leg-fiddle, was invented in Spain around A.D. 1470, and was further developed in Italy in the early Renaissance.[2] It is called *da gamba* because it is held between the knees or between the calves, according to size. The bass viol is the most important size of the family and that which is usually meant by viol without further specification. Save that its outline is rather smoother, it looks somewhat like a cello, which was also held between the calves in the days before the endpin was invented. It has six strings rather than four and it is bowed with the right hand palm-upward instead of palm-downward. The viol was, in King James's time, often used in consorts of several sizes, as for example in John Dowland's *Lachrimae, or Seaven Teares Figured in Seaven Passionate Pavans* of 1604. It was a much more respectable bowed instrument than the violin. The violin, which was more formally called *violino da braccio*, or arm-fiddle, because it was held on the shoulder, was then used mainly for dance music, and the violin band, the precursor of our orchestra, which included the alto, the viola and the bass, the violoncello, was only just beginning to appear.[3]

The Greek of the Septuagint follows the Hebrew of Isaiah 5:12 with κιθάρας καὶ ψαλτηρίου καὶ τυμπάνων καὶ αὐλῶν, *kitharas kai psaltēriou kai tympanōn kai aulōn*, lyre and psaltery, as is usual for kinnōr and nēvel, and drum and double-pipe. Jerome, however, in the Latin, has *cithara, et lyra, et tympanum, et tibia*. *Cithara* is his usual translation for kinnōr, as kithara is the Septuagint's, and why he suddenly changes to *lyra* for the nēvel, instead of his usual psalterium we have no way of telling. A likely suggestion is that he might have been influenced by the Targum, which has the Aramaic equivalent for kinnōr and nēvel, but instead of a word for drum has *qatros*, followed by *abuva*, the latter the normal Aramaic for chālīl. Qatros is similar to the name of one of Nebuchadrezzar's instruments, the *qaytros*, in Daniel 3. This, as we shall see, is always taken to be an attempt at Greek kithara and, like that word, is translated as harp by the AV in Daniel. If Jerome already had cithara for kinnōr, he could not use it again for qatros. Lyra in Greek was normally an alternative name for the smaller lyre, the *chelys*, so called because its body was traditionally made from a tortoise shell. This was the instrument used for less formal music making, for after-dinner song, for example, rather than for the professional bardic recitations for which the kithara was used. So perhaps Jerome decided to combine the Septuagint and the Targum, or perhaps the text of the Targum in his day had all five instruments, one of which was dropped by a later scribe.[4] If he decided to keep the tabret from the Septuagint, and he wanted also to include the qatros from the Targum, lyra would be a not unreasonable choice. This, in its turn, would leave the AV with little alternative, because it could not use harp twice, but to choose the name of another string instrument, preferably a respectable one, from those known to its readers, and hence the use of viol. For much the same reason, the Spanish translation of this passage uses *vihuela* and the French *luth,* both plucked instruments and both equally respectable, for the Spaniards used the vihuela, similar to the guitar of that period but larger, where the rest of Europe used the lute. The lute, with its pear-shaped back, was both a solo instrument and the first choice for accompanying a singer. Luther and the Italian translators keep more closely to the Hebrew with their usual German and Italian words for psaltery.

There is less reason for the AV to use "the noise of thy viols" in 14:11, save perhaps as a parallel to 5:12, and to try to make sense of a somewhat obscure verse, for although the word in the Hebrew is again nēvel, it does not appear in either LXX or Vulgate, both of which ignore any suggestion of music in this verse. Nor does it appear in the Targum.

The viol reappears in Amos 5:23, where the Hebrew has nēvel, the Targum kinnōr, LXX just instrument (*organōn*, the Greek for tool) and the Vulgate again has lyra. Nine verses later, however, both Hebrew and Aramaic are nēvel, Greek has organōn again, but Latin this time has psalterium, so that the previous use of Latin lyra can only be a partial explanation. Only Hebrew and AV are consistent, with respectively nēvel and viol every time, and we are still no wiser as to the reason for the use of viol, a word which appears only here and in 1 Maccabees 13:51, and nowhere else in the whole English text of the Bible.

Perhaps we should not be so surprised at this use of viol. It is part of the same general practice that has been going on for at least three thousand years. Whenever the translators, or in the case of the book of Daniel, which we shall meet shortly, the author, struck an unfamiliar word for a musical instrument, they simply reached for something with which their readers would be familiar. The earlier English translators did it all the time. Coverdale brought the lute into several psalms, the most respectable and best-known of all plucked instruments of his day, and also the shawm, the loudest of wind instruments and the mainstay of all outdoor ceremonies and celebrations. He used lute in the passage in Isaiah also. Wyclif brought the symfonye and croud into the party for the prodigal son in Luke 15:25. The symphony was a bagpipe-like string instrument, the ancestor of the hurdy-gurdy. The player had one hand on a short keyboard and with the other cranked a handle which turned a wheel to "bow" the strings so that one or more sounded a continuous drone while another played the melody. The crowd was the ancestor of the crwth, a bowed lyre—crowder was a common epithet for a minstrel and one which still survives as a surname. Tyndale brings in fydilles, in which Coverdale copies him, for instance in 1 Samuel 18:6. What is perhaps the more surprising is the consistency of translation, at least from Tyndale onwards, with the AV more often than not using the same words, often the same phrases, that Tyndale had used a century earlier.

Artists were different. When one wants to know what instruments were used in almost any period up to, but definitely not including the pre-Raphaelites who consistently tried, inaccurately and unsuccessfully, to revive the Middle Ages, one can simply look at the paintings of biblical scenes. The Elders of the Apocalypse, a favorite subject of the eleventh and twelfth centuries, play all the instruments then popular. The Assumption of the Virgin was a favorite excuse in the Renaissance to include every instrument the artist could think of. Psalm 150 has rung down the ages with whatever was closest at the time to the instruments named therein.

It is only very occasionally, strongly in the thirteenth century, and in our time with this book and those cited in the bibliography, that anyone has shown much interest in what the instruments really were. But to return to our subject.

Isaiah 16:11 substitutes harp for kinnōr as usual, as do 23:16 and 24:8, where the tabret is again the tambourine or timbrel.

In 18:3 the trumpet is the ram's horn, as it should be when sounding an alarm or a summons. The shōfār gādōl in 27:13, the great trumpet, is in legend, as we said in chapter 2, a special one. This is the other horn of the ram which Abraham sacrificed instead of Isaac. The left horn was heard from heaven at the Giving of the Law on Mount Sinai—the right horn, the larger, will be heard in times to come.[5] The times to come, in Hebrew thought, was the ingathering of the people, which was believed to precede the end of days.

In 30:29 the pipe is again the chālīl just as in 30:32 the tabrets and harps are those instruments to which we have become accustomed under those names.

In 38:20 we have, for the first time, the generic term stringed instruments, "The Lord *was ready* to save me: therefore we will sing my songs to the stringed instruments." Here it is not, as we might have hoped, *minnīm*, the word which we took to indicate that in Psalm 150:4. It is again words on the *ngn* root, וּבִגְנוֹתַי נְנַגֵּן, *ūn³ginōtai n³naggēn*. A closer, though less fluent translation of the text would be: The Lord to save me; and my stringed instruments (*n³ginotai*) we are touching (*n³naggen*) all the days of our life unto (or in) the house of the Lord. Nothing in the text about singing. Nor is there in LXX, which refers to blessing the Lord with psaltery, though the Latin does refer to song, *psalmos nos cantabimus*, we will sing our psalms. Perhaps the AV was trying to combine both ideas, *cantabimus* with *psaltēriou*. This all leaves us with this vexed, and vexing, question that comes up again and again: how limited is the meaning of the נגן, *ngn* words? Of a certainty, one could go through the whole length of the Hebrew Bible and find examples of words deriving from this root, and the allied נגע, *ngʿ*, to which one could assign a large number of meanings.[6] Many, but not all of them, are musical, and that is about as far as it is safe to go with any certainty.

There follows a series of references to singing. The first, 42:10, is a quotation from psalms, and therefore uses the word shīr which is constant there in that context, and in shīr hashīrīm, the Song of Songs. But those which follow, 42:11, 44:23, 48:20, 49:13, 51:11, 52:8 and 9, 54:1, and 55:12 all use a different word, *rinnāh*, which means a loud cry, "a ringing cry" according to the BDB.[7] These clearly culminate in 58:1, even though the *rnn* root, רנן, is not used in that verse, "Cry aloud . . . lift up thy voice like a trumpet", for indeed the ram's horn, the shōfār has a ringing cry.

Isaiah is one of the few books of the Bible where we have an independent cross-check on how our surviving Hebrew text may correspond with that of earlier times, for an almost complete copy of that book was among the Dead Sea Scrolls, as they are usually known, from the Essene communities based in and around Qumran and dating from the New Testament period. However, of the words and passages cited here, the only variant is a slight difference of spelling of one example of *rinnāh*, lengthening the *i*.

JEREMIAH

Jeremiah is on the whole too much concerned with howling and wailing to have much interest in music. His trumpet, whether an alarm or a summons to assembly or war, is always the ram's horn, in 4:5, 19, and 21, 6:1 and 17, 42:14, and 51:27.

The virgin's tabrets and dances in 31:4 are the normal frame drum, tōf, with māchōl, the sort of dance we have mostly met above, and again for dance in verse 13.

The pipes in 48:36 are the reed-pipe chālīl. It is surprising how seldom the chālīl appears. One would dearly like to know where it came from, and when, for it is never mentioned in the five books of Moses, nor in Joshua nor Judges. Not until Saul meets the group of prophets after he has been anointed by Samuel (1 Samuel 10:5) do we meet these pipes for the first time. We saw them again at Solomon's anointing (1 Kings 1:40), a passing reference in Psalm 87:7 (in the Hebrew though not in the AV), and in Isaiah 5:12 and 30:29, and then here. And that is all. For an instrument in such wide-spread use throughout the region, it seems odd that if it were to be used at all it would not be used much more frequently than this. Certainly it was common enough in the immediate post-biblical period for there are numerous illustrations of it in mosaics of the first few centuries A.D. and there are frequent references in the Talmud to its use and it appears in the Apocrypha. According to the Talmud it was used in the Temple, but only on twelve days in the year, always at a festival. Three occasions were during the seven days of Passover, one was at Shavuot, and eight were during Sukkot.[8] In the Gemara, this is expanded somewhat, saying that the Rabbis taught that there had been an *abūv,* as the chālīl is called in Aramaic, in the Temple. It was smooth, thin, made of reed, and from the time of Moses, but this last we may take with a grain of salt, for as we have just said there is no reference to it until Saul met the prophets.[9]

The origin of the aulos is unknown. Maybe the Greeks invented it, perhaps they picked it up as they traveled towards Greece through Central Asia. Perhaps it started in Egypt, where Hickmann suggests a date of around 1500 B.C. for the *māt,* the Egyptian equivalent.[10] However, the māt always appears both longer and narrower in bore than the aulos, as well as quite differently constructed, which suggests a different origin. The survival of the monaulos, the unpaired instrument of the same type, right across Asia, from Turkey to Japan (plate 9) gives some support to the Central Asian hypothesis.

LAMENTATIONS

Since this is also by Jeremiah it is not surprising that there are no references to music other than those mentioned above.

EZEKIEL

Ezekiel was one of the most mystical of the prophets, with a style which was later copied by St. John in Revelations, for while they did not both see the same visions, there are considerable similarities between them. Both mention instruments, but it would be with some caution that one took any of the references to apply to real life.

Ezekiel's first, 7:14, is to trumpet in the AV, though in the Hebrew it merely says that they blew a blast, but the words used, *tāk$^{ə c}$ū vatākō^{c}a*, are both variants of t^{ə}kī^{c}āh, the normal word for a shōfār call. The Targum uses the word qarna, the Aramaic equivalent of the Hebrew qeren, which we said above was not normally used in a musical sense, though we shall meet it again musically in Daniel. The Septuagint has salpinx and the Vulgate tuba, so it is clear that nobody had any doubt that the blast was blown on some sort of trumpet.

In 26:13 the harp is as usual the kinnōr, and is presumably a symbol of any symptoms of joy or pleasure in a general tirade of reproach. Unusually, although the Vulgate has cithara, the Septuagint has psaltērion.

28:13, on the other hand, is imbued with the vision of a mystic, and there is no suggestion that tabrets and pipes were really bejewelled. The AV here is recalling the pipe and tabor, the combination of a single musician playing the melody on a three-holed pipe with one hand while simultaneously playing the rhythm on a small drum with the other. This was the commonest dance band throughout Europe from the mid-thirteenth century onwards, one that survives to this day in southern France and northern Spain. It was still heard in England into the early years of the twentieth century and it has now been revived there and elsewhere, both for early music performance and for folk and folk-pop groups. On the pipe, three fingerholes, two for the fingers and one for the thumb, are sufficient for most dance tunes, which seldom modulate into different keys and which seldom exceed a range of a twelfth or so, an octave and a half.

One can cover that range with three holes because the pipe has a narrow enough bore that it plays easily in the upper octaves. The first note of the scale is the second harmonic, an octave above the pipe's fundamental. Opening the holes in sequence produces the next three notes of the scale, covering all three and blowing harder produces the third harmonic, and opening two fingerholes and then covering all again takes one to the octave or fourth harmonic. Doing this and playing a rhythm at the same time with the other hand on the drum, which hangs from the player's arm or shoulder, is a knack, but one that is only marginally more complex than that of steering an automobile while changing gear, and certainly no worse than playing different parts with each hand on the piano. The word translated tabret here seems to be the usual tōf, but the translators may have been moved towards pipe and tabor by the unusual word they translated as pipes, *ūn⁹kāveychā*. The initial *ū*- means and, and the terminal -*chā* means your, while the -*ey*- is because it is plural. *Nkv* is something pierced, and perhaps we have here a word that could mean some sort of flute, rather than a reed. However, the BDB denies any musical connotation. It describes *nekev* as a "technical term for jeweler's work, probably some hole or cavity".[11] Since a drum and a jeweler's cavity seem an inherently improbable coupling, and neither LXX or Vulg. seem aware of any musical association in this passage, speaking only of treasures and storehouses, it does look as though the AV may have been misled. A further complication is that according to the Kittel edition of the *Biblia Hebraica*, the Hebrew text may well be corrupt—they give two other renderings, one based on the Septuagint and the other on the Syriac.[12] Perhaps we should leave this passage as possibly musical but more probably relating only to jewelery and gold-work.

33:3, 4, 5, and 6 are much more straightforward. Here the watchman blows the shōfār, as in many other passages, a use that has remained a standard part of the shōfār's function to the present day. Here, at least, in a book full of mystical symbolism and visions, we have a musical reference from normal life.

In verse 32 no actual instrument is specified in English, Hebrew, or Latin in association with song and voice. LXX is the only source to specify an instrument with φωνὴ ψαλτηρίου, *phōnē psaltēriou*, the sound of the psaltery, presumably of the nēvel. The word used in Hebrew is *naggēn* which, as we have frequent occasion to note, is problematic in that it may refer to vocal music or to plucking strings.

DANIEL

In chapter 3 we have the most famous of all musical ensembles in the Bible, the royal orchestra of a foreign potentate, Nebuchadnezzar, king of Babylon. It is one that defeated the translators of the AV, not altogether surprisingly because to some extent at least it defeated the author of the book. The book of Daniel, as we have it, was written down long after the events it records and it was written not in Hebrew but mostly, and certainly the part that concerns us, in Aramaic. As a result there is no Targum, which might help us with a second opinion, for the Targum is a translation into Aramaic, and this book is already in that tongue. Nor is the Septuagint as much help as it might be because several of the Aramaic names of the instruments seem to be attempts at Greek names, so that the LXX were translating Aramaicized Greek back into Greek. And the final problem is that the list, which appears four times in chapter 3, in verses 5, 7, 10, and 15, differs slightly at each appearance. Of the seven terms for musical instruments, only the first and the last are the same in each of the four references, emphasizing the lack of certainty on the author's part. The second, מַשְׁרוֹקִיתָא, *mashrōqītā*, loses its *vāv* in verse 10, but the *vāv*, ו, and the *yōd*, י, are sometimes called vowel letters because they are often used to indicate which vowel should be inserted, here with vāv the long *ō*. The third, written as קִיתְרוֹס, *qaytrōs*, probably an attempt at Greek kithara, only has its vāv in verse 5 and loses its yōd in verse 15, again only a matter of vowel letters. Without the yōd it is the same qatros as in the Targum of Isaiah 5:12, discussed earlier in this chapter. One text suggests that it should always be spelled *kīthārōs*, even closer to the Greek term.[13] The fourth word, שַׂבְּכָא, *sabbᵉchā*, begins with a *sīn*, שׂ, in each verse except 5, where it begins with a *samech*, ס. The fifth, פְּסַנְתֵּרִין, is *pᵉsantērīn* everywhere except in verse 10 where the first letter is missing the dot in it, changing the *p* to *f*, again not an important matter, but in verse 7 the *t* is the sharper *tēt*, ט, rather than the aspirated *tāf*, ת.[14] The sixth, סוּמְפֹּנְיָה, *sūmpōnyāh*, is the worst treated for it is omitted entirely from verse 7 (which is clearly the most carelessly written verse of the four), and lacks its *m*, מ, in verse 10.

Let us first take each instrument and produce as near a translation as we can, and then see what we can do about identifications.

The first in each list is קַרְנָא, *qarnā* (AV cornet). At least we have an easy start, for qarnā is one of those words (the best known example is probably sack) which transcend linguistic barriers. There are great language families, such as the Indo-European, where one can follow word-roots from Sanskrit through Greek, Latin, and later European languages into English, and the Semitic, covering Arabic, Hebrew, Syriac, Aramaic, to name only two, and there are few connexions or common links between them. But qarnā is one that appears in both. It is qeren in Hebrew, *keras* in Greek, *cornu* in Latin, *Horn* in German (the *k* changing to a guttural *h* by Grimm's Law) and so into English. Always it means horn, both the horn of an animal and the animal horn that is blown. The LXX translated it not as keras but, perversely one might think, as salpinx each time, the long metal trumpet of the Greek armies. As one might expect, Jerome followed suit with tuba, the long metal trumpet of the Roman armies which is portrayed on Titus's Arch. The AV's cornet (today spelled with two *t*s to distinguish it from the modern brass instrument), as we said in Chapter 2, was a wooden instrument with fingerholes which was blown like a trumpet, the great virtuoso instrument of the Renaissance, used for elaborate divisions, as variations and elaborations were then called. It also frequently played the top line with voices in church, with sackbuts (which we shall meet very shortly) accompanying the lower voices. It was also used for tower music, performing hymns and other tunes, again with sackbuts, from a balcony in the tower of the town hall or of the main church in many cities across Europe— these were the direct ancestors of the Lutheran and other brass chorales. There is in the library of Christ Church, one of the greatest of the colleges of the University of Oxford and the site of the city's cathedral, barely a mile from where I write, a pair of cornetts which were bought to be played when King James visited Oxford. Since all the translators of this part of King James's Bible were professors and scholars of Oxford, it is not surprising that they adopted cornet for qarnā, but today we should be better advised to use the simpler horn.[15]

The second instrument is also the same each time, flute in AV and *mashrōqītā* in the Aramaic. The BDB suggests a derivation for this word, which appears in the Bible only these four times, from *shrq* which, in biblical Hebrew, becomes שָׁרַק, *shāraq*, a verb meaning 'hiss' or 'whistle' which we first met in Judges, and which they suggest might be the etymological origin of the Greek word, σῦριγξ, syrinx, the alternative name for the panpipe.[16] Certainly the LXX believed this and used syrinx each time; Vulgate uses *fistula*, a more general word for a flute or whistle. BDB gives, as it customarily does, all the known appearances of the word in the Bible, and although *mashrōqītā* does not appear anywhere else, other derivatives of *shāraq* are used for hissing in derision and, in Deborah's song in Judges 5:16 for the shepherd's pipe. Saʿadyah Gaon, a ninth-century A.D. Hebrew commentator on the Bible, suggests a link with Zechariah 10:8, where the AV's "I will hiss for them" could well mean whistle and could hark back to verses 2 and 3 in the same chapter, with their references to shepherds.

LXX uses kithara, as it normally does for kinnōr, for the third name, *qaytros,* and Vulgate follows suit in each verse. It is therefore logical for AV to use harp and for us to correct it to lyre.

Next comes the AV's sackbut, and here, as with cornett, we have a definite "no." Sackbut is English for trombone (*trombone* is an Italian word meaning big trumpet; the *-one* ending in Italian is an augmentative, to make the basic word, here *tromba,* larger). Sackbut was used for the trombone in English from the instrument's first appearance in the late Middle Ages up to the seventeenth or occasionally eighteenth century, when after a brief flirtation with double trumpet, meaning large as with double bass, the Italian name became the norm. Sackbut has returned into use today to distinguish between modern trombones, which retain the Italian name, and those reproductions of the Renaissance instruments which are made for early music performance. The reason for its use in the AV is that the word in the Aramaic is *sabbᵊchā,* and King James's translators had no idea of what it meant but just picked something familiar that sounded similar. The LXX has *sambykē* each time (Vulgate *sambuca*), and it is probable that it is that word that the author of Daniel was aiming at. Martin West cites a number of Greek descriptions and definitions of a somewhat unpopular and seldom-used instrument, concluding convincingly that it was a form of bow harp, with an illustration from a fifth century pot, very similar in appearance to the Ugandan *ennanga* in plate 14 here.[17] West uses the term arched harp, but that should be reserved for those harps whose neck arches over the soundbox, whereas the descriptions he cites, and the illustration, make it clear that it was a bow harp, with the neck curving up only slightly from the resonator.

Next comes psaltery. Again the assumption is that *pᵊsantērīn* is an attempt at Greek psaltērion, and that is the word used throughout by both LXX and Vulgate.

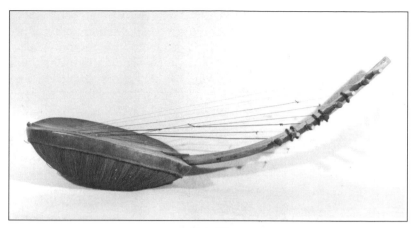

Plate 14
Bow harp, ennanga, from Uganda, similar to the Greek sambuca, and
to an Egyptian shoulder harp. Montagu Collection II 36.

Next comes dulcimer, except in verse 7, whence it is omitted. The Aramaic is *sūmpōnyāh*, an obvious attempt at Greek *symphonia*, which the LXX uses in verse 15, although omitting it from verses 5 and 10, and of course from 7. Certainly the Greek word does not mean a dulcimer; Wyclif and Coverdale simply transcribed it as symphonie, the hurdy-gurdy we described above. The dulcimer, an instrument which seems to have first appeared in Henry VIII's time in England, was, and still is, a form of psaltery whose wire strings were struck with light beaters instead of being plucked.[18] According to Liddell and Scott συμφωνία already had our modern meaning of "a union of many voices or instruments in concert:—a concert either of vocal or instrumental music," or "an agreeing together in sound" and so forth.[19] The Vulgate obviously decided to ignore scribal vagaries and uses *symphonia* in all four verses, including verse 7.

The most puzzling aspect of the use of *sūmpōnyāh* in verses 5, 10, and 15 is that it would seem to equate with the following phrase "and all kinds of musick", in the original וְכֹל זְנֵי זְמָרָא, *v°chol z°nēy z°mārā*. This does indeed mean "with all kinds of music", though if we were correct above in our understanding of *z°mārā*, music instrumental rather than vocal and perhaps indicating with additional wind instruments. How does that differ from *sūmpōnyāh*? We do not know.

So, what were these instruments? Here, thanks to the penchant of the Babylonians for monumental sculpture, we do have rather more and rather better information than for Israelite instruments. Unfortunately, Subhi Anwar Rashid's book on Mesopotamia in the great German series of the History of Music in Pictures tends to concentrate on the north of the area, with carvings and instruments from Nimrud and Nineveh, rather than from Babylon towards the south.[20] However, his illustrations from plate 129, about 200 years earlier than Nebuchadrezzar, to plate 153 will give a very good idea of what was available. There are vertical angle-harps, held with the soundbox projecting upwards, with many strings plucked with the fingers, horizontal harps, with the soundbox below, played with a plectrum, usually with rather fewer strings than the vertical harps if the carvings are to be trusted in this respect, divergently held double pipes like the aulos, parallel pipes like the zummāra, lyres of different shapes, frame drums both round and square, cymbals, trumpets which look as though they were metal, and bells. Almost any illustrated book on the history of music will have at least some illustrations of Mesopotamian reliefs. If one were to extend this research into the period when the text was written down, rather than when it happened, then as Rashid's plates from 154 onwards show, even more instruments become available, such as large kettle drums, panpipes (the syrinx or mashrōqītā), long-necked lutes, which might be what was intended by sabbᵊchā, in addition to the instruments already mentioned. If, as Canon Galpin suggests, "and all kinds of musick" was meant as an addition to the preceding list of instruments, which were already playing sūmpōnyāh in its Greek meaning of all together in concert, then these additional instruments which we see in Rashid's iconography could well have been included, *vᵊchol zᵊnēy zᵊmārā*.[21]

The most important aspect of the orchestra in the book of Daniel from our point of view is that it was a Babylonian orchestra, not an Israelite one, and thus, regrettably, one that can cast little light on all the other mentions of instruments in the Bible, though possibly with some influence on musical practices after the return from Exile in Babylon.

HOSEA

In Hosea 5:8 we have one of the rare examples of both types of trumpet in the same verse, the ram's horn in Giboa and the metal trumpet in Rama, blowing the one to the other about a mile and a half apart across the valleys, if Robinson and Smith's map of the environs of Jerusalem is to be trusted.[22] The trumpet to be set to the mouth in 8:1 is the shōfār.

JOEL

So also is Joel's trumpet in Zion (2:1 and 15), as is usual with alarms and assemblies.

AMOS

And again for Amos in 2:2 and 3:6. All three prophets are using the same symbolism for the same purposes.

In 5:23 and 6:5 we have quite a different mood, and here we have the second pair of translations of nēvel as a viol. In 5:23 there seems to have been considerable textual confusion over "the melody of thy viols", for while the Hebrew has *zimrat nᵊvāleychā*, the 'music of your nēvels', with the usual potential for confusion due to the use of zmr, the Targum has *nigun kinarach*, using ngn with its connotations of plucking, as well as a different instrument, the melody of your kinnōrs. The Septuagint has *psalmon organōn*, plucked instrument, or perhaps as Bagster's Septuagint translator has it somewhat freely, the music of thine instruments, and the Vulgate has *cantica lyræ tuæ*, the song of your lyre. It was, of course, the Vulgate's use of lyre in Isaiah that led to the AV's use of viol there.

In 6:5 both Hebrew and Targum are nēvel for "the sound of the viol" but LXX is organōn again. Vulgate goes back to its normal term for the nēvel and uses psalterii, whereas AV presumably decided to remain consistent. The whole meaning of the verse is depressing for us as musicians or interested in music, for the beginning of the sentence, of which verse 5 is only a part, runs from verse 1 "Woe to them . . ." and continues in verse 5 "that chant to the sound of the viol, *and* invent to themselves instruments of musick, like

David . . ."[23] In the second half of the verse, for "instruments of musick", the Hebrew is $k^\partial l\bar{e}y$-shīr, the tools of song, whereas the Targum has *manei z$^\partial$mara*, the playing of instruments or playing of music. LXX is unclear which half of the original verse is represented by the *phonē tōn organōn*, the sound of the instrument. The Vulgate has *vasa cantici*, tools of song as in the Hebrew.

The idea that the instruments were invented by King David was later taken up in 2 Chronicles 7:6—one needs to remember that although Chronicles is placed in its historical sequence in the King James Bible, it was written very much later, later than Amos or anything in the Bible except perhaps Daniel and Maccabees, so that ideas which we read later, as in this case, are sometimes resumed there. There is no earlier biblical suggestion that David invented, or made, instruments himself, though it is not unusual in other cultures for people such as shepherds to make their own instruments.

OBADIAH, JONAH, MICAH

There is no mention of music or instruments in any of these books. The word hissing appears in Micah 6:16 but this is derision, not whistling.

NAHUM

One might like to think that harness bells or plates such as we shall meet shortly in Zechariah might be included in 3:2, along with "the noise of a whip, and the noise of the rattling of wheels, and of the pransing [sic] horses, and of the jumping chariots", but there is no mention of them.

HABAKKUK

The last three words of the book, "my stringed instruments" is in Hebrew the one word *bingīnōtāy*, the ngn root that we have discussed in some detail above. The position of the rubric, which is omitted from both LXX and Vulgate, here as the final verse of Habakkuk's prayer was the genesis of Bathja Bayer's contention that

some of the psalm introductions may have slipped from the end of
one psalm to the beginning of a quite different one, an additional
complication here being that we have a prelude at the beginning of
chapter 3 as well as a postlude at the end.

ZEPHANIAH

1:16 is the ram's horn, as one would expect from its context, and the
hissing in 2:15 is again derision.

HAGGAI

He makes no mention of music.

ZECHARIAH

The trumpet in 9:14 is the shōfār as usual.

One is strongly inclined to take 10:8, "I will hiss for them, and
gather them", as whistle rather than hiss, for it is surely a summons,
just as one whistles to call people today. The Hebrew word, אֶשְׁרְקָה,
eshrᵊqāh is a form of shāraq just as mashrōqītā was, but whether
whistling from the mouth is meant or with a whistle, who can tell?—
the former seems the more likely.

In 14:20 we have the only definite evidence in the Bible for musical
horse harness. This is a clear reference back to Exodus 28:36, though
there is no apparent connexion between the gold plate on Aaron's
miter and these plates on a horse's bit. The AV has "upon the bells of
the horses" but the Hebrew is not pa'amōn nor any other word
which might mean bell but mᵊtsillōt, a word whose root is clearly
the tsil which much earlier we identified as meaning cymbal. These
are surely those plates of brass or bronze which hang from the
harness and which jingle and clash together as the horse moves. Targum however uses a word, כְּרוּבַת, kᵊrūvat which Jastrow translates
as a wrap or blanket.[24] The Septuagint uses the word for a horse's
bridle, or more specifically the bit, as does the Vulgate. A few years
ago I acquired some small bronze pellet bells from Luristan, not
unlike pomegranates (cf. Exodus 28:33–5), of much this period

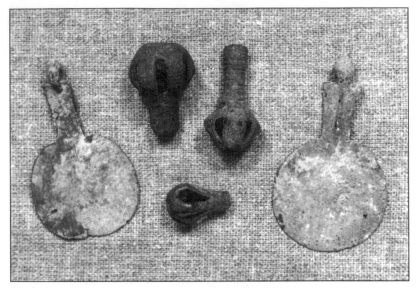

Plate 15
Pellet bells perhaps similar to pa'amōnīm (XI 14), and harness plates similar to
mᵊtsillōt (XI 16), all antiquities from Luristan. Montagu Collection.

though further to the east geographically. With them were two small thin bronze discs, exactly as one would expect these mᵊtsillot to be (plate 15) and it would certainly be much easier to engrave HOLINESS TO THE LORD (there are no capitals in the Hebrew, Greek, or Latin) on such plates than on a bell, though one must admit that, if Jastrow is correct in his translation, for which he offers no etymology, it would be easier still to embroider it on a horse-blanket.

There are no references in Malachi.

NOTES

1. Werner Bachmann, *The Origins of Bowing and the development of bowed instruments up to the thirteenth century,* translated Norma Deane (London: Oxford University Press, 1969).
2. Ian Woodfield, *The Early History of the Viol* (Cambridge: Cambridge University Press, 1984).

3. Peter Holman, *Four and Twenty Fiddlers: The Violin at the English Court 1540–1690* (Oxford: Clarendon Press, 1993).

4. I am grateful to my son Simon for the suggestion that qatros might have been present as an Aramaic gloss on either kinnōr or nēvel and that a later scribe could well have noticed that there was one instrument too many and deleted the wrong one.

5. *Pirke de Rabbi Eliezer*, translated and annotated Gerald Friedlander (London: Kegan Paul, Trench, Trubner & Co; New York: Bloch Publishing Company, 1916; reprinted New York: Judaic Studies Library 6, Sepher-Hermon Press, 1981), 31.

6. Francis Brown, S. R. Driver, and Charles A. Briggs, *A Hebrew and English Lexicon* (Oxford: Clarendon Press, 1907; reprinted 1975), 618–19, has two columns of them.

7. Brown, Driver, and Briggs, *Lexicon*, 943, *s.v.* רנן.

8. Mishnah, Jacob Neusner, *The Mishnah* (New Haven: Yale University Press, 1988), 811, Fifth Division, Holy Things, Arakhin, 2:3, III D.

9. Talmud, Sēder Kādāshīm, ʿArāchīn 10b.

10. Hans Hickmann, *Ägypten*, Musikgeschichte in Bildern II/1 (Leipzig: Deutscher Verlag für Musik, 1961), 104.

11. Brown, Driver, and Briggs, *Lexicon*, 666, *s.v.* נָקַב.

12. *Biblia Hebraica*, ed. Rudolf Kittel (Stuttgart: Württembergische Bibelanstalt, 7th ed., ed. A. Alt, O. Eissfeldt, and P. Kahle, 1951), 856.

13. In the notes to the *Biblia Hebraica* to verse 5, 1260.

14. The Hebrew alphabet has two letters which today sound s, the *samech*, ס, and the *sīn*, שׂ, which differs from *shīn* only by the position of a point above, before it for *shīn*, שׁ and after for *sīn*—we met above a case where the two may have been confused. Presumably there was once a difference in the sound between ס and שׂ. There are also two letters which sound t, *tēt*, ט, much the sharper of the two, and *tāf*, ת, which is aspirated to the extent that it is often transcribed as *th* as in sabbath.

15. For the lists of translators see A. C. Partridge, *English Biblical Translation*, The Language Library, ed. Eric Partridge and Simeon Potter (London: André Deutsch, 1973), 107.

16. Brown, Driver, and Briggs, *Lexicon*, 1117 for the Aramaic, *s.v.* שרק; 1056 for the Hebrew, *s.v.* שָׁרַק.

17. M. L. West, *Ancient Greek Music* (Oxford: Clarendon Press, 1992), 75–7 and plate 23

18. The Appalachian dulcimer is a special use of the name and should not be confused with the normal dulcimer. The latter is often called hammer dulcimer to avoid confusion with the Appalachian.

19. Henry George Liddell and Robert Scott, *A Greek-English Lexicon* (Oxford: University Press, 4th ed., 1855), 1346, *s.v.* συμφωνία.

20. Subhi Anwar Rashid, *Mesopotamien*, Musikgeschichte in Bildern II/2 (Leipzig: Deutscher Verlag für Musik, 1984).

21. Francis W. Galpin, *The Music of the Sumerians and their immediate successors the Babylonians and Assyrians* (Cambridge: University Press, 1936; reprinted Strasbourg: University Press, Librairie Heitz, 1955), 69.

22. James B. Pritchard, ed., *The Times Atlas of the Bible* (London: Times Books, 1987), 73. Unfortunately both place names seem to appear in more than one location!

23. I am grateful to Lynda Sayce for pointing out the link between verses 1 and 5, which I had missed.

24. Marcus Jastrow, *Dictionary of the Targumin, the Talmud Babli and Yerushalmi, and Midrashic Literature* (London: Luzac, 1903; reprinted New York: Judaica Press, 1989), 664, s.v. כְּרוּבְתָּא.

Chapter 6

The Apocrypha

The books of the Apocrypha are all late, dating from the last two or three centuries B.C. Some of them are further accounts of historical periods already covered while others are prophetical; the two books of Esdras are examples of each. Others are what are sometimes called Wisdom literature, for instance the Wisdom of Solomon and Ecclesiasticus, which because of the similarity of its name to Ecclesiastes is often called by its author's name, Ben Sirach, to avoid confusion. Some attempt to add further details to the canonical biblical books, others are quite simply good stories, and some combine the two as in the case of the three additions to Daniel. And two (in the Septuagint four) are late history, describing events which occurred too late to get into the Bible: the wars of the Maccabees from 168 B.C. against the Syrian Hellenistic occupiers who had desecrated the Temple. Their restoration of the Temple is the reason for the Jewish festival of Chanukah, which celebrates their feats and the eventual establishment of an independent Jewish state.

All the books have hovered, as it were, on the fringes of the Bible. They were not a part of the Jewish official text, although they exist only because they were included in the Septuagint, the translation into Greek for the Jews of Alexandria. They were adopted as canonical by the early Christian Church and they are still in the Vulgate and thence in other Roman Catholic Bibles without any distinction between them and other biblical books. There they are slotted into their appropriate places within the canon, rather than being set aside as a separate section as they in the LXX and in bibles of other churches. The Protestant and Reformed Churches have always been more hesitant about accepting them; they are often there but then only as a separate section between the two Testaments, Old and

New. They include stories well represented in European art, such as those of Susannah and the Elders and Judith and Holofernes. Although some of the books were originally written in Hebrew, most of these versions are lost and they survive today only in the Greek of the Septuagint, and of course in subsequent translation. There are comparatively few musical references.

ESDRAS

According to the introduction to the Bagster Septuagint, no Greek text of the second book of Esdras has survived and they therefore include only the first book.[1] This is the third Esdras in the Vulgate's enumeration because the Vulgate regards the Old Testament's Nehemiah as the second book of Ezra and then conflates the Apocryphal Esdras with the biblical Ezra, for the names are the same in Greek and Latin. Therefore the English Apocryphal Esdras 1 and 2 are the Vulgate's 3 and 4, the Latin of the fourth being its oldest surviving text.

1 Esdras's first mention, 4:63, is simply to "instruments of musick," but his second, 5:2, adds "tabrets and flutes." In the Greek these are tympanōn and aulos and in Latin tympanum and tibia. The first would be the same as the tōf and the second in each the reed-pipes or chālīl. Despite the large double reed used on the aulos, larger than that of our modern bassoon, there is an almost universal tendency to refer to them as flutes. Archeologists and museum curators alike look at them, see the reeds, which are often clearly visible in vase paintings and other illustrations, and then call them flutes without hesitation or consideration on the labels for the pots that illustrate them, or their statuettes, and write about them and caption their photographs again as flutes. With the pots themselves they are very careful always to give the correct Greek name for that particular type of bowl or cup, for it would be disgraceful to call a pelikē an amphora or vice versa, but it seems never to occur to them that it might be a good idea to use the right name for the musical instrument as well. Similarly, scholars translate the texts which refer to them equally unhesitatingly as flutes. Musicologists, understandably, get somewhat annoyed at this lack of proper scholarship and total disregard for the sound of music in antiquity.

In Esdras 5:42 and 59 and 62 to 66 we simply have repetitions of the parallel passages in Nehemiah 7:67 and Ezra 2:65, giving the numbers of the Temple servitors and of the singing men and women. There is a slight element of anything you can do I can do better, for while Ezra had 200 singing men and women, Nehemiah had 245 and although Esdras kept to that number in the Greek and in the English, in the Latin Apocryphal Esdras he acquired some extras and had 265. In verse 59 we have "musical instruments and trumpets; and the Levites the sons of Asaph had cymbals," here in the plural, not Asaph or one son alone as in the earlier books. Things were changing with the new generations and cymbal players multiplying. The trumpets as usual are salpinx and tuba. As so frequently with the LXX and Vulgate there is no way to tell whether this represents the shōfār or the metal chatsōtsᵊrāh, but it is unlikely that there was any change from the earlier accounts, which in Ezra was the metal trumpets.

In 2 Esdras, which is a more mystical and less narrative book, in 10:22 we are in the midst of one of the prophet's visions, where "Our psaltery is laid on the ground, our song is put to silence". This part of the book is very late, thought to be around A.D. 90, and there is no surviving Greek text. The Latin is *Et psalterium nostrum humiliatum est, et hymnus conticuit*—"our psaltery is humbled [thus on the ground] and song has become still [or silent]."

Tobit has nothing about music, regrettably for it is an enchanting story.

JUDITH

It is doubtful whether the story of Judith was ever intended to be believed as factual. It seems to be much more a retelling and updating of the story of Jael in Judges 4 and 5. It is set into the period of the Captivity in Babylon as a disguise from its own period, the troubled times of the second century B.C. which led up to the Maccabaean revolt, and it was probably written as a promise of future freedom from the oppression of the Asiatic Greeks. Thus Holofernes is greeted in the style of a much earlier period in 3:7 "with garlands, with dances, and with timbrels," μετὰ στεφάνων καὶ χορῶν καὶ τυμπάνων (*meta stephanōn kai chorōn kai tympanōn*), *cum coronis, et lampadibus, ducentes choros in tympanis, et tibiis,* "with garlands, torches, two hundred dancers with drums, and pipes." It is only the Vulgate which gives the number of two hundred for the dancers and adds the picturesque idea of a torch-light procession. Just as Deborah sang in triumph after Jael had slain Sisera, so Judith sang after she had killed Holofernes (16:2), tuning to God a new psalm, with timbrels and cymbals, again tympanois and kymbalois.

There is nothing musical in the additional chapters to Esther.

THE WISDOM OF SOLOMON

The strings of the psaltery are used symbolically in 19:18: "like as in a psaltery notes change the name of the tune, and yet are always sounds." The Greek ὥσπερ ἐν ψαλτηρίῳ φθόγγοι τοῦ ῥυθμοῦ τὸ ὄνομα διαλλάσσουσι, *hōsper en psaltēriō phthongoi tou rhythmou to onoma diallassousi* says much the same as the English save that it is the rhythm rather than the tune whose name is being changed. In the Latin, however, it is an organ whose sound is being changed. Music at this time, so far as we know, would normally be in one mode, using as it were (to employ our terms as an analogy) a single seven-note scale. If one were to change F to F sharp, or B to B flat, then one would have changed into a different mode or scale, with a different name. There were probably also different rhythmic modes (certainly there were in the Middle Ages), so that it makes little difference to the sense which word, tune or rhythm, one uses. Change the pitch of one string on the psaltery, or one key or pipe on the organ, and the tune or quality has changed "and yet are always sounds." By this time, shortly before the Christian era, some form of what we would call a psaltery might well have been possible. There is a variety of unclear instruments on the late Greek-style or Hellenistic pots of this period, some of which look as though they might be some form of psaltery, as well, of course, as the usual lyres. On the other hand, the coins which we used in plate 8 to show the two types of lyre, which we believe to be the kinnōr and the nēvel, dated from the Bar Kochba rebellion, a century or two later than this book. If both the instruments were still current in Bar Kochba's time (and how could his coiner know what they looked like to illustrate them if they were not?), then the psaltērion here may still be a lyre, probably the nēvel.

The organ was already established by this time and there is a number of small terracotta models of the hydraulis, as it was called, as well as clear illustrations in several Roman mosaics. It was called hydraulis because the air pressure was stabilized by water in a tank. If one blows air directly into an organ by pumping bellows, the pitch will be unstable because the harder one pumps the sharper the pitch, as every recorder player knows—blow hard, the pitch goes sharp, blow gently and it goes flat. A proper pneumatic organ has a second set of bellows as a reservoir, with lead weights lying on them to keep the pressure steady. One pumps air as strongly or as gently as one likes (nowadays with electric motors but originally with bellows) into that reservoir, and because its weights keep a uniform pressure of the air going to the pipes, the pitch does not fluctuate. Similarly, with the hydraulis, the primary bellows pumped air into a vessel where the air pressure was held steady by the weight of the surrounding water.[2] Jerome could well have been familiar with this type of instrument.

ECCLESIASTICUS OR THE WISDOM OF BEN SIRACH

In 9:4, the "woman that is a singer" is one of several women who are best avoided by those to whom Ben Sirach's advice is directed. She is more likely, as the AV margin points out, to have been an instrumentalist, and she was probably a string player, for the Greek is ψαλλούσης (*psallousēs*) and the Latin *psaltrice*, a woman who plucks. However later, in chapter 32, the author has several verses commending music, with higher praise than anywhere else in the Bible. From verse 3, "hinder not musick. Pour not out words where there is a musician, and shew not forth wisdom out of time. A concert of musick in a banquet of wine is as a signet of carbuncle set in gold. As a signet of an emerald set in a work of gold, so is the melody of musick with pleasant wine." The Greek and Latin (in 35:3 to 6 in LXX, for this is one of the places where AV and LXX are not precisely parallel) are simply μουσικὰ and *musica*, with no precise form specified. He says, too, in AV 40:20, that "wine and musick rejoice the heart" and that "the pipe and the psaltery make sweet melody" (40:21), though he prefers "a love of wisdom" and "a pleasant tongue." Αὐλὸς, aulos and tibia, and ψαλτήριον, psaltērion, are the pipe and psaltery and, again, mousika is music.

In 45:9 we are back in a repeat of Exodus 28:33–5 and 39:24–6 with the High Priest's robe, with its twined-linen pomegranates and golden bells, with the same Greek and Latin words as in Exodus, κώδων, kōdōn, and tintinnabulum, meaning as before either small clapper bells or pellet bells.

We continue in much the same vein of reminiscence in Ecclesiasticus 47:9, and here as in his warning against loose women, the root of the word for singers is the same *psal-* so that we may be dealing with string players, though one must remember the discussion above about the very name psalm. The Latin is *cantores* but while the AV goes on to refer to making sweet melody by their voices, both Vulgate and LXX refer not to voices but to their sound. The question of whether the music was vocal or instrumental, or of course both, thus has to remain open. Reminiscent too of the Old Testament is "the sons of Aaron . . . sounding the silver trumpets" in 50:16, though the silver is only the AV's memory of Numbers 10:2, for the description in the Greek and Latin is as it was in those versions of Numbers: "of beaten work." The AV translators would obviously want to keep this reference parallel with the original passage.

Baruch has no mention of music, nor has the Song of the Three Holy Children even though the song itself, adopted into the church service as the Benedicite, is one of the finest of all the psalms of praise to the Almighty. Nor have the other two additions to the book of Daniel, the History of Susannah and the highly entertaining story of Bel and the Dragon. The Prayer of Manasses, like the Apocryphal Esdras, is regarded as less canonical by the Vulgate and is relegated to an appendix at the back of the book, as it is in the LXX also.

MACCABEES

With Maccabees we are once again in historical narration, something of a shock return to reality from the beauties and entertainments of the extra episodes of Daniel's career in Babylon. The LXX has four books of Maccabees, in a decreasing order of historical fact. Only the first two were taken into the church's canon of the Apocrypha, and of these the second is much less reliable and less factual than the first. It has many additional details to the story, all clearly the creation of the author's imagination, with only one musical reference, to the Greek army of Nicanor advancing (15:25) with "trumpets and songs," both of which are plural in the Greek, the trumpets being, as they would have been in any Greek army, the salpinges.

The events of the revolt are told much more simply in 1 Maccabees. The first reference, in 3:45, seems to be the origin of 2 Esdras 10:22, with the "joy was taken from Jacob, and the pipe with the harp ceased." The instruments are the familiar αὐλὸς and κινύρα. The use of kinyra, a transliteration of Hebrew kinnōr, is sure indication that the text was originally in either Hebrew or Aramaic, for had it been in Greek from the beginning the word the AV translates as harp would have been far more likely to have been κιθάρα, kithara, the Greek name for the instrument. In verse 54 Judas's army sounded with trumpets, most probably shōfār in the original, though one must remember that Judas and his brothers were priests and so entitled to use the priestly chatsōtsᵊrōt as in Numbers 10:8 and 9, but we have no way of telling which it was because all that we have is the usual σάλπιγξ, salpinx in the Greek and tuba in the Latin.

In 4:13 the trumpets are again salpinx, and also in verse 40 where they blow a battle call as in Numbers 31:6 where the Hebrew text firmly says chatsōtsᵊrōt, the silver trumpets.

The rededication of the Temple in 4:54 involved the Temple orchestra, much as we have met it above, though now ἐν ᾠδαῖς καὶ κιθάραις καὶ κινύραις καὶ ἐν κυμβάλοις, "songs, and citherns, and harps, and cymbals." The songs really were songs, for the Greek is ōdais or odes, and the Latin *canticis*. The cittern, as it is more usually spelled today, was a very popular instrument in Elizabethan and Jacobean England and thus contemporary with the King James Bible. It was a plucked instrument, flat-backed and wire strung and so holding its tuning better than the lute, which was both gut strung and more lightly constructed with a delicate bowl-shaped body. As a result, while the cittern was used for some formal music making, for example in Thomas Morley's *Consort Lessons*, it was also used in all sorts of informal contexts for casual music. It was much used in barbers' shops because it could be reached down off its hook where it hung on the wall, ready to play while waiting for a chair to be free, and in taverns to be plucked at a moment's whim. A lute, on the other hand, would need several minutes to tune, by which time the conversation would have changed, the previous customer completed, or the desire to sing drowned in another pot of ale. This is the only time that the cittern is mentioned in the Bible and it is here as a translation of κιθάρα, Latin *citharis.* The Latin *cinyris* for the third term, κινύρα, is simply a transliteration of the Greek, for Greek *upsilon* or *u* always becomes a *y* in Latin as it does in English, just as kinyra is a Greek transliteration of kinnōr. Κύμβαλον of course is cymbals. The reason for using cittern was clearly again the problem of translating two terms for lyre, kithara and kinyra, and the impossibility of using harp for both. Why we here have cithern, whereas in Isaiah 5:12 we had viol as the solution to a similar problem, we cannot tell but the likely explanation is simply that it was a different team of translators: Isaiah was translated in Oxford and the Apocrypha was translated in Cambridge.[3] This discrepancy between Isaiah and Maccabees was probably so minor a matter that it failed to catch anyone's attention at the more general discussions when the texts came to the reviewing panel made up of members of each of the companies who had worked on the different part of the Bible. One should probably not draw any conclusions about life in the two universities in the early seventeenth century from the use of the respectable chamber-music viol in Oxford as distinct from the barber-shop and tavern cittern in Cambridge.

The external façade of the Temple was decorated for the occasion (4:57) "with crowns of gold and with shields." Crowns is στεφάνος, *stephanos* which can also mean a wreath (it was translated in the AV as garlands in Judith 3:7 above), and wreaths (or garlands) of gold seem more likely as celebrations of victory than crowns, though either is possible. The shields, according to legend, were those of the conquered Greek armies, hung there as trophies and as further signs of victory. The Septuagint uses, of course, the Greek name for a shield ἀσπιδίσκαις, *aspidiskais* and the Vulgate the Latin *scutulis.* The Greek *aspis* was a round shield with a protruding boss in the center, looking very like the *kempul* and the gongs that we see hanging from the cross-bars of stands in the Javanese gamelan. The *-diskais* is a diminutive, suggesting that they were small shields. The question that concerns us is, were they struck?

There is a great deal of evidence for the use of the gong in ancient Greece, for instance in the Eleusinian mysteries, under the name of ἠχεῖον or χαλκὸς ἠχεῖον. *Ēcheion* was a gong, from ἠχέω, *ēcheō,* to sound, ring, or echo, and *chalkos* means copper or, more likely in this context, bronze. There is also both Greek and Roman evidence for the use of the shield as a gong. The Corybantic dance, for example, was one in which soldiers struck each other's shields with their swords. It preserves the legends of the birth of Zeus when the κορυβάντες, the priests of Cybele, beat on their shields to drown his infant cries lest his father Kronos should hear him and eat him as he had eaten all his previous children. The dancers were also known as κούρητες, *kourētes*, the young men attending his mother, who was known as Rhea as well as Cybele. Many cities seem to have claimed to be the place where Zeus was born and issued coins showing this scene.[4] A bronze disc, which is probably itself such a shield-gong, was found in the Idean Cave, one of the oldest claimants to be the site of Zeus's birth and therefore a major cult center.[5] The disc, sometimes known as the Melkart Shield and preserved in the museum in Heraklion, dates from the eighth or ninth century B.C. It is heavily decorated in the Assyrian style and shows the kourētes as winged figures beating on shields, one each side of a Zeus who is a young man. He is thus rather older than on the coins referred to above, which are of later date and which all show him as a baby. The Idean cave also contained a number of other shield-gongs, or *kourētic tympana* as they are sometimes referred to, though the others are not so elaborately decorated as this one. The *ēcheion* were also used at the Zeus cult site at Dodona in mainland Greece, presumably as a result of this tradition of the use of gongs at his birth, though these seem to have been mainly cauldrons in shape, like those buried in the walls of Greek and Roman theaters as amplifiers.

The Romans had a procession in which the *salii* marched or danced through the streets beating special figure-eight shaped shields. There is at least one Roman, or Romano-British, bronze gong surviving, preserved in the Wiltshire Archaeological Society Museum in Devizes in England (plate 16). It was found at Westbury-on-Trym in the late nineteenth century and was initially catalogued as a tray, though subsequently labeled on display as a gong.[6] Further doubt was cast on this by Sir Ian Richmond, a leading authority on Romano-British archeology, who suggested that it was the base of a document box.[7] It is quite small, a little over 11 inches in diameter, between 28 and 29 cm, flat-faced with five concentric rings as decoration on the face, and a turned-back rim about 5/8 inch, or 17 mm, in depth. The thickness of the metal is not uniform, varying from 0.8 mm to 2.0 mm. The rim is partly corroded and broken away, but one suspension hole survives, important evidence that it probably was a gong. It could be hung like a gong, it looks like a gong, it would sound like a gong, though it was not, of course, possible to strike an

Plate 16
Roman or Romano-British gong from Westbury-on-Trym, Wiltshire, found c. 1880.
Wiltshire Archaeological and Natural History Society, Devizes, 620.

object of this age or rarity to hear how it sounded, and it may well have been a gong. By comparison with modern instruments of a similar size and shape in my own collection, the sound would have been more a "dong" than the deep resonant boom of our modern orchestral instruments. It is much the size of a small shield or aspidiskais, though flat-faced without the central boss.

Nor, of course, is beating on shields confined to the ancient world; Zulu warriors did the same in the nineteenth-century wars against the British, and there are many examples of shields made especially to be struck while accompanying dancing.[8]

It is, incidentally, certain that the gong did not originate in the Orient, for the Chinese stated quite positively that they acquired it from the West around the sixth century A.D.[9]

We shall return to this matter with 1 Corinthians 13:1, but we should emphasize here that St. Paul's reference there to the gong is proof that it was known to the Greeks, for if it were unknown in first or second-century Corinth there would have been no point in using it as a simile. We may assume, too, that it was known to Paul in Palestine for the gong remained associated with Cybele and her cult which, under various names, was widespread throughout Asia Minor and the Near East into his own time.

Returning from this digression to the Maccabees, we cannot answer the question whether their trophy shields were struck, though one can certainly say that they could have been. Josephus, unfortunately, does not mention them, though he does expand somewhat on the story of the rededication, noting that it became the eight-day festival of lights, known in Hebrew as Chanukah.[10]

In 1 Maccabees 5:31 and 33 the trumpets are as usual salpinx and tuba, and also in 6:33. It is not wholly clear in the text which side is sounding trumpets, but the probability seems to be Judas's army for 5:33 and the Greek armies in 5:31 and 6:33. Both are likely to have been the metal trumpets, but if Josephus's description of the chatsōtsᵊrōt as "a little less than a cubit long" is correct, the Hellenistic instruments, judging from the illustrations on Greek pots, were more than twice that length and therefore rather different in sound.[11] Only one allegedly Greek salpinx has been found in modern times. It is about five feet long, around three cubits, differs in almost all respects save length from those shown on the pots, and has no definite archeological provenance.[12] It is slightly longer than the full-size coach-horn of the nineteenth century, which is still heard today at horse-shows, and the modern bugle if it were uncoiled and straightened out, and it is therefore capable of at least half a dozen notes, a much wider range than the chatsōtsᵊrāh. The only other surviving salpinges that I know of come from Cyprus and date from the late Cypro-archaic period. These are all of pottery and although they are the same shape as those illustrated on the Greek pots, with the characteristic bottle-bell (the Boston salpinx has a conically flaring bell), they are all very short. The one in the Ashmolean Museum in Oxford is only just over a foot long, not much more than half a cubit.[13]

The trumpets in 7:45 are certainly the chatsōts³rōt for "sounding an alarm after them with their trumpets" would be better translated as sounding after them the signal trumpets. In 9:12 and 13 we clearly have again the trumpets of both armies, though with no distinction of terminology since both are indeed trumpets. In 9:39 there may have been some attempt at distinction for, since this is a Hellenistic bridal party, we have "drums, and instruments of musick" instead of the more usual timbrels or tabrets for tympanon, as the AV margin points out. The margin also suggests that musicians might have been better for *musikon* than instruments.

Apart from two more references to trumpets, 16:8, specified as "holy trumpets," or priestly trumpets in the Greek, and so clearly chatsōts³rōt, and 2 Macc. 15:25, the Greeks' trumpets which we mentioned at the beginning of the discussion of Maccabees, our final musical note is in 1 Macc. 13:51, again a restoration of Jerusalem, ἐν κινύραις, καὶ ἐν κυμβάλοις, καὶ ἐν να΄βλαις, καὶ ἐν ὕμνοις, καὶ ἐν ᾠδαῖς, "with harps, and cymbals, and with viols, and hymns, and songs." The harp as usual is κινύρα, and again *cinyris*, the Greek and Latin for kinnōr, and cymbals is kymbalois. But nablais, the Greek equivalent of the nēvel, this time is viols, as it was in Isaiah and Amos, and not citherns as one might have expected from the previous example in this book. There is another question here, also: what is the difference, if any, between ὕμνοις, the word we took over unchanged into English as hymns, and ᾠδαῖς, also unchanged in English as odes, here in the Latin *hymnis* and *canticis*, and in the AV hymns and songs? Appropriately enough for our final reference for the older part of the Bible, we can only say, as so often before, we do not know.

NOTES

1. *The Septuagint Version of the Old Testament and Apocrypha* (London: Samuel Bagster and Sons, n.d.), 'The Apocrypha', I.

2. Full details, with much illustration and translation of all the early texts, will be found in Jean Perrot, *The Organ from its Invention in the Hellenistic Period to the end of the Thirteenth Century*, translated Norma Deane (London: Oxford University Press, 1971).

3. A. C. Partridge, *English Biblical Translation*, The Language Library, ed. Eric Partridge and Simeon Potter (London: André Deutsch, 1973), 107.

4. A. B. Cook, *Zeus, a Study in Ancient Religion* (Cambridge: Cambridge University Press, 1914–40), vol. 1, 1914, 150–153, illustrates a number of these. The Greek and Roman deities were each known by a variety of names, reflecting local custom and belief.

5. Also illustrated by Cook, facing p. 644. It appears also in Georg Kinsky, *Musikgeschichte in Bildern* (Leipzig: Breitkopf und Härtel, 1930, and published also in English, French, and Italian by other houses with the same illustrations and pagination at the same date), 9 fig. 5, and in Friedrich Behn, *Musikleben im Altertum und frühen Mittelalter* (Stuttgart: Hiersemann, 1954), Taf. 34, Abb. 80. Both also show a number of the other instruments mentioned in this book.

6. Mrs M. E. Cunnington and the Rev. E. H. Goddard, *Catalogue of the Antiquities in the Museum of the Wiltshire Archaeological and Natural History Society at Devizes*, Part II (Devizes: The Society at the Museum, 1911), 71, no. 620 pl. xl.1. Also recorded in Mrs M. E. Cunnington and the Rev. E. H. Goddard, "Notes on other objects in the Westbury Collection," *Wiltshire Archaeological Magazine*, no. CXIII, vol. XXXVI (June 1910; so on the cover, but 1909 incorrectly on the title page): 464–77, 476, pl. ix fig. 2. Described in Jeremy Montagu, "What is a Gong?" *Man*, 1965:5, fig. 1.

7. Personal communication.

8. For example, a wooden dance shield with its beater from the Wapare people of Tanzania in the Ethnographic Museum in Göteborg in Sweden, 33.11.141 a & b, which produces two distinct pitches when struck and which has a vertical slot beside the integral handle which improves the sound but which would render it useless as a shield for battle, thus proving that it was made specifically for musical use. I am grateful to the late William Fagg for first telling me about this instrument, and to Karl Erik Larsson for permitting me to investigate its sound.

9. Jaap Kunst, "A hypothesis about the origin of the gong," *Ethnos* 1 & 2 (1947): 79–85 and 147, quoting (147) the Chinese encyclopaedia *Ku Chin T'u Shu Chi Ch'eng*.

10. Flavius Josephus, *Antiquities of the Jews*, translated William Whiston (London: Printed by W. Bowyer for the Author to be sold by John Whiston, Bookseller, 1736; reprinted Peabody, Mass.: Hendrickson, 1987), 328; book 12, chapter 7, paragraph 6 (316–25).

11. Josephus, *Antiquities,* 99; book 3, chapter 12, paragraph 6 (291).

12. Lacey D. Caskey, "Archaeological Notes: Recent Acquisitions of the Museum of Fine Arts, Boston," *Archaeological Institute of America Bulletin* XLI (1937): 525–31.

13. Catalog no. 1937.158. Others have been seen passing through the sale rooms at Sotheby's in London.

Chapter Seven

The New Testament

There is much less mention of music or of instruments in the New Testament than in the Old, probably because there is much less occasion for it in narratives such as the Gospels and the Acts, and certainly less occasion in the letters of encouragement and exhortation that make up the Epistles. Such mentions as there are come mostly as similes and examples, and there are few which describe actual use.

THE GOSPEL ACCORDING TO ST. MATTHEW

The first musical note comes in Matthew 6:2, and here the Greek is slightly different from the Latin or English, for where the AV has "Therefore when thou doest *thine* alms, do not sound a trumpet before thee", the Greek says μὴ σαλπίσῃς ἔμπροσθέν σου, *mē salpisēs emprosthen sou*, or don't trumpet it, don't make a noise about your generosity, rather than referring to any actual use of a trumpet. In 11:17 where "we have piped to you, and ye have not danced", the piping, ηὐλήσαμεν, *ēulēsamen*, derives from αὐλέω, *auleō*, to play the aulos, so that we have the chālīl again. The dancing, ὠρχήσασθε, *ōrchēsasthe*, comes from *orcheomai*, to dance.

In 24:31 we have a direct reference back to, and a link with Isaiah 27:13, which is concealed in the AV. Isaiah said that "the great trumpet shall be blown", in the LXX σάλπιοῦσι τῇ σάλπιγγι τῇ μεγάλῃ, *salpiousi tē salpingi tē megalē* whereas in the AV Matthew refers to "a great sound of a trumpet," σάλπιγγος φωνῆς μεγάλης, *salpingos phōnēs megalēs*. However, *phōnēs*, the word for sound, is missing from many early sources of the Greek text, including the fourth-century

Codex Sinaiticus, the oldest source of the New Testament that we have.[1] This suggests that what Matthew originally wrote might have been much closer to what Isaiah said than the text we have today, and that it may have been a deliberate quotation to help relate what was new to what was already familiar and accepted. All four Gospel authors were well versed in Scriptures, and such references and quotations would be immediately recognized by their initial readership in the days before the Church spread to all nations. In this way they follow Jesus's own practice, recognizing how effective it is when the new provides links to the old and familiar. This, too, is why we so often get references to the fulfilment of the prophecies. In the early days of Christianity, the link between the older and the newer scriptures was an essential tool in spreading the word and converting the unbelievers.

ST. LUKE

Luke 7:32 repeats "we have piped unto you" (there are no musical references in Mark) and while we still have the same word for piping in the Greek as in Matthew 11:17, ηὐλήσαμεν, Jerome when translating it in the Vulgate writes *cantavimus vobis tibiis*, we have played to you (or sung to you) on *tibiis*. Instead of *cecinimus*, which he had used in Matthew and which is part of the word *cano*, I sing, he changes to a different, though related, word for singing, *canto. Cano* seems, according to Lewis and Short, to be a somewhat earlier word than *canto*, relating possibly to the cry of a cock.[2] As in English, it was used for bird-song and other animal cries, and thus applied less overtly to human song than *canto*, though both were used interchangeably, especially in literary works. Tibiis, the plural of tibia, were the Roman equivalent of the Greek aulos.

When the prodigal son returned, not only did his father kill the fatted calf; he also provided the "musick and dancing" which his elder son was so surprised and affronted to hear in 15:25 as he came in from the fields. In both Greek and Latin we have the same words, *symphoniam, et chorum. Symphonia* is literally a playing together. From Classical times onwards it simply came to mean music, though, as we saw in Daniel 3, it does seem sometimes to be used in contrast with, or as a supplement to, *mousikon. Chorus* is always dance—our modern meaning of massed voices is a later concept.

There are no further references in the Gospels, nor are there any in the Acts of the Apostles, save for one fascinating speculation: was Judas Iscariot an aulos player? In John 12:6 and 13:29 the AV refers to the fact that Judas "had the bag"—he was the bagman and was responsible for the apostles' common stock of money and did the marketing for their daily food supplies and other needs. Sir John Stainer points out that the "bag" which is referred to in these verses is, in the Greek, γλωσσόκομον, *glōssokomon*.[3] The -komos half comes from a word meaning to take care of something, and glōsso- (or glōtto—the choice of one or the other is a difference of Greek dialect) means a tongue, in musical terms the tongue or reed of an instrument. In classical Greek, *glōssokomeion* was the box in which aulos players kept their reeds, just as our oboists and bassoonists have boxes in which they keep their reeds to protect them. Reeds are delicate objects and easily damaged, so no sensible players keep them loose in the instrument case—always they have a special, often fitted box in which they will be safe.

Had Judas been an aulos player and did he use his old reed box as something in which to carry the apostles' money, perhaps to keep it safe and to keep it separate from any money of his own? Stainer raises the possibility but we, like him, can never know for certain. We can only wonder why, if he were not a musician, the Evangelist should have chosen that comparatively rare word, one that is used in only one other place in Scripture, rather than any of the other more common terms (and there are several available) for Judas's cash-box. The earlier use, again for a money-chest, was in LXX, in 2 Chronicles 24:8, 10, and 11, where it was the chest which Joash put out to collect money for the repair of the Temple. Maybe *glōssokomos* by this late date had taken on the meaning of any box or other container, perhaps especially one for money, so that the translations by Wyclif as a purse and most other translators as a bag are correct. It is, otherwise, an interesting speculation, for this may add some slight information about Judas, of whose background we otherwise know practically nothing.

THE EPISTLES OF ST. PAUL TO THE CORINTHIANS

St. Paul uses one of the most interesting references we have as a simile in 1 Corinthians 13:1, "Though I speak with the tongues of men and of angels, and have not charity, I am become *as* sounding brass, or a tinkling cymbal." Here he is calling on Psalm 150:5 as his scriptural parallel, which suggests that the Corinthians are likely to have had some familiarity with the Old Testament, or at least with the Book of Psalms. He is not quoting it as we have it in the AV but very naturally, as one would expect when he was writing to the people of the Greek city of Corinth, he is quoting the psalm as it stands in the Greek of the Septuagint. He was writing in Greek for Greeks, and it is logical that he should have cited the psalm in that language. The LXX text of the psalm for "upon the loud cymbals" and "upon the high sounding cymbals" is ἐν κυμβάλοις εὐήχοις, *en kymbalois euēchois* and ἐν κυμβάλοις ἀλαλαγμοῦ, *en kymbalois alalagmou*. What St. Paul wrote was χαλκὸς ἠχῶν ἢ κύμβαλον ἀλαλάζον, *chalkos ēchōn ē kymbalon alalazon*, sounding bronze or clanging cymbal. He substitutes *chalkos* for *kymbalon* in the first phrase but leaves the rest much the same. His *ēchōn* means sounding. The prefix *eu-*, added for the Psalter's *euēchois*, means good, hence Wyclif's "sownynge wel" and Coverdale's rather nicer "well-tuned", which is preserved in the Book of Common Prayer. The different ending, *-ois* instead of *-on*, is only because of a different grammatical position.[4] The psalm's ἀλαλαγμοῦ (*alalagmou*) becomes St. Paul's ἀλαλάζον (*alalazon*). Both relate to a basic meaning of *"repeating frequently the cry* alalá, as soldiers used to do on entering battle."[5] It relates also to the Latin *ululare*, our ululation, a sound produced by moving the tongue within the mouth while uttering a wordless cry—children imitate it by moving the hand in front of the open mouth. It can be argued, as we did above in Chapter 3, that there is a connexion with hallel and hallelujah, though as we said there, that word can also be explained lexically.[6]

In Latin St. Paul's text is *aes sonans*, again sounding bronze, and *aut cymbalum tinniens*, from which Tyndale got tynklyng, perhaps by assonance, in which he was followed by AV, though *tinniens* can better mean ringing.[7] We have discussed the chalkos ēchōn above and shown that it represents the gong. Since both gongs and cymbals were known and used in Greece, the use of chalkos ēchōn allows Paul to make a stronger antithesis between the two instruments than was possible for the Psalmist. It also allowed him both to cite an ancient and respected text, whether or not it was known to his Corinthian readers—we have no way of knowing how much scriptural background was available to gentile proselytes—and at the same time to include a local and up-to-date reference, a circumstance always pleasing to any author.

The Corinthians had been known from Classical times for their arts, including music and dancing, and for a love of luxury, so that it is not surprising that St. Paul continues with musical metaphors in 1 Corinthians 14:7 and 8. The "pipe and harp" are aulos and kithara, the two most important Greek instruments, both appearing frequently on the painted pottery and bronze statuettes which had always been a feature of the Corinthian export trade. The trumpet in verse 8 is the salpinx, in the Vulgate the tuba, each the basic military signal instrument, as is appropriate to the context.

In the next chapter, 15:52, "the last trump" again is salpinx. *Eschatē*, the word used for last, appears in a number of places in the New Testament, always meaning the last of all before the arrival of the Messiah and the end of days. It is this reference to which Isaiah's great trumpet, shōfār gādōl (27:13), is linked in the AV margin, though the margin here in Corinthians links back to Matthew 24:31 and ahead to 1 Thessalonians 4:16. Of all four, it is this one in Corinthians which is the best known, both for its beauty of language and for its setting by Handel in *Messiah*, with the rest of the verse, beginning "for the trumpet shall sound".

THE EPISTLES TO THE THESSALONIANS AND HEBREWS

Our next reference is that to which we have just referred, 1 Thess. 4:16, σάλπιγγι Θεοῦ, *salpingi Theou*, "the trump of God." St. Paul refers again to the trumpet, in Hebrews 12:19. Here both AV and Vulgate have "the sound of a trumpet," whereas the original Greek is stronger: σάλπιγγος ἤχω, *salpingos ēchō*, the loud, or to use our word which derives from this Greek word, the echoing trumpet.

None of the other Epistles have any musical references.

THE REVELATION OF ST. JOHN THE DIVINE

In this last book of the Bible we return to a mystic visionary, writing in the same tradition as Isaiah and Ezekiel. Most of his references are to the trumpet and these are invariably the military trumpets, the

Greek salpinx and the Roman tuba, as with the "great voice" in 1:10, and the "first . . . voice" in 4:1.

His "four *and* twenty elders" and their "harps" in 5:8 are of enormous importance to any historian of musical instruments, for they are a constant attraction to artists. We see them in manuscripts, paintings, and carvings from the tenth century onwards and while in some cases, as in John's text, each has the same instrument, in many others each has a different instrument. Especially in the earlier periods, the tenth to the twelfth centuries, it is they, even more than the Psalmist and his musicians, who can tell us what were the instruments of the artist's time and place, what they looked like, and how they were played. In John's text each one of the Elders has a kithara, the Greek lyre, that most respected of all instruments, sacred to Apollo, played by Orpheus and Homer and all the great bards and poets who followed them, and known to and recognized by all who loved music and poetry, for all poems were sung to the lyre in those days.

In some of the early Spanish Mozarabic manuscripts we see other instruments. Perhaps the earliest European illustration of any bowed instrument, huge spade-like fiddles with semi-circular bows, is a Beatus Apocalypse manuscript, dating from around 925.[8] The first oval fiddles appear in other Mozarabic Beatus manuscripts.[9] Others show sharply triangular harp-psalteries, sometimes as well as rebecs.[10] Some of the best-known and, for the instrument historian, the most important illustrations of the Elders are the magnificently carved porticos of the great twelfth-century cathedrals and churches of northern Spain and southern France, which have a dazzling array of instruments of all varieties, mostly but not invariably string instruments, showing us the full range of instruments used in that locality at that period. Examples are Carboeiro, Gargilesse, Leon, Moissac, Oloron, Perazancas, Ripoll, and above all others that greatest center for pilgrimages, Santiago de Compostela.[11] These carvings are three-dimensional and thus in some cases even more informative than the drawings and paintings of the psalters and other liturgical texts. Those at Gargilesse are so deeply carved that Laurence Wright was able to climb up ladders and peer behind the figures and establish, for the first time ever (for no such instruments survive) that the medieval rebec did not always have the rounded back that we know from sixteenth-century illustrations, but often had flat backs, like the Turkish *karadeniz kemence* (Black Sea fiddle) or had backs keeled like a boat, like a Moroccan *rebab andaluz.* Our sole knowledge of many other medieval instruments comes from the illustrations of the Elders of the Apocalypse.

Neither the Elders nor their harps are supposed to be real people in the text of the Apocalypse—they are part of the vision of heaven and of the final days. But that vision cannot be made real to the hearers and readers of the Revelation unless it can be made manifest. Only by portraying real people and real instruments on the porticos, the arches surrounding the entrance doors, and in the manuscripts, can ordinary people approach the visions of heaven. And this vision is made the more real if the harps which the Elders hold or play (there are examples of each) are those instruments which we know on earth. To St. John, neither the harps nor the trumpets which he saw and heard in his visions were necessarily related to those on earth. Some of the instruments in the Bible are instruments of our world, and others are those of the world to come. Some are the harps, pipes, and trumpets of men (Revelations 18:22) and some, Revelations 15:2, are "the harps of God."

NOTES

1. *Novum Testamentum Graece,* ed. Alexander Souter, editio altera penitus reformata (Oxonii: E Typographeo Clarendoniano, 1947), 24.45, fn. 31.

2. Charlton T. Lewis and Charles Short, *A Latin Dictionary* (Oxford: Clarendon Press, 1879), 279 and 281, *s.vv. cano* and *canto.*

3. John Stainer, *The Music of the Bible with some account of the Development of Modern Musical Instruments from Ancient Types; revised edition with Additional Illustrations and Supplementary Notes by Francis W. Galpin* (London: Novello, 1914; reprinted New York: Da Capo Press, 1970), 95–6.

4. Many languages change words according to grammatical context far more than we do in English. Greek and Latin change the ends of nouns and adjectives according to whether they are subject or object and so forth. Greek, Latin, Hebrew, like English, change for singular and plural. Hebrew changes for pronouns, his, our, my and so on all producing different endings. To a great extent words have been simplified in this book, often using the basic singular form, which makes comparison and cross-reference easier. Only when we are quoting the whole context, of which this is one example, do we need the exact wording.

5. Joseph Henry Thayer, *A Greek-English Lexicon of the New Testament, being Grimm's Wilke's Clavis Novi Testamenti Translated Revised and Enlarged* (Edinburgh: T. & T. Clark, 4th ed., 1901), 25, *s.v. ἀλαλάζω.*

6. Hallel means praise, the -u- is the imperative you plural, and -jah is the Lord, so Praise ye the Lord. Nevertheless, the final form of the word, and its use, fit well with the Greek and Latin.

7. Perhaps we need to repeat here that although Greek chalkos and Latin aes can each mean either brass or bronze, the use at this date of bronze was more common than that of brass, and without doubt beaten bronze makes a far better sound than beaten brass.

8. Werner Bachmann, *The Origins of Bowing and the Development of Bowed Instruments up to the Thirteenth Century,* translated Norma Deane (London: Oxford University Press, 1969), plate 1: Madrid Biblioteca Nacional, Hh 58, fol. 127r, illustrating Revelations 15:2.

9. E.g. Bachmann, *Bowing,* plate 3, Madrid, Academia de la Historia, Sig. 33, fol. 177, 11th century, illustrating Rev. 14:2.

10. E.g. Tilman Seebass, *Musikdarstellung und Psalterillustration im früheren Mittelalter* (Bern: Francke, 1973), Abb. 57, Burgo de Osma, Archivo de la Catedral, Cod. 1, fol. 73v, dated 1086, and Abb. 49, Oxford, Bodleian Library, Bodley 352, fol. 6, 11th century.

11. All but Gargilesse are illustrated by Seebass. Several, especially Santiago, appear in many other books. Gargilesse was published by Laurence Wright, "Sculptures of Medieval Fiddles at Gargilesse," *Galpin Society Journal* XXXII (1979): 66–76.

Chapter 8

How Were the
Instruments Used?

We have said very little about the playing technique of any of the instruments we have discussed. At least one requires no special effort on the part of the player: the pa'amōnīm, the small clapper bells or pellet bells on the High Priest's robe (Exodus 28:33–5 and 39:25). All he had to do was to walk, and they sounded—that was their purpose "that his sound shall be heard . . ."

RATTLES—SHALISHĪM AND MᵊNAʿANᵊʿĪM

Rattles are only a little more complex—one has to shake them, but then they sound without further trouble, though shaking them to sound rhythmically is rather more difficult. A rhythm, such as that of the maracas or cabaca of the Latin-American dance band, is quite easy, for no great precision is required. A general shlsh on the beat is adequate, and this may well be all that was required for the shalishīm (1 Samuel 18:6) and mᵊnaʿanᵊʿīm (2 Sam. 6:5). It is unlikely that anything so precise and as tricky to execute as the rhythm that Gustav Holst demands from the sleigh-bells in *The Perfect Fool* was required in biblical times. The sistrum, if that is what the shalishīm were, was also probably simply shaken, as it still is in the Ethiopian Coptic church. However, because there is little or no archeological evidence for the sistrum in the biblical area, we have to say that the identification of the shalishīm remains uncertain—they were probably rattles but of what sort we cannot say. Nor can we even know whether the word is plural (the -*īm* ending is that of a masculine plural noun) because, like many rattles, there was a number of pellets or other elements rattling together, or whether several shalishīm were being used at the same time.

This same question applies to mᵊnaʿanᵊʿīm. These are much more certainly rattles, as we noted above from the etymology of the word, and very probably, as Bathja Bayer has pointed out from the finds in the area, made of pottery.[1] She includes sketches of several types which have been found archeologically and Joachim Braun includes photographs of these and more.[2] He also has a photograph of a pottery figurine which appears to be holding one of these types of rattle under his arm, though he misinterprets it as a drum, for which it is really rather too small.[3] Some would have been hand-held, and several are waisted to make this easier; others look as though they had been attached to something, with a suspension loop at the top, perhaps as we attach pellet bells to costumes or to leggings. Some may have been toys, for rattles are always a favorite plaything for children, but there is no reason why others should not have been used by dancers or anyone else as they are in many areas. They are less likely to have been used as ritual instruments, but on the one occasion when they are mentioned in the Bible, the ark was being transported towards David's city and he and others were probably dancing in celebration as they accompanied it, with all the joyful sounds they could command, as they did when it was moved again.

CYMBALS—MᵊTSILTAYĪM

Cymbals are not too difficult to play. While not, one hopes, simply banged together—a technique which produces both an unpleasant sound and broken instruments as inexperienced marching bandsmen rapidly discover today—the technique of the slightly sliding clash is not difficult to acquire. The full potential of our modern orchestral instruments requires much more experience and skill than is immediately apparent, including a secure grip, but with as little contact with, or pressure on the cymbals themselves as possible, combined with totally relaxed wrists at the moment of impact. It is unlikely that such advanced technique would have been required or even possible on the small instruments of the period. The very small cymbals might have been fixed on the thumb and fingers, as they are in Egypt and Morocco today. The very slightly larger but thicker instruments, about two or three inches in diameter, would have been played one in each hand. They were probably struck edge to edge as such cymbals often are in India and Tibet, rather than face to face like the larger ones, producing a clear, bell-like, ringing sound. The larger cymbals, such as that in plate 12, would have been played much like ours. Some were held with the plates vertical, as we do, and some were held with the plates horizontal. There is a number of pottery cymbal-playing figurines surviving, and both the techniques are illustrated. With neither was the sound likely to have been anywhere near as loud as with our much larger modern instruments, and this again suggests the Coverdale's well-tuned and Wyclif's well-sounding are better translations than the AV's loud. There is some difference in sound between the vertical and horizontal holds and certainly the grip is different, for with the plates vertical the cymbals were held much as we do, but with the plates horizontal, the thumb of each hand is uppermost. The upper cymbal hangs below the little finger, the lower cymbal rests on the thumb. The implication is a more immediately face-to-face impact of the cymbals and, for the safety of the instruments themselves, a more gentle and therefore quieter one than with the other grip, and perhaps more frequent. It would seem more appropriate than the other grip for marking the rhythm, for example, as we suggested in Chapter 3 might have been a function in 1 Chronicles 16:5.

If we are correct in our interpretation of St. Paul's "sounding brass", the gong must have been known, though of course possibly only in Corinth rather than in ancient Israel, for there is no point in making a comparison with something unless the readers recognize the object to which one is referring. However, we have no information at all about the musical use of gongs other than the examples noted above of the Roman salii, the Greek korybantes and, in legend, the Cretan kouretes, none of which is relevant for the Bible. Presumably, if they were known, they were simply struck as in those examples. The only known surviving gongs from the classical period are all quite small, a foot or so in diameter, and thus their sound cannot have been as loud as those we know today. Since the cymbals of that period were also quite small, the gong would have contrasted markedly with them nevertheless.

/

DRUMS—TUPPĪM

Drums require far more skill, especially in Eastern areas where playing techniques are much more subtle than they are in our own culture. The variety of tone color and pitch elicited from a single drum in the East far transcends that which is required in any ordinary drumming in our music. This is partly because players on all the high-art drums in that part of the world, and even on the simpler dance drums also, use their fingers, whereas we use beaters, and however skilled and subtle in their technique our timpanists may be, they cannot approach the range of sonorities that the best *tabla, donbek, darabukke,* or *bendir* and *duff* players can elicit with their fingers. In Europe in the Middle Ages, as it still is throughout the Near and Middle East, the frame drum or timbre was held vertically, with the frame in the palm of the hand, the drumhead facing outwards, and the hand supporting the drum from below with the fingers of that hand on the drumhead. This is quite different from the way we hold the tambourine today, which is from the side rather than from below and with the thumb on the head, rather than the fingers. With our type of grip, the holding hand can do nothing (save shake the drum) for the fingers cannot reach the head. With the oriental underhand grip, because the drum is securely held between the thumb and the fold of the palm, the fingers are free to produce the lighter rhythmic strokes on the head near the rim, while the other hand can play anywhere on the head or on the rim itself, producing sharp sounds akin to our side-drummer's rim shots and hoop cracks. In addition, the fingers of the holding hand can exert pressure on the head, so raising its pitch, producing a variation of pitch in addition to the tonal variations produced by the various types and locations of strokes mentioned. A skilled player of the bendir and other frame drums of this region today can provide a wide and ever-changing range of sounds to accompany dance and song and there is no reason to doubt that Miriam's women, Jephthah's daughter, or any other biblical players of the tōf were equally skilled and equally able to produce a large and ever-changing range of sonorities as well as of rhythms.

A form of drum used all over that area today, but for which there is little or no evidence in the biblical period, is that known as *darabukke* or *donbek* among other names. Donbek is clearly onomatopoeic—the deep don- of a stroke in the middle of the head, and the sharp -bek of a rim shot or a lighter tap near the rim. These drums are often called goblet drums for they resemble a great wine glass, the upper part the bowl, with the skin over the open end, contracting to a narrow waist and flaring somewhat, depending on type and area of origin, towards the foot. They are traditionally made of earthenware, or of rather finer pottery in Morocco, and of wood, often highly decorated, in Persia. The cup shape and contracted waist ties the contained air of the upper body to the vibration of the head, rather like our timpani, which aids the effect of the don- part of the sound. The use of pottery for the shell adds very considerably to the tone and volume because, as Laurence Picken pointed out, striking a drumhead releases only a finite amount of energy: the less that is wasted by any plastic deformation or vibration of the shell, the more there is that is free to come out as sound.[4] Pottery is an ideal material in this respect. As can be heard today all over that area, the more modern metal-shelled darabukke gives a sharp incisive sound but does not compare with the traditional pottery for depth of tone. One reason that the Persian donbek often has its wooden shell covered with ivory and mother-of-pearl set in black mastic is that this clamps the wood and restricts its vibration and therefore increases its sonority.

Playing technique is similar to that of the frame drum, though it can be considerably more elaborate because the drum is usually played in a seated position, with the shell resting across the thigh, or, when standing, with the drum gripped between the arm and the side of the body, thus allowing greater freedom to the hand which would otherwise be holding it.[5] The coupling of contained air to the drumhead allows greater control of pitch than on the frame drum and a really skilled donbek player can even play scales on the drum and, like an Indian *tabla* player, play both rhythmically and melodically. Unfortunately, there is not sufficient evidence to suggest with any certainty that this type of drum was a biblical instrument.

METAL TRUMPETS—CHATSŌTS°RŌT

Experiment with reproductions of Tut'ankhamūn's trumpets shows that they could produce three notes, but it also shows that only two were really useful. Of those, the lowest note can be dull and poorly centered, though with practice it can be made to ring. It can be inflected, especially downwards, by altering the lip tension, as is usual with the lower notes of any trumpet-type instrument. The middle note is excellent and would carry across any battlefield or encampment, two of the uses which Moses specifies. The highest note requires greater lip pressure than is comfortable on these instruments and would seem to risk some deformation of the metal as well as a likelihood of cutting the player's lips. However, there are two cautions involved here, even if, as I believe one should, one accepts this type of trumpet as the model for the chatsōts⁹rōt rather than the Roman-style trumpet, which had a much more modern-style mouthpiece, carved on Titus's Arch. One is that Tut'ankhamūn's trumpets may have been made as grave goods, and therefore not exactly the same as trumpets would have been for practical use—however, signs of wear on them do suggest that they had had at least some use and therefore were real trumpets. The other is that we do not know what type of blowing technique was used, and especially what form of embouchure, the position of the player's lips. Almost certainly the experiments recorded, Hickmann's, Kirby's (neither of whom provided any information in this respect), and certainly my own, were made with the modern technique of curling the lips in towards the teeth, just as we are taught today to play all our trumpets and horns.[6] If one adopts the everted embouchure used, for example, on Tibetan trumpets, on the Australian *didgeridu,* and on some African horns, with the lips protruding outwards so that the opposed vibrating areas of the lips are the softer inner surfaces, results are quite different. Only the lowest note can be produced, with quite wide inflection of pitch but with little evidence of ringing tone. Nevertheless the sound would carry well and the amount of deflection of pitch would allow quite an elaborate signal code to be established—even allow the trumpets to play with the singers, a matter on which we expressed some doubt above, if the vocal range were limited to a compass of around a fifth.

Perhaps one should explain what is meant by inflection and deflection in this context. Brass players know that by altering the tension of the lips and the manner of blowing (there is a good deal of debate between players of different schools and acousticians over just what really happens), one can sound different overtones of the natural pitch of the instrument (which are sometimes referred to as harmonics, though acousticians argue about that also). On the bugle, for example, one produces the octave of the fundamental, traditionally written as middle C but sounding according to the physical length of the instrument. Above it comes the fifth, written as G, then

C again, followed by E and the G sitting above the top line of the treble stave, each of which is a well-centered, discrete pitch. With valves, on modern horns and trumpets, and with a slide on trombones, one can obtain notes between these "natural" sounds. These "natural" pitches can be varied to some extent by the way in which one blows, raised a little, lowered usually a little more, until the pitch shifts with a jump to the next "natural" pitch. Such variation is called deflection, lip-bending, blue notes, and by various other terms, and it is much easier over the lowest notes of the range than in the upper, where it is more difficult, though with suitably designed instruments this was how all Baroque brass music was played. In the low range, where "natural" notes are an octave apart, players can produce notes in this way which are theoretically absent from the instrument's range, and do so just with the lip, without the use of valves, handstopping, or any other artificial aids. Two Haydn symphonies, among many other works, depend on this ability.[7]

It is possible that only one note was ever used. The prescribed use in Numbers 10 was as signal instruments for movement and war and, as Samuel Morse amply demonstrated, one can construct as elaborate a code as one wishes on a single note by using adequate rhythmic variation. However, as we shall see in the following section, pitch variation is traditional on the shōfār and there is no logical reason to exclude it from the chatsōts³rōt.

RAM'S HORN—SHŌFĀR

The shōfār or ram's horn can, in the same way, deflect its lowest note but the extreme narrowness of its bore makes any such behavior much more difficult in the upper register. Equally, the very small mouthpiece makes it difficult to use everted lips though it does encourage the use of an embouchure set in to the red of both lips (*einsetzen* as it is called in German orchestral horn playing terminology). As with the Renaissance cornett, this technique prevents excessive back pressure and promotes freedom of tone as well as greater relaxation and, partly as a result, the use of less air and therefore the ability to sustain notes for much longer.

In post-biblical times, the shōfār was a general signal instrument, and was also used as a means of appealing to God in times of catastrophe, including fire, flood, famine, drought, and even raging inflation.[8] Today in Jerusalem a mechanical simulacrum, which replaces the shōfār so that it can be heard over the whole city, announces the advent of the Sabbath. The principal use, throughout the Jewish world, is for Rosh haShanah, the New Year, as the talmudic references here suggest. The Rabbis of the Talmud spent much time debating who could blow and what should be blown. The consensus of the Mishnah was that the obligation is on everyone to blow for themselves.[9] However, Rabban Gamaliel's dictum, that one may fulfill the obligation by hearing the shofar blown by an officiant of the congregation, was generally accepted.[10] Thus today someone, such as the rabbi or the reader for the congregation, or another suitable member, blows on behalf of the community and provided that one listens with the intent to fulfil the commandment, this suffices.[11] Women are allowed to blow,[12] though only for other women,[13] as are children, and it is a commandment to help and encourage both of them to do so and to teach them.

Shōfᵊrōt are still used throughout the Jewish world. Examples from Israel, Morocco, Persia, Germany, and Poland are illustrated here (plate 5). Ashkenazim, the Western Jews, use the shōfār only at Rosh haShanah and Yom Kippur (the Day of Atonement), to signal the beginning and the end of the ten days of reflection and repentance, and during the preceding month of Ellul, as a warning of the approach of those solemn days, but the Sephardim, the Southern and Oriental Jews, use them on many other occasions, both ritual and secular, for celebrations and to signal the arrival of the Sabbath. Most are made today from the horn of a ram, but, as may be seen here, shōfᵊrōt made for different communities differ in detail. Some, for example the Moroccan, have a well-shaped mouthpiece carved in the tip of the horn. Others, for example the Persian, simply have the tip cut off flat, though with the rough corrugations of the natural horn scraped off. Some, for example the Central and Eastern European, have the wider end decoratively carved. Others leave it plain or have simpler shaping. Some, especially those made in Israel in the early years of the twentieth century, have a form of ladder carved under the keel. Inscriptions and other decorative engraving may be used, and these were common in Germany and Poland in the seventeenth century. The example of that type shown here. at the bottom left of plate 5, has Ps. 81:3, meaning "Blow up the trumpet in the new moon, in the time appointed, on our solemn feast day", engraved on it (with several spelling mistakes!). The first two words of the verse are missing from one side of the horn, and the last two from the other, showing that, as permitted, a section at least six inches long has been cut off to remove a lateral split, and a new mouthpiece has been crudely shaped.

The use of any separate mouthpiece is forbidden under the general prohibition, mentioned above, of covering the mouthpiece with any other material. Nevertheless, this is sometimes seen in America if the special skill has not been acquired of blowing with the very small embouchure hole of the natural shōfār. Some Reform synagogues have even used a conventional modern trumpet instead of a shōfār, but this would not be permitted in any more traditional community.

We have no surviving shōfᵊrōt earlier than around A.D. 1250, but these are sufficiently similar to the later ones, though usually left with some of the twist of the natural horn, that perhaps we may assume that tradition is strong enough that those of the biblical period were also similar. The shōfār is made today by scraping away all the rough outer part of the horn (the statement in the Mishnah quoted in Chapter 2 confirms that the horns were scraped in the second century A.D., too), heating it to straighten the narrow end and perhaps eliminate all the twist, and cutting off enough of the tip to leave at the tip a flat surface a centimeter or so wide. A straight hole is then bored down from the center of this flat surface, through the solid end of the horn, until it meets the natural cavity. The bell end is left with some of the natural hook, either in a twisted curve or flattened into the same plane as the tip. That the ram's horn is curved goes back to the Mishnah and, according to tradition, this is because, when the shōfār is blown on Rosh haShanah to commence the ten days of penitence before the whole-day fast of the Day of Atonement, its shape is bent to remind the hearers to bend their hearts to God. The horn is then softened by heat and the narrow end slightly opened out as a mouthpiece. The mouthpiece is so small that it is placed at the side of the mouth where the lips are narrowest.

As for what is blown on the shōfār, confusion is indeed confounded. The rabbis argued this fiercely in the Talmud.[14] They realized that none of them knew what one of the original calls, the yᵊbaba, had been and they agreed to follow Rabbi Abbahu's decision, made around A.D. 300 in Caesarea, to substitute the shᵊvārīm for it. They disputed whether one should blow a tᵊkī'āh or a tᵊrū'āh, and settled the matter by deciding to blow both as well as each, as we shall see below. As if this were not bad enough, their descriptions of each of the calls are so vague as to be totally incomprehensible to anyone who tries to follow them as an instruction manual. The earliest surviving notation is that of the thirteenth-century *Codex Adler* in the Jewish Theological Seminary of America.[15] This is no more than a series of squiggly lines, but it clearly represents the same tradition as that of today. The tᵊkīʿāh is a single squiggle longer than each of the three squiggles for the shᵊvārīm, and the tᵊrūʿāh is more wiggly than the others, but unfortunately this tells us nothing precise. Since hardly any two shōfār blowers blow exactly the same calls as each other today, and since some are so radically different from others that only the names bear any resemblance to each other, it is plain that there is no possible common link to the biblical, or even the Talmudic periods save in the names of the calls and the order in which they are blown. There is even a break between the Ashkenazic and the Sephardic traditions, for while both agree that each cycle of calls ends with an extended call, the Ashkenazim end with a tᵊkīʿāh gᵊdōlāh (a great tᵊkīʿāh or trumpet blast) whereas the Sephardim end with a tᵊrūʿāh gᵊdōlāh (a great tᵊrūʿāh or trumpet call or alarm). At least one author refused to believe that there was such a difference and had the temerity to change tᵊrūʿāh gᵊdōlāh in a quotation by a better scholar, Rabbi Francis Lyon Cohen, to tᵊkīʿāh gᵊdōlāh, believing that it was incorrect.[16] The differences today between the many various tᵊkīʿōt and tᵊrūʿōt are simply those between different traditions and between different teachers or exemplars. Any recorded archive, including my own, contains many examples of each, all different.

Because of the very irregular bore, a very narrow cylindrical tube through the solid end leading to the very irregular conoid of the natural cavity, narrowly ovoid in section, the overtones are seldom harmonic. The first is usually between a narrow fourth and a wide sixth from the lowest note, and the next, not always used or achieved, between a fourth and a fifth higher. The lowest note can easily be inflected downwards by altering the lip tension, often over a range of most of an octave though with some deterioration of tone quality, and certainly sufficiently for the drop of a whole tone noted below.

There are today, and have been at least since the days of the Mishnah in the second century, three basic calls, tᵊkīʿāh, tᵊrūʿāh, and that which became sh³vārīm, which are blown today in a specified order and combination. While I know of many varying traditions, the following is what I was taught to blow for each of these basic calls. It is very similar to that given as the "correct" calls in the British United Synagogue book of liturgical music, the *Voice of Prayer and Praise*.[17] That is printed on a five-line staff with treble clef and key signature, but because there is no intention to indicate actual pitches, which will vary according to the size and acoustical characteristics of the shōfār, I have used here a staff with an x indicating each of the "natural" notes; the other pitches are inflected from these (music example 1).

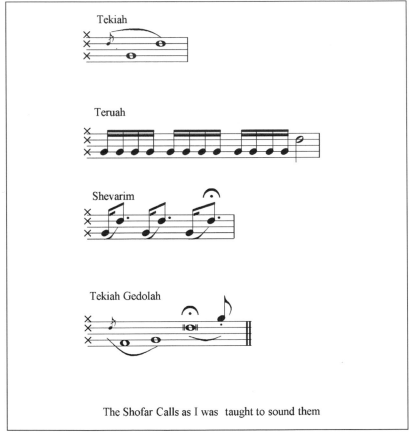

The Shofar Calls as I was taught to sound them

Music Example 1

The lower note is that obtained as the lower "natural" pitch, and the upper as the first overtone of that pitch. The flipped note at the end of the tᵊkīʿāh gᵊdōlāh is the next overtone, achieved by a sudden push from the diaphragm as well as by altered lip tension. The lowered lower note at the beginning of that call is achieved by relaxing the lips. Alfred Sendrey says that this is irregular and that F. L. Cohen must have heard it played by some local performer and should not have quoted it.[18] He was wrong because many of us do it as a matter of course, certainly in Britain and one would presume elsewhere. It is done as easily as natural horn players played the low F sharp on the third leger line in the Trio of the "Scherzo" of Beethoven's 7th Symphony.[19]

There is a tendency to assume that all tᵊkīʿōt, all tᵊrūʿōt, and all shᵊvārīm, are the same, but this is because most writers on the subject are Jewish and they go to the same synagogue every year and they hear the same blower, or his pupil, each year. Only by interviewing a number of blowers, recording their calls, and building up the archive mentioned above, has it been possible to discover the breadth and range of calls used.[20] Very briefly, they range from narrow inflections, covering a semitone or less, of one pitch, produced by varying the lip tension, to two or three distinct overtones covering a range of more than an octave. Study of a comparatively limited number of shōfār blowers suggests that the former technique is prevalent among the Sephardim and the latter among the Ashkenazim. Certainly at least two Ashkenazi instruction manuals firmly specify the latter technique of distinct overtones.[21]

Music example 2 shows a small selection of different ways of blowing each of the three basic calls. Again a single line is used for each pitch, with deflections of that pitch shown above or below the line. There is no intention in any of these musical examples to indicate any precise durations. This is an aspect which has been argued and disputed since Talmudic times. It is generally accepted, but often ignored in practice since what is important is to produce clear notes, that the two tᵊkīʿōt of each line (for which see below) should equal in length the middle call. Thus the tᵊkīʿōt surrounding shᵊvārīm-tᵊrūʿāh will be longer than the other tᵊkīʿōt and those surrounding tᵊrūʿāh will be slightly longer than those surrounding shᵊvārīm. Many authorities say that there should be nine notes in tᵊrūʿāh; I can only say that I was taught three groups of four and that that number also appears in print in several authoritative sources.

Music Example 2

The prescription of what should be blown is, verbally, precise in every Jewish community of whatever persuasion. As will have become apparent, what is blown, acoustically, differs widely. Does this matter? No, provided that the sound is clear, reasonably consistent, and within the parameters described above and in the next paragraph. Every shōfār blower remembers with gratitude the pronouncement of Rabbi Simeon ben Gamaliel: "Whether its sound is thin or thick or choked, it is valid, since all sounds emitted by a shofar are valid."[22]

The sequence of calls blown today on Rosh haShanah is: *tᵊkīʿāh—shᵊvārīm-tᵊrūʿāh—tᵊkīʿāh* (three times); *tᵊkīʿāh—shᵊvārīm—tᵊkīʿāh* (three times); *tᵊkīʿāh—tᵊrūʿāh—tᵊkīʿāh* (three times), the third time blowing *tᵊkīʿāh gᵊdōlāh* (in Ashkenazi communities, but *tᵊrūʿāh gᵊdōlāh* among the Sephardim) instead of the last *tᵊkīʿāh*. This whole sequence comes three times and is followed at the end of the service with a sufficient number of calls to bring the total to 100. We have of course no evidence at all on how this corresponded with the commandment to Moses for Rosh haShanah in Leviticus 23:24, as "Speak unto the children of Israel, saying, In the seventh month, in the first day of the month, shall ye have a sabbath, a memorial of blowing of trumpets, an holy convocation." This is repeated, with slight variation in Numbers 29:1 as, "And in the seventh month, on the first day of the month, ye shall have an holy convocation; ye shall do no servile work: it is a day of blowing the trumpets unto you." It does, however, follow the Talmudic interpretation of that commandment and it is as near as we can ever expect to get to what was done, first in the forty years in the wilderness, and thereafter in the Temple until its destruction.

What calls were used at Jericho and elsewhere we have no way of knowing. Presumably, one day we shall all hear the sound that was heard at Sinai.

SHELL TRUMPETS

An instrument not mentioned in the Bible but found archeologically in the Holy Land is the shell trumpet or conch. Some ten examples have been found so far.[23] The best known are those from Hazor, Tel Qasile, and Tel Shiqmona.[24] It seems more probable that most conch trumpets were associated with the Philistine Dagon cult than anything which is our concern—Tel Qasile is certainly a Philistine temple site. While Tel Shiqmona, on the slopes of mount Carmel, was a Phoenician site, Joachim Braun states that the conch is one of several which come from the later Hellenistic stratum.[25] Bathja Bayer suggests that for Hazor, which is a Jewish site and fairly well inland, the pagan religious influence, for which one might blame Jezebel, could be responsible.

WOODWINDS—CHĀLĪL

Among woodwind instruments, the single-reed, geminate parallel pipes present no problem. The commonest varieties have five or six fingerholes in each pipe and are played by covering the equivalent holes on each pipe by the same finger: the forefinger of the upper hand covers the uppermost hole on each pipe, that in the further pipe with the tip of the finger and that in the nearer with the middle phalange, and so on down the instrument. The two pipes may be lashed together with twine or luted with wax, or, as in the one next to the right on plate 10, which was bought at the source of the Jordan, with both. The two ancient Egyptian instruments which Hickmann illustrates are missing their mouthpieces.[26] These are smaller pieces of cane in the side of which a tongue is slit from the surface so that it remains attached to the cane at one end but is otherwise free to vibrate as a reed—the tongue is broken off each mouthpiece on the left-hand example on the plate. The whole of the mouthpiece is taken into the mouth, since otherwise the player's lips would hold the reed to the mouthpiece and prevent it from vibrating. The reason for using twin pipes is that when they are very slightly out of tune with each other, the vibrations set up between them help to reinforce the sound, which is thus both stronger and more aurally interesting than the sound of either pipe alone.

There is more problem with the double-reed geminate divergent pipes illustrated on plate 4. Again five or six holes in each pipe seems to have been the norm, though we have much less evidence because fewer such pipes have survived and, unlike the single-reed pipes, none are in use at the present day. One surviving archeological example, the so-called Lady Maket pipes have three holes in one pipe and four in the other.[27] The nearest surviving relatives today, the Sardinian *launeddas*, have four holes in each pipe, though these have several significant differences from the aulos: the bores are narrower, the reeds are single, like those of the zummāra, and one of the pipes is attached to a third drone-pipe.[28] We are mainly dependent on iconography for details of the aulos, most of which is either Greek, or in the later post-biblical periods in Israel, from Greek- or Roman-influenced mosaics.[29] All the illustrations show the players with one hand on each pipe. Most have the two hands about the same distance down from the player's mouth on each pipe. So how did they cover all the holes? If they left holes open below the hands, this would cause no acoustical problem though it would limit the range because it would mean that only the upper notes of the pipes were being played. One cannot, however, effectively stop finger-holes when there are holes open nearer the mouth than those stopped because it is the uppermost open hole which determines the pitch; closing holes below it has little effect. And yet many illustrations show the hands near or towards the lower end of the pipes, presumably with open holes above and with only three fingers apparently being used to cover holes which, again, severely limits the range. There is never any suggestion in these illustrations that the hands cover holes on both pipes as with the parallel pipes, nor that both hands cover the holes on one pipe, leaving the other to sound as a drone. Nor does one often see one hand appreciably lower down on one pipe and higher on the other, which would imply that each pipe covered a different melodic range. This remains an unsolved problem.

Most double-reeds in this part of the world today are made from flattened plant stems, a natural tube that was originally cylindrical but which has been flattened to make two opposed sides which beat against each other. There is little use even today of reeds made, like our oboe and bassoon reeds, of two separated blades. The nearest two-bladed reeds, geographically, are those used on the *gralla* and *dulzaina* in northern Spain—all those in North Africa, the Middle and Near East, the Balkans, and from Central Asia right across to the Far East use the flattened plant stem, the type of plant varying from one area to another according to the botanical geography. The clearest and most comprehensive description of the construction of such reeds will be found in Laurence Picken's *Folk Musical Instruments of Turkey*, already referred to in this chapter.[30]

While using fingers to stop holes in both pipes simultaneously, as with the parallel pipes, can only produce unisons, or all-but unisons, playing with a hand on each pipe can also produce two-part music, either two lines moving in parallel or two distinct lines. The third possibility, if one pipe has holes and the other does not, is to play a single part against a drone, but for that we have no evidence even though such parallel pipes, one with fingerholes and the other without, are common today in neighboring areas (though not, apparently, in the Holy Land). We can only say that since we know nothing whatever of the music of this area and period, any of these are possible.

We have discussed reed instruments, both single-reed and double-reed.[31] What about flutes? The word only appears twice in the AV: the first time in Daniel 3 in all four verses listing Nebuchadrezzar's band, and the second in the Apocryphal 1 Esdras 5:2, again the account of a foreign band. This is borne out by the archeological relics, which also indicate that there must have been less use of flutes than of reeds. Certainly the transverse flute was unknown; it did not arrive in this area before about the 11th century A.D. and first appears in the illuminations of Byzantine manuscripts of that date.[32] There is some late evidence for small whistles but these are fragmentary and almost certainly irrelevant, for they are not much bigger than toys, unless perhaps they represent the *mashrōqītā*. If flutes were used at all, and we noted in Chapter 2 the possibility of flutes of some sort with the shepherds, they are most likely to have been of the *nay* or *kaval* type, sometimes called rim-flutes or end-blown flutes. There is no duct, like that of our recorder—one simply blows against the edge or rim of the top of the tube, holding the instrument somewhat obliquely downwards with the top partly between the lips. Such instruments are still widely used, much more commonly than transverse flutes, especially in the Near and Middle East and North Africa, and they are far more expressive than duct or whistle flutes because, by slightly varying the angle of blowing and so covering the end of the tube more or less with the lips, one can play loudly or softly at will, as one can on the transverse flute. On the duct flute, on the other hand, because the angle of incidence of the air on to the voicing edge is fixed by the instrument, one can get louder or softer only by also going sharp or flat, higher or lower in pitch. Whether such end-blown flutes were used in Israel as well as in Egypt, whence examples survive, and Mesopotamia we cannot be sure, even though the names chālīl and ʿūgāv could apply equally well to them.[33] There is no contemporary iconographic evidence for them, whereas there is for the reed instruments. Also flutes on the whole are less suited to some of the occasions on which the chālīl were used, such as by ecstatic prophets and coronations.

Nor, save for one late carving, an altar to Dionysus which is hardly relevant to the Bible, is there any evidence for the syrinx or pan-pipe.[34] However this is so simple an instrument that it cannot be excluded, for it is known as an instrument world-wide, from antiquity to the present day, from the Americas through Oceania, Asia, and Africa to Europe. It is often simply a raft of reeds, each a different length so that each produces a different pitch, usually each closed at the lower end, which makes it easier to blow. It is played much as we would play a mouth-organ or harmonica, moving the reeds to and fro as required in front of the mouth as one blows across their tops, just as one blows across the top of a bottle. But, once again, there is no evidence for its presence in ancient Israel.

STRING INSTRUMENTS—NĒVEL AND KINNŌR

With the strings we come, as we have seen already, into an area with rather more evidence for their appearance, their use, and their construction, even if much of it is contradictory.

So how were they played? When playing with the fingers, as Josephus told us was done with the nēvel, the likeliest technique is plucking with both hands, as indeed one of the Roman references cited by Bayer suggests: Ovid in his *Arts of Love* recommends ladies to "learn to sweep with both hands the pleasant nablas."[35] When playing with a plectrum, as both Josephus and Ovid tell us was done on the kinnōr (the Latin cithara in Ovid's case) one can pluck individual notes just as one can with the fingers, but one can also use a form of autoharp technique by stopping the strings that one does not wish to sound with the fingers of one hand and then sweeping the plectrum across all the strings with the other so that only those left free to vibrate will sound. This can also be done with the fingers but not quite so effectively as with the plectrum.

We have, as the reader may have noticed, a serious conflict here. There is no reason to doubt either Josephus or Ovid—both lived within the period in which these instruments were in use. But in 1 Samuel 16:16 they were searching the length and breadth of the country to find someone who could play the kinnōr בְּיָדוֹ, bᵊyādō. Does this really mean with his hand? Bayer suggests, as we noted above, that it may well not mean that.[36] Certainly even the most cursory glance at any biblical concordance will show innumerable instances where hand is used to represent strength, power, or skill, and a more careful search could surely produce even more meanings. However, we also have the problem of time, and of the possibilities that fashions and techniques change over time. The kinnōr is clearly very much older than the nēvel, which first appears in Samuel's time, and there is no reason why an instrument which was played with the hand in Saul's and David's time should not, by Josephus's day, have been played with a plectrum, especially if it were found in the meanwhile that a newer instrument, the nēvel, was better suited to finger playing and that the older one went well with a plectrum. This could especially be true if there were a change in string materials—Rabbi Joshua is also late, contemporary with Josephus, and his distinction between the materials that we quoted in Chapter 3 may not have been true most of a thousand years earlier. An example nearer our own time is the mandolin. In Vivaldi's time, and probably as late as Mozart's and Beethoven's, both of whom wrote for it, it had gut strings and was plucked with the fingers—today, as later in the nineteenth century, it has steel strings and is played with a plectrum.

Finally, what would have been played on either kinnōr or nēvel (which surely we can now accept was the larger lyre, with more strings, thicker and lower-pitched than those of the kinnōr)? The kinnōr was clearly used as a solo instrument, either by itself or with a voice. What it played we cannot tell; we can get some idea what it sounded like by listening to recordings from Kenya, Uganda, and Ethiopia where the lyre is still in common use—the music will be entirely different, but the noise, the sound of the music, will be not unlike. We can also get an idea of what sort of music it played by listening to recordings of present-day bards from other cultures, whatever instrument they use. Any bard accompanies himself with simple passages, working them up to something more elaborate for dramatic moments, and interpolating longer virtuostic passages while reminding himself of, or making up, the next part of the story, and of course while the hat or bowl is going round the audience, a part of the performance where audience participation is both essential and universal. The nēvel, however, appears only once as a solo instrument, in Psalm 144:9, plus the somewhat enigmatic reference in Isaiah 14:11 and the two references in Amos 5:23 and 6:5, both of which seem rather more symbolic than actual. Otherwise it appears always with other instruments, probably in an accompanying role, which again increases the probability of it being a lower-pitched instrument.

Later, after the return from the Babylonian exile, where Ezra and Nehemiah had acquired new ideas for running the Temple services, both were absorbed into the Temple orchestra. Again this provides evidence that the nēvel was lower pitched than the kinnōr for there were nine or more kinnōrōt against two nēvalīm, or no more than six nēvalīm however many more kinnōrōt there were. For exactly the same reasons, we have fewer cellos and basses in an orchestra than we do violins. What they played in the Temple we have no idea, but it would seem unlikely that it was in unison. We have no way of telling whether higher-pitched and lower-pitched instruments played the same music in parallel octaves, but again it would seem unlikely, especially if one instrument were plectrum-played and the other fingered. A guess, and it can never be more (and even that much is rash), is a basic, fairly simple melody on the lower-pitched, twelve-note instrument, with some quicker elaboration and decoration around those notes on the higher-pitched, plectrum-played one.

Was the larger limited to twelve notes, one from each string, and the other to ten? Not necessarily. One can, and people do, stop a string with a finger close to the yoke, either using the fingernail or the pad of the finger or pinching the string between finger and thumb, and so shortening its sounding length and raising the pitch. This technique is limited to a semitone or maybe a tone, according to the length of the string. However, since we do not know whether musical practice of that period recognized anything analogous to modulation into different keys or modes, or even the concept of keys, we cannot know whether such techniques were used. Unlike the Greeks, the Hebrews left us no works on musical theory, scales, or temperaments, and any ostensible performances of "Music of the Bible" are nothing more than the results of the performers' imagination and powers of guesswork.

Even all that we have written here about the musical instruments amounts to little more. As the Preacher said (Ecclesiastes 8:17), "though a wise *man* thinks to know *it*, yet he shall not be able to find *it*." He was not always so discouraging, for he did also say (9:7), "Go thy way, eat thy bread with joy, and drink thy wine with a merry heart; for God now accepteth thy works."

NOTES

1. Bathja Bayer, "Mena'an'im—Pottery Rattles," *Tatzlil* 4 (1964): 19–22, in Hebrew with English summary, 65.

2. Bayer, 18. Joachim Braun, *Die Musikkultur Altisraels/Palästinas: Studien zu archäologischen, schriftlichen und vergleichenden Quellen*, Abb. III/5–3 to –12.

3. Braun, *Musikkultur*, Abb. II/2A–1.

4. Laurence Picken, *Folk Musical Instruments of Turkey* (London: Oxford University Press, 1975), 61.

5. It is a drum of this type in this latter position, under the arm, which Dr. Braun postulates in his Abb. II/2A–1

6. Hans Hickmann, *La Trompette dans l'Égypte Ancienne* (Cairo: Institut français d'archéologie orientale, 1946); Percival Kirby, "Ancient Egyptian Trumpets," *Music Book: Volume VII of Hinrichsen's Musical Yearbook* (London: Hinrichsen, 1952), 250–5, and "The Trumpets of Tut-ankh-amen and their Successors," *Journal of the Royal Anthropological Institute* 77 (1947): 33–45. I regret that although I knew them both, I never thought to ask them about this while they were still alive.

7. Symphony 51 in B♭, slow movement, bars 9–12 and 78–81, and Symphony 61 in D, first movement, bars 160–7. There are many shorter examples throughout the orchestral repertoire.

8. Talmud, Sēder Mō'ēd, Ta'anīth 14a.

9. Talmud, Sēder Kādāshīm, 'Arāchīn, 2b, "All are obliged to sound the shofar" [Soncino translation from the Davka CD-ROM] towards the bottom of the page, quoting Mishnah, Sēder Mō'ēd, Rōsh haShānāh, 4:9, the penultimate sentence of that tractate, "So, everyone and all has the duty [to blow]."

10. Mishnah, Sēder Mō'ēd, Rōsh haShānāh, 4:9, final sentence. Jacob Neusner, *The Mishnah* (New Haven and London: Yale University Press, 1988), 307, 4:9, G and H.

11. Talmud, Mō'ēd, Rōsh haShānāh 29a.

12. Rōsh haShānāh 33a.

13. Rōsh haShānāh 29a.

14. Rōsh haShānāh 33b, 34a, and 34b.

15. Illustrated in Alfred Sendrey, *Music in Ancient Israel* (New York: Philosophical Library, 1969), 351.

16. Francis L. Cohen's notation in his article "Shofar" in the old *Jewish Encyclopedia*, ed. Isidor Singer (New York and London: Funk and Wagnall, 1901–6), vol X1, 1905, 306, was quoted but changed by Alfred Sendrey, 354.

17. Rabbi Francis L. Cohen and David M. Davis, arr. and ed., *Qōl Rinnāh v°Tōdāh: The Voice of Prayer & Praise* (London: The United Synagogue, 3rd ed., 1933), 180.

18. Sendrey, 353, note (x).

19. In the second horn part from bar 181 leading to letter C, and wherever that figure reappears. This is always better done by lipping than by hand-stopping.

20. Details are included in Jeremy Montagu, "Kōl haShōfār," forthcoming.

21. F. L. Cohen & D. M. Davis, *VPP&P*; David Hausdorff, *Kol HaShofar* (New York: Folkways, 33 rpm disc LP FR 8922, 1957), with accompanying notes.

22. Talmud, Rōsh haShānāh, 27b.

23. Joachim Braun, *Musikkultur,* 137–40 and Abb. IV/5–1 and –2.

24. Batya Bayer, "The Conch-Horn of Hazor," *Tatzlil* 3 (1963): 140–2, in Hebrew; English summary, 209; Braun, *Musikkultur,* Abb. IV/5–1 and –2 for Hazor and Shiqmona; Amīhāi Mazār, *Tel Qasīle* (Tel-Avīv: Mūsēiōn Ha'Āretz, 1983), 19, in Hebrew only, photo on p. 25, for that instrument.

25. Braun, *Musikkultur,* 139.

26. Hans Hickmann, *Ägypten,* Musikgeschichte in Bildern II/1 (Leipzig: Deutscher Verlag für Musik, 1961), Abb. 86.

27. John Stainer, *The Music of the Bible with some account of the Development of Modern Musical Instruments from Ancient Types; revised edition with Additional Illustrations and Supplementary Notes by Francis W. Galpin* (London: Novello, 1914; reprinted New York: Da Capo Press, 1970), 114 in Galpin's additional notes.

28. Andreas Fridolin Weis Bentzon, *The Launeddas: a Sardinian Folk Music Instrument,* Acta Ethnomusicologica Danica I (Copenhagen: Akademisk Forlag, 1969).

29. For example, Kathleen Schlesinger, *The Greek Aulos* (London: Methuen, 1939); Ze'ev Weiss and Ehud Netzer, *Promise and Redemption: a Synagogue Mosaic from Sepphoris* (Jerusalem: The Israel Museum, 1996), also illustrated in Braun, *Musikkultur,* Abb. V/5–4.

30. Picken, *Turkey,* 356–63 and 476.

31. Considerable detail on many such reed pipes, both single-reed and double-reed, will be found in the relevant volume of the catalogue of my own collection of musical instruments, also published by Scarecrow Press.

32. Joachim Braun, "Musical Instruments in Byzantine illuminated manuscripts," *Early Music* 8:3 (July 1980): 312–27.

33. There is a very fine bronze example in the British Museum as well as two of reed. R. D. Anderson, *Catalogue of Egyptian Antiquities in the British Museum: III Musical Instruments* (London: British Museum Publications, 1976), 64–6, nos. 96, 97, and 98, catalog nos. 12742, 6385, and 54480.

34. Braun, *Musikkultur,* Abb. V/5–1.

35. Publius Ovidius Naso, *Ars amatoria,* 3, 327–8; cited by Bathja Bayer, "The Biblical Nebel," *Yuval* I (1968): 89–131, 124.

36. Bayer, "Nebel," 92, fn. 16: "but since *be-yadô* is also very probably not 'with his hand', it only furthers our contention that the enquiry on this celebrated scene should be re-opened."

Bibliography

EARLY TEXTS

The Bible. The editions mainly used for this book are:

Hebrew
Biblia Sacra Polyglotta: Textus Archetypos Versionesque Præcipuas. . . . Londini: Samuelis Bagster et Ff., *regno* Gulielmus IV.
Biblia Hebraica, ed. Rudolf Kittel. 7th ed., ed. A. Alt, O. Eissfeldt, and P. Kahle Stuttgart: Württembergische Bibelanstalt, 1951
Tanach included with Soncino Talmud on CD-Rom. Chicago: Davka Corporation, 1991–6, and various printed editions.

Hebrew & Aramaic
Mikraot Gedolot. Warsaw: 1866; reprinted Tel-Aviv: Shiloh and Pardes, 1958.

Greek
The Septuagint Version of the Old Testament and Apocrypha. London: Samuel Bagster and Sons, n.d.
Novum Testamentum Graece, ed. Alexander Souter, editio altera penitus reformata. Oxonii: E Typographeo Clarendoniano, 1947.

Latin
Biblia Sacra Vulgatæ Editionis Sixti V. Pont. Max. jussu recognita et Clementis VIII auctoritate edita. 5th ed. Tornaci Nerviorum: Desclée, Lefebvre & Soc, 1894.

English
The Holy Bible, (Authorized Version or King James Bible). Robert Barker, 1611 and later printings. I have used mainly a volume which includes the Apocrypha and the Book of Common Prayer. Cambridge: John Archdeacon for Cambridge University Press, 1769 for the Bible, 1770 for the Book of Common Prayer.

Biblia the Bible, that is, the holy Scripture of the Olde and Newe Testament, tr. out of Douche and Lat. Cologne [?]: 1535, by Miles Coverdale; reprinted as *The Coverdale Bible 1535.* Folkestone: Dawson, 1975.

The Byble, translated by Thomas Matthew. Antwerp [?]: for R. Grafton and E. Whitchurch, 1537; known as The Matthew Bible but mainly William Tyndale's work with some books by Miles Coverdale.

The New Testament 1526. London: The British Library, 2000, a reprint of William Tyndale's translation, retaining the original language and spelling, unlike some other versions available.

The Holy Bible containing the Old and New Testaments with the Apocryphal Books in the earliest English versions made from the Latin Vulgate by John Wycliffe and his Followers, ed. Rev. Josiah Forshall and Sir Frederick Madden. Oxford: Oxford University Press, 1850.

The English Hexapla exhibiting the Six Important English Translations of the New Testament Scriptures. London: Samuel Bagster and Sons, 1841.

The Booke of the Common Prayer, 1549, which retains Miles Coverdale's translation of the Psalter. I have used mainly the Cambridge printing of 1770 cited above as *The Holy Bible.*

Wright, William Aldis, ed. *The Hexaplar Psalter being the Book of Psalms in Six English Versions.* Cambridge: Cambridge University Press, 1911.

OTHER EARLY TEXTS

Josephus, Flavius. *The Works of Josephus.* Translated William Whiston. London: Printed by W. Bowyer for the Author to be sold by John Whiston, Bookseller, 1736; reprinted Peabody, Mass.: Hendrickson, 1987, of which pp. 1–26 are Josephus's account of his life, and 27–542 are *The Antiquities of the Jews.*

————. *Jewish Antiquities.* Translated Ralph Marcus in the Loeb Classical Library, with Greek and English on facing pages. Cambridge, Mass.: Harvard University Press, reprinted in nine volumes, 1998.

Ovidius Naso, Publius. *Ars amatoria.*

The Mishnah, *Shishāh sidrēi Mishnāh.* I have used an edition published in Jerusalem: Hōrev, 1998 (in Hebrew).

The Mishnah, translated Herbert Danby. Oxford: Oxford University Press, 1933.

The Mishnah, A New Translation, Jacob Neusner. New Haven: Yale University Press, 1988.

Pirke de Rabbi Eliezer. Translated and annotated Gerald Friedlander. London: Kegan Paul, Trench, Trubner & Co; and New York: Bloch Publishing Company, 1916; reprinted New York: Judaic Studies Library 6, Sepher-Hermon Press, 1981.

The Talmud, *Talmud Bavli: The Babylonian Talmud.* The Soncino edition, London: Soncino Press, 1965ff., on CD-ROM. Chicago: Davka Corporation,

1991–6, in Aramaic and English, and including the Hebrew Bible in Hebrew and English.

Talmud Bavli. Photolitho copy of a Vilna edition, probably that of Romm; reprinted Jerusalem: Tōrāh LᵃˁĀm, 1968, in Hebrew and Aramaic.

MODERN TEXTS

Agnon, S. Y. *Days of* Awe. New York: Schocken, 1948.

Anderson, R. D. *Catalogue of Egyptian Antiquities in the British Museum: III Musical Instruments.* London: British Museum Publications, 1976.

Bachmann, Werner. *The Origins of Bowing and the Development of Bowed Instruments up to the Thirteenth Century.* Translated Norma Deane. London: Oxford University Press, 1969.

Baines, Anthony. "Fifteenth-century Instruments in Tinctoris's *De Inventione et Usu Musicae.*" *Galpin Society Journal* III (1950): 19–26.

Bayer, Bathja. "The Biblical Nebel." *Yuval* I (1968): 89–131.

Bayer, Batya. "The Conch-Horn of Hazor." *Tatzlil* 3 (1963): 140–2.

Bayer, Bathyah. *The Material Relics of Music in Ancient Palestine and its Environs: an Archeological Inventory.* Tel-Aviv: Israel Music Institute, 1963.

Bayer, Bathja. "Mena'an'im—Pottery Rattles." *Tatzlil* 4 (1964): 19–22.

Bayer, Bathja. "Nᵊgīnāh vᵊzimrāh." *Entsīqlōpedyāh Miqra'īt Ōtsar Hayᵊdiōt 'al HaMiqra Ūtᵊqufātō (Encyclopaedia Biblica, Thesaurus Rerum Biblicanum Alphabetico Ordine Digestus).* Jerusalem: Mōssad Bī'ālīq, 1964– , vol. 5, 1968, 755–82.

Bayer, Bathja. "The Titles of the Psalms—A Renewed Investigation of an Old Problem." *Yuval* IV (1982): 29–123.

Becker, Heinz. *Zur Entwicklungsgeschichte der antiken und mittelalterlichen Rohrblattinstrumente.* Hamburg: Musikverlag Hans Sikorski, 1966.

Behn, Friedrich. *Musikleben im Altertum und frühen Mittelalter.* Stuttgart: Hiersemann, 1954.

Bentzon, Andreas Fridolin Weis. *The Launeddas: a Sardinian Folk Music Instrument.* Acta Ethnomusicologica Danica I. Copenhagen: Akademisk Forlag, 1969.

Braun, Joachim. "Musical Instruments in Byzantine illuminated manuscripts." *Early Music* 8:3 (July 1980): 312–27.

———. *Die Musikkultur Altisraels/Palästinas: Studien zu archäologischen, schriftlichen und vergleichenden Quellen.* Freiburg: Universitätsverlag; Göttingen: Vandenhoek & Ruprecht, 1999.

Bright, John. *A History of Israel.* 2nd ed. London: SCM Press, 1972.

Brown, Francis, S. R. Driver, and Charles A. Briggs. *A Hebrew and English Lexicon of the Old Testament.* Oxford: Clarendon Press, 1907; reprinted 1975.

Caskey, Lacey D. "Archaeological Notes: Recent Acquisitions of the Museum of Fine Arts, Boston." *Archaeological Institute of America Bulletin* XLI (1937): 525–31.

The Chicago Manual of Style. 14th ed. Chicago: University of Chicago Press, 1993.

Cohen, Francis L. "Shofar." *The Jewish Encyclopedia*, ed. Isidor Singer. New York and London: Funk and Wagnall, 1901–6, vol. XI, 1905, 301–6.

Cohen, Rabbi Francis L., and David M. Davis, arr. and ed. *Qōl Rinnāh vᵊTōdāh: The Voice of Prayer & Praise*. 3rd ed. London: The United Synagogue, 1933.

Collins, Nina L. "Who Wanted a Translation of the Pentateuch into Greek?" *Journal of Semitic Studies*, Supplement 11: *Jewish Ways of Reading the Bible*, ed. George J. Brooke. Oxford: Oxford University Press on behalf of the University of Manchester, 2000, 20–57.

Cook, A. B. *Zeus, a Study in Ancient Religion*. Cambridge: Cambridge University Press, 1914–40, specifically vol. 1, 1914.

Cunnington, Mrs M. E., and the Rev. E. H. Goddard. *Catalogue of the Antiquities in the Museum of the Wiltshire Archaeological and Natural History Society at Devizes*, Part II. Devizes: The Society at the Museum, 1911.

Cunnington, Mrs M. E., and the Rev. E. H. Goddard. "Notes on other objects in the Westbury Collection." *Wiltshire Archaeological Magazine*, no. CXIII, vol. XXXVI (June 1910): 464–77.

Edwards, I. E. S. *Treasures of Tutankhamun*. London: British Museum, 1972.

Galpin, Francis W. *The Music of the Sumerians and their immediate successors the Babylonians and Assyrians*. Cambridge: University Press, 1936; reprinted Strasbourg: University Press, Librairie Heitz, 1955.

Ginzberg, Louis. *The Legends of the Jews*. Translated Henrietta Szold. Philadelphia: Jewish Publication Society of America, 1909–41; reproduced on CD-ROM, Chicago: Davka Corporation, 1998, specifically vol. 1, 1909 & 1998.

Hausdorff, David. *Kol HaShofar*. New York: Folkways, 33 rpm disc LP FR 8922, 1957.

Hayashi, Kenzō, Shigeo Kishibe, Ryōichi Taki, and Sukehiro Shiba, for the Shōsōin Office. *Musical Instruments in the Shōsōin*. Tokyo: Nihon Keizai Shimbun Sha, 1967.

Hickmann, Hans. *Ägypten, Musikgeschichte in Bildern II/1*. Leipzig: Deutscher Verlag für Musik, 1961.

———. *La Trompette dans l'Égypte Ancienne*. Cairo: Institut français d'archéologie orientale, 1946.

Hodges, Henry. *Artifacts: an Introduction to Early Materials and Technology*. London: John Baker, 1964.

Hofman, Shlomo. *Miqra'ey Musica*. Tel-Aviv: Israel Music Institute, 1974.

———. *Music in the Talmud*. Tel-Aviv: Israel Music Institute, 1989.

Holman, Peter. *Four and Twenty Fiddlers: The Violin at the English Court 1540–1690*. Oxford: Clarendon Press, 1993.

Jastrow, Marcus. *Dictionary of the Targumin, the Talmud Babli and Yerushalmi, and Midrashic Literature*. London: Luzac, 1903; reprinted New York: Judaica Press, 1989.

Kinsky, Georg. *Musikgeschichte in Bildern*. Leipzig: Breitkopf und Härtel, 1930; and published also in English, French, and Italian by other houses with the same illustrations and pagination at the same date.

Kirby, Percival. "Ancient Egyptian Trumpets." *Music Book: Volume VII of Hinrichsen's Musical Yearbook*. London: Hinrichsen, 1952, 250–5.

———. "The Trumpets of Tut-ankh-amen and their Successors." *Journal of the Royal Anthropological Institute* 77 (1947): 33–45.

Kunst, Jaap. "A hypothesis about the origin of the gong." *Ethnos* 1 & 2 (1947): 79–85 and 147.

Lewis, Charlton T. and Charles Short. *A Latin Dictionary*. Oxford: Clarendon Press, 1879.

Liddell, Henry George and Robert Scott. *A Greek-English Lexicon*. 4th ed. Oxford: Oxford University Press, 1855.

Manniche, Lisa. *Musical Instruments from the Tomb of Tutʿankhamūn*, Tutʿankhamūn's Tomb Series VI. Oxford: Griffith Institute, 1976.

Mazār, Amīhāi. *Tel-Qasīle*. Tel-Avīv: Mūsēiōn Ha'Āretz, 1983.

Meucci, Renato. "Roman Military Instruments and the *Lituus*." *Galpin Society Journal* XLII (1989): 85–97.

Montagu, Jeremy, *Timpani and Percussion*, New Haven and London: Yale University Press, 2002.

———. *The Montagu Collection Annotated Catalogue*, 4:2: "Reed Instruments." Lanham, Md.: Scarecrow Press, 2001.

———. "Kōl HaShōfār." Conference paper, publication forthcoming.

———. "One of Tutankhamon's Trumpets." *Galpin Society Journal* XXIX (1976): 115–7; reprinted with the same title, *The Journal of Egyptian Archaeology* 64 (1978): 133–4.

———. "What is a Gong?" *Man* (1965:5): 18–21.

Ó Suilleabháin, Micheál. "The Bodhran." *Treoir*, vol. 6 no. 2 (1974): 4–7, and no. 5 (1974): 6–10.

Page, Christopher. "Biblical Instruments in Medieval Manuscript Illustration." *Early Music* 5:3 (July 1977): 299–309; reprinted in Christopher Page, *Music and Instruments of the Middle Ages: Studies on Texts and Performance*. Aldershot: Variorum, 1977.

Partridge, A. C. *English Biblical Translation*. The Language Library, ed. Eric Partridge and Simeon Potter. London: André Deutsch, 1973.

Pepys, Samuel. *Diaries*. The original manuscript is in the Pepys Library, Magdalene College, University of Cambridge; the most authoritative modern edition is ed. Robert C. Latham and William Matthews. London: G. Bell and Sons, 1971; reprinted London: HarperCollins, 1995.

Perrot, Jean. *The Organ from its Invention in the Hellenistic Period to the end of the Thirteenth Century*. Translated Norma Deane. London: Oxford University Press, 1971.

Picken, Laurence. *Folk Musical Instruments of Turkey*. London: Oxford University Press, 1975.

————. *Music from the Tang Court*. London: Oxford University Press, 1981.

Pritchard, James B., ed. *The Times Atlas of the Bible*. London: Times Books, 1987.

Rashid, Subhi Anwar. *Mesopotamien, Musikgeschichte in Bildern* II/2. Leipzig: Deutscher Verlag für Musik, 1984.

Sachs, Curt. *History of Musical Instruments*. New York: W. W. Norton, and London: J. M. Dent, 1940.

Sadie, Stanley, ed., *The New Grove Dictionary of Musical Instruments*. London: Macmillan, 1984.

Schlesinger, Kathleen. *The Greek Aulos*. London: Methuen, 1939.

Seebass, Tilman. *Musikdarstellung und Psalterillustration im früheren Mittelalter*. Bern: Francke Verlag, 1973.

Sendrey, Alfred. *Music in Ancient Israel*. New York: Philosophical Library, and London: Vision, 1969.

Shanks, Hershel. *Jerusalem: An Archaeological Biography*. New York: Random House, 1995.

Smith, William, ed. *Dictionary of Greek and Roman Antiquities*. 2nd ed. London: Walton and Maberly, and John Murray, 1853.

Stainer, John. *Music of the Bible with some account of the Development of Modern Musical Instruments from Ancient Types; revised edition with Additional Illustrations and Supplementary Notes by Francis W. Galpin*. London: Novello, 1914; reprinted New York: Da Capo Press, 1970.

Thayer, Joseph Henry. *A Greek-English Lexicon of the New Testament, being Grimm's Wilke's Clavis Novi Testamenti Translated Revised and Enlarged*. 4th ed. Edinburgh: T. & T. Clark, 1901.

Weiss, Ze'ev, and Ehud Netzer. *Promise and Redemption: a Synagogue Mosaic from Sepphoris*. Jerusalem: The Israel Museum, 1996.

West, M. L. *Ancient Greek Music*. Oxford: Clarendon Press, 1992.

Wiengreen, J. *Introduction to the Critical Study of the Text of the Hebrew Bible*. Oxford: Clarendon Press, 1982.

Wigram, George V. *The Englishman's Hebrew and Chaldee Concordance of the Old Testament*. London: Samuel Bagster, 1843; 5th ed. reprinted Grand Rapids, Mich.: Zondervan, 1970.

Woodfield, Ian. *The Early History of the Viol*. Cambridge: Cambridge University Press, 1984.

Wright, Laurence. "Sculptures of Medieval Fiddles at Gargilesse." *Galpin Society Journal* XXXII (1979): 66–76.

Young, Robert. *Analytical Concordance to the Holy Bible*. Edinburgh: George Adam Young, 1879; 8th ed. 1939; reprinted by various publishers, mine Guildford and London: Lutterworth Press for the United Society for Christian Literature, 1979.

Ziegler, Christiane. *Catalogue des instruments de musique égyptiens, Musée du Louvre, Département des antiquités égyptiennes*. Paris: Éditions de la Réunion des Musées Nationaux, 1979.

Index of Biblical Citations

Quadrilingual Index of
Musical References

King James	Vulgate	Septuagint	Hebrew
Genesis	**Genesis**	**Γενεσις**	**בראשית**
4:21 harp, organ	cithara, organum	ψαλτήριον, κιθάρα	כנור, עוגב
31:27 songs,tabret, harp	cantici, tympanum, cithara	μουσικῇ, τύμπανον, κιθάρα	שרים, תף, כנור
Exodus	**Exodus**	**Εξοδος**	**שמות**
15:20 timbrel, dances	tympanum, chori	τύμπανον, χοροί	תף, מחלת
19:13 trumpet	buccina	σάλπιγξ	יבל
19:16 voice of the trumpet	clangor buccinæ	φωνὴ σάλπιγγος	קל שפר
19:19 voice of the trumpet	sonitus buccinæ	φωνὴ σάλπιγγος	קל השפר
27:2 horn	cornu	κέρας	קרן
28:33-5 bell	tintinnabulum	κώδων	פעמן
39:25 bell	tintinnabulum	———	פעמן
Leviticus	**Leviticus**	**Λευιτικον**	**ויקרא**
23:24 memorial of blowing of trumpets	memoriale clangentibus tubis	μνημόσυνον σάλπιγγων	זכרון תרועה
25:9 trumpet of the jubile	buccina mense septimo	σάλπιγξ	שופר
Numbers	**Numeri**	**Αριθμοι**	**במדבר**
10:2f trumpets	tubæ	σάλπιγγες	חצצרת
29:1 day of blowing the trumpets	dies clangoris tubarum	ἡμέρα σημασία σάλπιγγες σημασιῶν	יום תרועה
31:6 trumpets	tubæ	**Ιησους Ναυη**	חצצרות
Joshua	**Josue**	σαλπίσητε τῇ σάλπιγγι	**יהושע**
6:4 seven trumpets of ram's horns	septem buccinas quarum usus est		שבעה שופרות היובלים
6:5 ram's horns, trumpet	jubilæo tubæ	———	קרן היובל, שופר
6:6 seven trumpets of rams' horns	septem jubilæorum buccinas	ἐπτὰ σάλπιγγας ἱερὰς	שבעה שופרות יובלים
6:8 seven trumpets of rams' horns, trumpets	septem buccinis	———	שבעה שופרות היובלים, שופרות
6:9 trumpets	buccinis	σαλπίζοντες	שופרות, שופרות
6:13 seven trumpets of rams' horns, trumpets	septem buccinas quarum in jubilæo usus est, buccinis	σάλπιγγας, σάλπιγξι	שבעה שופרות היובלים, שופרות
6:16 trumpets	buccinis	ἐσάλπισαν	שופרות
6:20 trumpets, sound of trumpet	tubis	σάλπιγξιν, σάλπιγγων	שופרות, קול השופר
Judges	**Judicum**	**Κριται**	**שפטים**
5:16 bleatings of the flocks	sibilos gregum	συρισμοῦ ἀγελῶν	שרקות עדרים
7:16 trumpet	tuba	κέρας	שופרות
7:18 trumpet, trumpets	tuba, clangite	κερατίνας σαλπίζειν	שופר, שופרות
7:19 trumpets	buccina	κερατίνῃ, κερατίναις	שופרות
7:20 trumpets	tuba	κέρας	שופרות
7:22 trumpets	buccina	κέρας	שופרות
11:34 timbrels & dances	tympanis et choris	τυμπάνοις & χοροῖς	תפים, מחלות
First Samuel	**Primus Regum**	**Βασιλειων Α'**	**שמואל א**
2:1 horn	cornu	κέρας	קרן
10:5 tabret, psaltery, pipe, harp	psalterium,tympanum, tibiam, citharam	νάβλα, τύμπανον, αὐλὸς, κινύρα	נבל, תף, חליל, כנור
13:3 blew the trumpet	cecinit buccina	σάλπιγγι σαλπίζε	תקע בשופר

King James	Vulgate	Septuagint	Hebrew
16:1 horn	cornu	κέρας	קרן
16:16 harp	psallere cithara	ψάλλειν ἐν κινύρᾳ	מנגן בכנור, נגן בידו
16:23 harp and played with his hand	citharam et percutiebat manu sua	κινύρα, καὶ ἔψαλλεν ἐν χειρὶ	כנור ,ונגן בידו
18:6 tabrets, joy, instruments of music	tympanis lætitiæ, sistris	τυμπάνοις, χαρμοσύνῃ, κυμβάλοις	תפים , שמחה, שלשים
18:10 played with hand	psallebat manu sua	---	מנגן בידו
19:9 played with hand	psallebat manu sua	ἔψάλλε χερσὶν	מנגן ביד
21:11 sing in dances	cantabant per choros	ἐξῆρχον χορεύουσαι	יענו במחלות
29:5 sing in dances	cantabant per choros	ἐξῆρχον ἐν χοροῖς	יענו-לו במחלות
Second Samuel	**Secundus Regum**	**Βασιλειων Β'**	**שמואל ב**
2.28 trumpet	buccina	σάλπιγγι	שופר
6:5 fir wood, harps, psalteries, timbrels, cornets, cymbals	omnibus lignis, citharis, lyris, tympanis, sistris, cymbalis	ὀργάνοις ἡρμοσμένοις ἰσχύϊ, ᾠδαῖς, κινύραις, νάβλαις, τυμπάνοις, κυμβάλοις, αὐλοῖς	עצי ברושים, כנרות, נבלים, תפים, מענענים, צלצלים
6:14 danced with all his might	saltabat totis viribus	ἀνεκρούετο ἐν ὀργάνοις ἡρμοσμένοις	מכרכר בכל-עז
6:15 sound of the trumpet	clangore buccinæ	φωνῆς σάλπιγγος	קול-שופר
6:16 leaping & dancing	subsilientem atque saltantem	ὀρχούμενον καὶ ἀνακρουόμενον	מפזז ומכרכר
15:10 trumpet	buccina	κερατίνῃ	שפר
18:16 trumpet	buccina	κερατίνῃ	שפר
19:35 singing men and singing women	cantorum atque cantatricum	ἀδόντων καὶ ἀδουσῶν	שרים ושרות
20:1 trumpet	buccina	κερατίνῃ	שופר
20:22 trumpet	tuba	κερατίνῃ	שפר
22:3 horn	cornu	κέρας	קרן
First Kings	**Tertius Regum**	**Βασιλειων Γ'**	**מלכים א**
1:34 trumpet	buccina	κερατίνῃ	שופר
1:39 trumpet	buccina	κερατίνῃ	שופר
1:40 piped with pipes	canentium tibiis	ἐχόρευον ἐν χοροῖς	מחללים בחללים
1:41 trumpet	tuba	κερατίνῃ	שופר
10:12 almug trees, harps, psalteries	lignis thyinis citharas, lyras	ξύλα πελεκητὰ νάβλας, κινύρας	עצי אלמגים כנרות, נבלים
Second Kings	**Quartus Regum**	**Βασιλειων Δ'**	**מלכים ב**
3:15 minstrel	psaltem	ψάλλοντα	מנגן
9:13 trumpets	tuba	κερατίνῃ	שופר
11:14 trumpeters, blew with trumpets	tubas, tubis canentem	σάλπιγγες σάλπιγξι	החצצרות חצצרות
12:13 trumpets	tubæ	σάλπιγγες	חצצרות
First Chronicles	**1 Paralipomenon**	**Παραλειπομενων Α'**	**דברי הימים א**
13:8 singing, harps, psalteries, timbrels, cymbals, trumpets	canticis, citharis, psalteriis, tympanis, cymbalis, tubis	ψαλτῳδοῖς, κινύραις, νάβλαις, τυμπάνοις, κυμβάλοις, σάλπιγξι	שירים, כנרות, נבלים, תפים, מצלתים, חצצרות
15:16 instruments of musick, psalteries, harps, cymbals	organis musicorum nablis, lyris, cymbalis	ὀργάνοις, νάβλαις, κινύραις, κυμβάλοις	כלי-שיר, נבלים, כנרות, מצלתים
15:19 cymbals of	cymbalis æneis	κυμβάλοις χαλκοῖς	מצלתים נחשת

	King James	Vulgate	Septuagint	Hebrew
	brass			
15:20	psalteries on Alamoth	nablis arcana	νάβλαις ἐπὶ ἀλαιμώθ	נבלים על־עלמות
15:21	harps on the Sheminith	citharis pro octava	κινύραις ἀμασενὶθ	כנרות על־השמינית
15:24	trumpets	tubis	σάλπιγγιν	חצצרות
15:27	master of the song	princeps prophetiæ	ἄρχων τῶν ᾠδῶν	השר המשא
15:28	sound of the cornet, trumpets, cymbals, psalteries, harps	sonitu buccinæ, tubis, cymbalis, nablis, citharis	φωνῇ σωφὲρ, σάλπιγξι, κυμβάλοις, νάβλαις, κινύραις	קול שופר, חצוצרות, מצלתים, נבלים, כנרות
16:5	psalteries, harps, cymbals	organa psalterii, lyras, cymbalis	ὀργάνοις, νάβλαις, κινύραις, κυμβάλοις	נבלים, כנורות, מצלתים
16:6	trumpet	tuba	σάλπιγξι	חצצרות
16:42	trumpets, cymbals, musical instruments	tuba, cymbala, omnia musicorum organa	σάλπιγγος, κύμβαλα, ὄργανα	חצצרות, מצלתים, כלי־שיר
23:5	instruments which I made	organis quæ fecerat	ὀργάνοις οἷς ἐποίησε	כלים אשר עשיתי
25:1	harps, psalteries, cymbals	citharis, psalteriis, cymbalis	κινύραις, νάβλαις, κυμβάλοις	כנרות, נבלים, מצלתים
25:3	harp	cithara	κινύρᾳ	כנור
25:5	horn	cornu	κέρας	קרן
25:6	cymbals, psalteries, harps	cymbalis, psalteriis, citharis	κυμβάλοις, ναβλαις, κινύραις	מצלתים, נבלים, כנות
Second Chronicles		**2 Paralipomenon**	**Παραλειπομενων Β'**	דברי הימים ב
5:12	cymbals, psalteries, harps, 120 trumpets	cymbalis, psalteriis, citharis, 120 tubis	κυμβάλοις, νάβλαις, κινύραις, 120 σάλπιγξι	מצלתים, נבלים, כנרות, 120 חצצרות
5:13	trumpets, cymbals, instruments of music	tubis, cymbalis, organis, diversi generis musicorum	φωνὴν ἐν σάλπιγξι, κυμβάλοις, ὀργάνοις τῶν ᾠδῶν	קול בחצצרות, ובמצלתים, ובכלי השיר
7:6	instruments of music, trumpets	organis, tubis	ὀργάνοις ᾠδῶν, σάλπιγξι	כלי־שיר, מחצצרים
9:11	algum trees, harps, psalteries	lignis thyinis, citharas, psalteria	ξύλα πεύκινα, κιθάρας, νάβλας	עצי־האלגומים כנרות, נבלים
13:14	trumpet	tuba	σάλπιγξι	חצצרות
13:15	shout	vociferati	ἐβόησαν	ויריעו
15:14	trumpets, cornets	tubæ, buccinarum	σάλπιγξι, κερατίναις	חצצרות, שופרות
20:28	psalteries, harps, trumpets	psalteriis, citharis, tubis	νάβλαις, κινύραις, σάλπιγξιν	נבלים, כנרות, חצצרות
23:13	trumpet, instruments of musick	tubis, diversi generis organis	σάλπιγξι, ὀργάνοις ᾠδοὶ	חצצרות, כלי השיר
29:25	cymbals, psalteries, harps	cymbalis, psalteriis, citharis	κυμβάλοις, νάβλαις, κινύραις	מצלתים, נבלים כנרות
29:26	instruments of David, trumpets	organa David, tubas	ὀργάνοις Δαυὶδ, σάλπιγξι	כלי דויד, חצצרות
30:21	loud instruments	organa	ὀργάνοις	בכלי עז
35:25	singing men and singing women	cantores atque cantatrices	ἄρχοντες καὶ ἄρχουσαι	השרים והשרות

King James	Vulgate	Septuagint	Hebrew
Ezra	**Primus Esdræ**	**Εσδρας**	**עזרא**
2:65 200 singing men & singing women	cantores atque cantatrices ducenti	ᾄδοντες καὶ ᾄδουσαι διακόσιοι	משוררים ומשוררות מאתים
Nehemiah	**Secundus Esdræ**	**Νεεμιας**	**נחמיה**
4:18 trumpet	buccina	κερατίνῃ	שופר
4:20 trumpets	tubæ	κερατίνης	שופר
7:67 245 singing men & singing women	cantores et cantatrices 245	ᾄδοντες καὶ ᾄδουσαι 245	משוררים ומשוררות מאתים ואבעים
12:27 singing, cymbals, psalteries, harps	cantico, cymbalis, psalteriis, citharis	ᾠδαῖς, κυμβαλίζοντες, ψαλτήρια, κινύραι	שיר, מצלתים, נבלים, כנרות
Job	**Job**	**Ιωβ**	**איוב**
21:12 timbrel and harp, sound of the organ	tympanum et cithara, sonitum organi	ψαλτήριον καὶ κιθάραν, φωνῇ ψαλμοῦ	תף וכנור, קול עוגב
30:31 harp, organ	cithara, organum	κιθάρα, ψαλμός	כנר, עגב
39:24 trumpet	tubae	σάλπιγξ	שופר
39:25 trumpets	buccinam	σάλπιγγος	שפר
Psalms	**Psalmorum**	**Ψαλμοι**	**תהלים**
3 title A Psalm of David	Psalmus David [AV numbers]	Ψαλμὸς τῷ Δαυὶδ [AV numbers]	מזמור לדוד
4 title To the chief Musician on Neginoth, a Psalm of David	In finem in carminibus, Psalmus David	Εἰς τὸ τέλος, ἐν ψαλμοῖς ᾠδὴ τῷ Δαυίδ	למנצח בנגינות מזמור לדוד
6 title on Neginoth upon Sheminith	carminibus... pro octava psalmus cantici	ὕμνοις ὑπὲρ τῆς ὀγδόης	בנגינות על-השמינית
30 titl psalm & song	in cithara; in psalterio	ψαλμὸς ᾠδῆς	מזמור שיר
33:2 harp, psaltery & instrument of ten strings	decem chordarum	κιθάρα, ψαλτηρίῳ δεκαχόρδῳ	כנור, נבל עשור
33:3 Sing unto him a new song; play skilfully with a loud noise	Cantate ei canticum novum; bene psallite ei in vociferatione	ᾄσατε αὐτῷ ᾆσμα καινόν, καλῶς ψάλατε ἐν ἀλαλαγμῷ	שירו-לו שיר חדש, היטיבו נגן בתרועה
43:4 harp	cithara	κιθάρᾳ	כנור
46 titl song upon Alamoth	pro arcanis, psalmus	ὑπὲρ τῶν κρυφίων ψαλμός	על-עלמות שיר
47:5 sound of trumpet	voce tubæ	φωνῇ σάλπιγγος	קול שופר
47:6 sing praises	psallite	ψάλατε	זמרו
49:4 harp	psalterium	ψαλτηρίῳ	כנור
54 titl on Neginoth Maschil	in carminibus intellectus	ὕμνοις συνέσεως	בנגינת משכיל
57:8 psaltery and harp	psalterium et cithara	ψαλτήριον καὶ κιθάρα	נבל וכנור
58 titl Al-taschith, Michtam	ne disperdas, in tituli inscriptionem	μὴ διαφθείρῃς εἰς στηλογραφίαν	אל-תשחת, מכתם
61 titl upon Neginah	in hymnis	ἐν ὕμνοις	על-נגינת
67 titl on neginoth	in hymnis	ἐν ὕμνοις	בנגינת
68:25 singers, players on instruments, damsels with timbrels	principes conjuncti psallentibus, juvencularum tympanistriarum	ἄρχοντες, ἐχόμενοι ψαλλόντων, νεανίδων τυμπανιστριῶν	שרים אחר נגנים בתוך עלמות תופפות
71:22 psaltery, harp	vasis psalmi, cithara	σκεύει ψαλμοῦ, κιθάρᾳ	נבל, כנור
76 tit on Neginoth	in laudibus	ἐν ὕμνοις	בנגינת
81:2 Take a psalm,	Sumite psalmum,	Λάβετε ψαλμὸν,	שאו-זמרה, תף,

	King James	Vulgate	Septuagint	Hebrew
	timbrel, harp, psaltery	tympanum, psalterium, cithara	τύμπανον, ψαλτήριον τερπνὸν, κιθάρας	כנור, נבל
81:3	Blow up the trumpet in the new moon	Buccinate in Neomenia tuba	Σαλπίσατε ἐν νεομηνίᾳ σάλπιγγι	תקעו בחדש שופר
89:15	joyful sound	jubilationem	γινώσκων ἀλαλαγμόν	תרועה
89:17	our horn	cornu nostrum	κέρας ἡμῶν	קרננו
92:3	upon an instrument of ten strings and upon the psaltery; upon the harp with a solemn sound	in decachordo, psalterio; cum cantico, et cithara	ἐν δεκαχόρδῳ ψαλτηρίῳ, μετ᾽ ᾠδῆς ἐν κιθάρᾳ	עלי־עשור ועלי־נבל עלי הגיון בכנור
95:2	joyful noise with psalms	psalmis jubilemus	ψαλμοῖς ἀλαλάξωμεν	בזמרות נריע
98:5	with the harp and the voice of a psalm	in cithara et voce psalmi	ἐν κιθάρᾳ καὶ φωνῇ ψαλμοῦ	בכנור וקול זמרה
98:6	with trumpets and sound of cornet	in tubis ductilibus, et voce tubæ corneæ	ἐν σάλπιγξιν ἐλαταῖς καὶ φωνῇ σάλπιγγος κερατίνης	בחצצרות וקול שופר
108:2	psaltery and harp	psalterium et cithara	ψαλτήριον καὶ κιθάρα	נבל וכנור
137:2	our harps	organa nostra	ὄργανα ἡμῶν	כנרותינו
144:9	upon a psaltery & an instrument of ten strings	in psalterio, decachordo	ἐν ψαλτηρίῳ δεκαχόρδῳ	בנבל עשור
147:7	harp	cithara	κιθάρᾳ	כנור
149:3	dance, timbrel, harp	choro, tympano, psalterio	χορῷ, τυμπάνῳ, ψαλτηρίῳ	מחול, תף, כנור
150:3	sound of the trumpet, psaltery and harp	sono tubæ, psalterio et cithara	ἤχῳ σάλπιγγος, ψαλτηρίῳ καὶ κιθάρᾳ	תקע שופר, נבל וכנור
150:4	timbrel & dance, stringed instruments & organs	tympano et choro, chordis et organo	τυμπάνῳ καὶ χορῷ, χορδαῖς καὶ ὀργάνῳ	תף ומחול מנים ועוגב
150:5	loud cymbals, high-sounding cymbals	cymbalis benesonantibus, cymbalis jubilationis	κυμβάλοις εὐήχοις, κυμβάλοις ἀλαλαγμοῦ	צלצלי־שמע צלצלי־תרועה
	Ecclesiastes	**Ecclesiastes**	**Εκκλησιαστης**	קהלת
2:8	men singers, women singers, musical instruments	cantores et cantatrices	ᾄδοντας καὶ ᾀδούσας	שרים ושרות ותענוגת
3:4	to dance	saltandi	τοῦ ὀρχήσασθαι	עת רקוד
	Isaiah	**Isaiæ**	**Ησαιας**	ישעיהו
5:12	harp, viol, tabret, pipe	cithara, lyra, tympanum, tibia	κιθάρας, ψαλτηρίου, τυμπάνων, αὐλῶν	כנור, נבל, תף, חליל
14:11	thy viol	---	---	נבליך
16:11	harp	cithara	κιθάρα	כנור
18:3	trumpet	tuba	σάλπιγξ	שופר
23:16	harp	cithara	κιθάρα	כנור
24:8	tabrets, harp	tympanorum, citharæ	τυμπάνων, κιθάρας	תפים , כנור
27:13	great trumpet	tuba magna	σάλπιγγι τῇ μεγάλῃ	שופר גדול
30:29	pipe	tibia	αὐλὸς	חליל
30:32	with tabrets and harps	in tympanis, citharis	μετὰ τυμπάνων καὶ κιθάρας	בתפים ובכנרות

King James	Vulgate	Septuagint	Hebrew
38:20 stringed instruments	psalmos	ψαλτηρίου	נגינותי ננגן
58:1 trumpet	tuba	σάλπιγγι	שופר
Jeremiah	**Jereremiæ**	**Ιερεμιας**	ירמיהו
4:5 trumpet	tuba	σάλπιγγι	שופר
4:19 trumpet	buccinæ	σάλπιγγος	שופר
4:21 trumpet	buccinæ	σαλπίγγων	שופר
6:1 trumpet	buccina	σάλπιγγι	שופר
6:17 trumpet	tubæ	σάλπιγγος	שופר
31:4 tabrets, dances	tympanis, choro	τύμπανον	תף, מחול
31:13 dance	choro	---	מחול
42:14 trumpet	tubæ	σάλπιγγος	שופר
48:36 pipes	tibiæ	αὐλοὶ	חלילים
51:27 trumpet	buccina	σάλπιγγι	שופר
Ezekiel	**Ezechielis**	**Ιεζεκιηλ**	יחזקאל
7:14 they have blown the trumpet	canite tuba	σαλπίσατε ἐν σάλπιγγι	תקעו בתקוע
26:13 harps	cithararum	ψαλτηρίων	כנור
28:13 thy tabrets, thy pipes	----	_	תפיך וגנקביך
33:4,5,6 trumpet	buccina	σάλπιγξ	שופר
Daniel	**Danielis**	**Δανιηλ**	דניאל
3:5 sound of the cornet, flute, harp, sackbut, psaltery, dulcimer, and all kinds of musick	sonitum tubæ, et fistulæ, et citharæ, sambucæ, et psalterii, et symphoniæ, et universi generis musicorum	φωνῆς σάλπιγγος, σύριγγός τε, καὶ κιθάρας, σαμβύκης τε, καὶ ψαλτηρίου, καὶ παντὸς γένους μουσικῶν	קל קרנא משרוקיתא קיתרוס סבכא פסנתרין סומפניה וכל זני זמרא
3:7 sound of the cornet, flute, harp, sackbut, psaltery, and all kinds of musick	sonitum tubæ, fistulæ, et citharæ, sambucæ, et psalterii, et symphoniæ, et omnis generis musicorum	φωνῆς τῆς σάλπιγγος, σύριγγός τε, καὶ κιθάρας, σαμβύκης τε, καὶ ψαλτηρίου, καὶ παντὸς γένους μουσικῶν	קל קרנא משרוקיתא קיתרוס, שבכא פסנתרין וכל זני זמרא
3:10 sound of the cornet, flute, harp, sackbut, psaltery, and dulcimer, and all kinds of musick	sonitum tubæ, fistulæ, et citharæ, sambucæ, et psalterii, et symphoniæ, et universi generis musicorum	φωνῆς τῆς σάλπιγγος, σύριγγός τε, καὶ κιθάρας, σαμβύκης, καὶ ψαλτηρίου, καὶ παντὸς γένους μουσικῶν	קל קרנא משרוקיתא קיתרוס, שבכא, פסנתרין וסיפניה וכל זני זמרא
3:15 sound of the cornet, flute, harp, sackbut, psaltery, and dulcimer, and all kinds of musick	sonitum tubæ, fistulæ, citharæ, sambucæ, et psalterii, et symphoniæ, omnisque generis musicorum	φωνῆς τῆς σάλπιγγος, σύριγγός τε, καὶ κιθάρας, σαμβύκης τε, καὶ ψαλτηρίου, καὶ συμφωνίας, καὶ παντὸς γένους μουσικῶν	קל קרנא משרוקיתא קיתרוס שבכא, פסנתרין וסומפניה וכל זני זמרא
Hosea	**Osee**	**Ωσηε**	הושע
5:8 trumpet, cornet	buccina, tuba	σάλπιγγι	שופר, חצצרה
8:1 trumpet	tuba	---	שפר
Joel	**Joel**	**Ιωηλ**	יואל
2:1 trumpet	tuba	σάλπιγγι	שופר
2:15 trumpet	tuba	σάλπιγγι	שופר
Amos	**Amos**	**Αμως**	עמוס
2:2 trumpet	tuba	σάλπιγγος	שופר
3:6 trumpet	tuba	σάλπιγξ	שופר
5:23 thy viols	lyræ tuæ	ψαλμὸν ὀργάνων σου	נבליך

	King James	Vulgate	Septuagint	Hebrew
6:5	viol, instruments of musick	psalterii, vasa cantici	φωνὴν τῶν ὀργάνων	נבל, כלי־שיר
	Habbakuk	**Habacuc**	**Αμβακουμ**	הבקוק
end	stringed instruments	psalmis canentem	ᾠδῇ αὐτοῦ	בנגינותי
	Zephaniah	**Sophoniæ**	**Σοφονιας**	צפניה
1:16	a day of the trumpet	dies tubæ	ἡμέρα σάλπιγξ	יום שופר
	Zechariah	**Zachariæ**	**Ζαχαριας**	זכריה
9:14	trumpet	tuba	σάλπιγγι	שופר
10:8	I will hiss	sibilabo	σημανῶ	אשרקה
14:20	bells of the horses	frenum equi	ἐπὶ τὸν χαλινὸν τοῦ ἵππου	מצלות הסוס
				The End of the Hebrew Bible
	Apocrypha **First Esdras**	**Esdræ Tertius**	**Apocrypha** **Εσδρας Α'**	
4:63	with instruments of musick	cum musicis	μετὰ μουσικῶν	
5:2	with musick [instruments], tabrets, flutes	cum musicis, tympanis, tibiis	μετὰ μουσικῶν, τυμπάνων, αὐλῶν	
5:42	Singing men & singing women 245	cantores et cantatrices 245	ψάλται καὶ ψαλτῴδοὶ 245	
5:59	musical instruments and trumpets, cymbals	tubis, cymbala	μουσικῶν καὶ σαλπίγγων, κύμβαλα	
5:62ff	sounded trumpets	tuba cecinerunt, tubis	ἐσάλπισαν, σαλπίγ-γων [no LXX]	
	Second Esdras	**Esdræ Quartus**		
10:22	psaltery	psalterium		
	Judith	**Judith**	**Ιουδιθ**	
3:7	dances & timbrels	choros in tympanis et tibiis	χορῶν καὶ τυμπάνων	
16:2	timbrels, cymbals	tympanis et cymbalis	τυμπάνοις,κυμβάλοις	
	Wisdom of Solomon	**Sapientiæ**	**Σοφια Σαλωμων**	
19:18	like as in a psaltery notes change the name of the tune, and yet are always sounds	sicut in organo qualitatis sonus inmutatur, et omnia suum sonum custodiunt	ὥσπερ ἐν ψαλτηρίῳ φθόγγοι τοῦ ῥυθμοῦ τὸ ὄνομα διαλλάσσουσι, πάντοτε μένοντα ἤχῳ	
	Ecclesiasticus	**Ecclesiasticus**	**Σοφια Σειραχ**	
9:4	woman singer	saltatrice	ψαλλούσης	
32:3	hinder not musick	non impedias musicam	μὴ ἐμποδίσῃς μουσικά	
32:4	musician	---	ακρόαμα	
32:5	concert of musick	comparatio musicorum	σύγκριμα μουσικῶν	
32:6	melody of musick	numerus musicorum	μέλος μουσικῶν	
40:20	wine & musick	vinum et musica	οἶνος καὶ μουσικὰ	
40:21	pipe & psaltery	tibiæ et psalterium	αὐλὸς καὶ ψαλτήριον	
45:9	pomegranates and many golden bells round	tintinnabulis aureis plurimus in gyro	ῥοΐσκοις χρυσοῖς κώδωσι πλείστοις κυκλόθεν	

King James	Vulgate	Septuagint	Tyndale
about			
47:9 singers	cantores	ψαλτῳδοὶς	
50:16 silver trumpets	tubis productilibus	σάλπιγξιν ἐλαταῖς	
First Maccabees	**Machabæorum I**	**Μακκαβαιων Α'**	
3:45 pipe with harp	tibia et cithara	αὐλὸς καὶ κινύρα	
3:54 trumpets	tubis	σάλπιγξ	
4:13 trumpets	tuba	ἐσάλπισαν	
4:40 trumpets	tubis	σάλπιγξ	
4:54 songs, citherns, harps, cymbals	canticis, citharis, cinyris, cymbalis	ᾠδαῖς, κιθάραις, κινύραις, κυμβάλοις	
4:57 crowns of gold and with shields	coronis aureis, et scutulis	στεφάνοις χρυσοῖς καὶ ἀσπιδίσκαις	
5:31 trumpets	tuba	σάλπιγξι	
5:33 trumpets	tubis	σάλπιγξι	
6:33 trumpets	tubis	σάλπιγξι	
7:45 trumpets	tubis	σάλπιγξι	
9:12/3 trumpets	tubis	σάλπιγξι	
9:39 drums, instruments of musick	tympanis, musicis	τυμπάνων, μουσικῶν	
13:51 harps, cymbals, viols, hymns, songs	cinyris, cymbalis, nablis, hymnis, canticis	κινύραις, κυμβάλοις, νάβλαις, ὕμνοις, ᾠδαῖς	
16:8 holy trumpets	sacris tubis	ἱεραῖς σάλπιγξι	
Second Maccabees	**Machabæorum II**	**Μακκαβαιων Β'**	
15:25 trumpets & songs	tubis et canticis	σαλπίγγων καὶ παιάνων	
The New Testament	**Novum JesuChristi Testamentum**	**Η Καινη Διαθηκη**	**New Testament Tyndale, 1526**
Matthew	**Matthæum**	**Ματθιον**	**Mathew**
6:2 trumpet	tuba	σαλπίσῃς	trompet
11:17 we have piped unto you and ye have not danced	cecinimus vobis, et non saltastis	ηὐλήσαμεν ὑμῖν, καὶ οὐκ ὠρχήσασθε	we have pyped unto you, and ye have not daunsed
24:31 great sound of a trumpet	tuba, et voce magna	σάλπιγγος [φωνῆς] μεγάλης	greate voyce of a tromp
Luke	**Lucam**	**Λουκαν**	**Luke**
7:32 we have piped unto you and ye have not danced	cantavimus vobis tibiis, et non saltastis	ηὐλήσαμεν ὑμῖν, καὶ οὐκ ὠρχήσασθε	we have pyped unto you, and ye have nott daunsed
15:25 musick and dancing	symphoniam, et chorum	συμφωνίας καὶ χορῶν	minstrelcy, and daunsynge
John	**Joannem**	**Ιωαννην**	**Jhon**
12:6 had the bag	loculos habens	γλωσσόκομον ἔχων	kept the bagge
13:29 Judas had the bag	loculos habebat Judas	γλωσσόκομον εἶχεν ὁ Ἰούδας	Judas had the bagge
First Corinthians	**Ad Corinthios I**	**Προς Κορινθους Α'**	**Fyrst Corrinthians**
13:1 sounding brass, or a tinkling cymbal	æs sonans, aut cymbalum tinniens	χαλκὸς ἠχῶν ἢ κύμβαλον ἀλαλάζον	soundynge brasse: and as a tynklynge Cynball
14:7 pipe, harp; piped, harped	tibia, cithara; canitur citharizatur	αὐλὸς, κιθάρα; αὐλούμενον, κιθαριζόμενον	pype, harpe; pyped, harped
14:8 trumpet	tuba	σάλπιγξ	trompe
15:52 last trump: for the trumpet shall sound	novissima tuba, canet enim tuba	ἐσχάτη σάλπιγγι· σαλπίσει γὰρ	last trompe, for the trompe shall blowe

King James	Vulgate	Septuagint	Tyndale
First Thessalonians	**Thessalonicenses I**	**Θεσσαλονικεις Α'**	**Fyrst Tessalonians**
4:16 trump of God	tuba Dei	σάλπιγγι Θεοῦ	trompe of God
Hebrews	**Hebræos**	**Εβραιους**	**Hebrues**
12:19 sound of a trumpet	tubæ sonum	σάλπιγγος ἤχῳ	sounde of a trompe
Revelation of St. John the Divine	**Apocalypsis Beati Joannis Apostoli**	**Αποκαλυψις Ιωαννου του Θεολογου**	**Revelacion off sanct Jhon the devine**
1:10 trumpet	tubæ	σάλπιγγος	trompe
4:1 trumpet	tubæ	σάλπιγγος	trompet
5:8 harps	citharas	κιθάραν	harpes
8:2 seven trumpets	septem tubæ	ἑπτὰ σάλπιγγες	vij. trompettes
8:6 seven trumpets	septem tubas	ἑπτὰ σάλπιγγας	vij trompettes
8:13 trumpet	tuba	σάλπιγγος	trompe
9:14 trumpet	tubam	σάλπιγγα	trompe
14:2 harpers harping with their harps	citharœdorum citharizantium in citharis suis	κιθαρῳδῶν κιθαριζόντων ἐν ταῖς κιθάραις αὐτῶν	harpers harpynge with their harpes
15:2 harps of God	citharas Dei	κιθάρας τοῦ Θεοῦ	harpes of God
18:22 voice of harpers, and musicians, and of pipers, and trumpeters, shall be heard no more at all in thee;	vox citharœdorum, et musicorum, et tibia canentium, et tuba non audietur in te amplius :	φωνὴ κιθαρῳδῶν καὶ μουσικῶν καὶ αὐλητῶν καὶ σαλπιστῶν οὐ μὴ ἀκουσθῇ ἐν σοὶ ἔτι·	voyce off harpers, and musicions, and off pypers, and trompetters, shalbe herde no more in the:

General Index